W9-BKW-498

The Historians' Paradox

The Historians' Paradox

The Study of History in Our Time

Peter Charles Hoffer

NEW YORK UNIVERSITY PRESS

New York and London

NEW YORK UNIVERSITY PRESS
New York and London
www.nyupress.org

Library of Congress Cataloging-in-Publication Data

Hoffer, Peter Charles, 1944–
The historians' paradox : the study of history in our time /
Peter Charles Hoffer.
p. cm.
Includes bibliographical references and index.
ISBN-13: 978-0-8147-3714-9 (hbk. : alk. paper)
ISBN-10: 0-8147-3714-5 (hbk. : alk. paper)
1. History—Philosophy. I. Title.
D16.8.H6265   2008
901—dc22   2008022994

New York University Press books are printed on acid-free paper,
and their binding materials are chosen for strength and durability.
We strive to use environmentally responsible suppliers and materials
to the greatest extent possible in publishing our books.

Manufactured in the United States of America
c 10 9 8 7 6 5 4 3 2 1
p 10 9 8 7 6 5 4 3 2 1

Contents

HISTORIAN, n. A broad-gauge gossip.

—Ambrose Bierce (1911)

The crucial problem to be tackled is: what can be a genuine philosophy of history?

—Jacques Maritain (1957)

In large part, historians' claims to seriousness, originalism, and objectivity depend upon their ability to convince their peers that they have avoided sophistry . . . the artifice and appeal to the emotions with which rhetoric is normally associated.

—Hayden White (1976)

But I would have them whom the lightness or foolery of the argument may offend to consider that mine is not the first of this kind, but the same thing that has been often practiced even by great authors.

—Erasmus, *In Praise of Folly* (1509)

Preface

How do we know what happened in the past? We cannot go back. Even historians who truly believe that in some future time historians would have assembled enough facts to understand with certainty how it was "then," like the German historian Wilhelm Dilthey, admit that "the explanation of historical connections . . . cannot justify itself by incontestable proofs when confronted with historical skepticism." How do you *know* you have got it right?

Is it folly, then, to research and write history? And greater folly to propose a theory of how history is possible at all? If so, this folly has its uses. Desiderius Erasmus of Rotterdam, in the Low Countries, was one of the most learned men of the Renaissance. On a visit to English scholar Thomas More, whose intellect matched Erasmus's own and whose dry wit could appreciate Erasmus's brand of gentle satire, Erasmus composed a brilliant essay, *In Praise of Folly* (1509). In it, he lambasted notable scholars who wore their erudition as ostentatiously as they wore their academic gowns. But at the end of this razor-sharp proof that we could not know about the past, he asked pardon for taking the "liberty was ever permitted to all men's wits, to make their smart, witty reflections on the common errors of mankind."

It is easy to demolish the very *idea* of historical knowing but impossible to demolish the *importance* of historical knowing. For who can know the past, forever gone, and who can ignore the past, always with us? In the 1980s and 1990s, history became the focal point of a national struggle here and abroad, a centerpiece of the pervasive and highly partisan culture wars. American political divisions overlapped cultural divisions about homosexuality, religion and science, and reproductive rights. *Liberal* and *conservative* came to mean one's stances on art and learning as well as the economy and the role of government in our lives. College campuses, once havens of civil discourse, became armed camps as faculty, administration, and students debated hate speech codes, academic freedom, and affirmative action. In more recent days of cable pundits and anonymous bloggers dueling over history, the value of owning history increases at the same time as our confidence in history as a way of knowing crumbles.

Historical knowledge thus presents a paradox—the more it is required, the less reliable it has become. Perhaps we should just embrace the paradox that we historians cannot know what we proclaim to know. After all, a paradox is an educated person's delight. It frames humor and inspires wonder. For this reason the famous lyricist W. S. Gilbert favored plots of "topsy turvy"—logical puzzles—for his operettas: for example, the logical illogicality of *The Mikado*. Koko, in prison for the serious offense of "flirting," for which the punishment is death, is named Lord High Executioner. To carry out his office, he would first have to chop off his own head— a task he is not eager to perform even if he could. The **paradox** (from here on, every bolded word is defined in the glossary at the end of the book) lies in the illogical twisting of time and space—an unreal world, to be sure, but so close to our own that we can understand and appreciate it. Like history.

To reconcile this paradox—that history is impossible but necessary—I propose here a practical, working **philosophy of history** for our time. The project is something of a valedictory for me. As I near the end of my active teaching career, I find myself reflecting on the wisdom my teachers offered me, abetted by my own interaction with nearly four generations of students and colleagues. Over this course of time, I have taught in one form or another the "historical methods" course and written about methods in workbooks and book-length critical essays. It is time that I try to pull the threads together into a single garment. Of course, one size will never fit all, and the following pages reflect both personal opinions and political perspectives that not every reader will share. It will not take long for anyone sensitized by *The Daily Show* and *The O'Reilly Factor* to figure out where I stand.

I explored the "dark side" of historical practice in my *Past Imperfect: Facts, Fictions, and Fraud in American History* (2004), and I am grateful to PublicAffairs, my publisher, and Clive Priddle, my editor at PublicAffairs, for permission to retrofit and reuse small portions of that book. I hope that this essay complements that one, offering hope to new generations of historians and readers of history. In 1988, Peter Novick ended the introduction to his *That Noble Dream*: "The book's aim is to provoke my fellow historians to greater self-consciousness about the nature of our work" and "to offer those outside of the historical profession a greater understanding of what we're up to." A noble objective, surely. To that I can only humbly add that *The Historians' Paradox* aims to extend this project.

Last but not least, I want to thank the folks who were kind enough to read and comment on early drafts of this book—Steve Allen, Farley Chase, N. E. H. Hull, Derek Krissoff, Marlie Wasserman, Thom Whigham, and Michael Winship. The attendees at the University of Georgia Department of History faculty colloquium read and critiqued the introduction and chapter 7. Two editors at New York University Press saw value in the work in its finished state. Deborah Gershenowitz, a fellow historian as well as a senior editor at the press, and editor-in-chief Eric Zinner shaped the final version with enthusiasm and good humor. Scholar teachers the press asked to referee the manuscript, Peter Onuf and Claire Potter, substantially improved it with their comments. I am blessed to have a life partner and two sons who love history and write it, and I dedicate the book to them: Natalie Hull, Williamjames Hoffer, and Louis Hoffer.

Introduction

Why History Is Impossible, Yet Necessary All the Same

Now that I am old, the most intriguing aspect of history turns out to be neither the study of history nor history itself . . . but rather the study of the history of historical study.

—Carl Becker (1938)

Early in my career of teaching history at the college level, nearly forty years ago, I found myself writing and lecturing confidently, positive about something I could never really know, trying to take my students and readers back to a time and place where I had never been, asking them to believe what I said and wrote about it. I supported my writing and teaching with voluminous citations to authorities who in retrospect had engaged in the same impossible task. We call this exercising the historical imagination, as if by some magic of naming an impossible act we can perform it. At the same time, I knew that if my travel back through time and space was impossible it was nonetheless necessary, for what is a people without a history? They do not exist. Historians bring to life what is dead—surely the most impossible of all quests, yet the most humane. Without history, a people have no identity, no present as well as no past.

Perhaps I should have known better. Who can even claim to master a subject that is forever receding from our sight? In a wrenchingly honest appraisal of a life doing history, Oscar Handlin wrote of knowing about the past as one knew the way to a mountain's top. "We know now that no simple journey will bring us to the summit. Indeed, we cannot be sure where the summit lies, or in fact whether it exists at all, for our valley is high enough to reveal the complexity of the surrounding ranges."

The increasing elaboration of theories of history and methods of historical research in the 1960s and after was no help. Borrowing social science theories, quantitative methods, and literary devices could not provide the certainty, or even the promise of certainty, of historical knowledge that Handlin sought. As Allan Megill has prefaced his learned essay *Historical Knowledge, Historical Error* (2007): "It is not my intention to offer a theory of historical writing, because I do not think that a single theory, either of historical writing in general or of historical epistemology [knowing], can be offered. At any rate, no *acceptable* theory can be offered [italics in original]." What then?

A century ago, historians—and their audiences—had little trouble with the notion that history was possible. It was a science. The French historian Fustel de Coulanges lectured his colleagues in 1862, "History is something more than a pastime. . . . It is not pursued merely to entertain our curiosity or to fill the pigeonholes of our memory. History is and should be a science." His German contemporary Leopold von Ranke put it even more simply when he ordered his students to report on the past "as it actually happened." J. B. Bury, a professor of history at Cambridge University, taught his students forty years later, "It has not yet become superfluous to insist that history is a science, no less and no more." The library and the archive were laboratories, and historical evidence rigorously tested and objectively presented could be used to prove, or disprove, hypotheses about the past. In fact, the first seminar room in the first graduate program in American history at the Johns Hopkins University in 1880 was designed to look like a laboratory.

The yearning for **truth** in history persists. As British historical giant G. R. Elton wrote in *The Practice of History* (1967), the historian's "instinctive familiarity with evidence results in a useful and necessary sense which extends his range beyond the strict confines of the evidence, even his guesses bear the stamp of truth because they fit the reality of the situation." The well-attuned professional historian's "hunch is based on an expert understanding of what can, what must have happened." We can be confident, for Elton assures us that the "principles and practice of historical research" yield truth.

But such claims of totally logical and **objective** historical inquiry, whether based on the analogy to science or a simple faith in expertise, cannot be credited without some suspicion that they are self-serving. After all, they found the historian's authority on what amounts to nothing more than the authority of the historian. But the historian is a person living in a time and place, not an objective observer. One can even retranslate von Ranke's famous aphorism to mean that historians "wanted" to show the past as it happened, not that they could. What stopped them? The fact that the historian was a historical actor. As Carl Becker told the American Historical Association (AHA) in 1931, "It must then be obvious that living history, the ideal series of events that we affirm and hold in memory, since it is so intimately associated with what we are doing and with what we hope to do, cannot be precisely the same for all at any given time, or the same for one generation as for another. . . . Each of us is subject to the limitations of time and place." In short, the "reality of the situation" may be ours more than the evidence's.

Becker was one of the first of the **relativists.** He tells us that we are part of the history that we write and teach. Our choices of subject, our selection and arrangement of evidence, our emphasis and nuance, are not reducible to a science. Relative to our own training and the world around us, our history tells our own story as well as the stories of times gone by. Everyman is a historian every time he reads his heating bills. As the basis for a philosophy of history, however, Becker's formula is as suspect as Elton's faith in expertise. Too often, everyman is not a reliable factfinder or weigher of fact. Everyman's hopes and fears, his biases and blindness, his expectations all shape how he reads that heating bill. The Monty Python "Dead Parrot" sketch, in which the owner of a pet store confronts an irate customer, demonstrates how everyman regards facts as conveniences.

> Customer: 'Ello, I wish to register a complaint. . . . I wish to complain about this parrot what I purchased not half an hour ago from this very boutique.
>
> Owner: Oh yes, the, uh, the Norwegian Blue. . . . What's, uh . . . What's wrong with it?
>
> Customer: I'll tell you what's wrong with it, my lad. 'E's dead, that's what's wrong with it!
>
> Owner: No, no, 'e's uh, . . . he's resting.
>
> Customer: Look, matey, I know a dead parrot when I see one, and I'm looking at one right now. . . . 'ELLO POLLY! Testing! Testing! Testing! Testing! This is your nine o'clock alarm call! . . . Now that's what I call a dead parrot.
>
> Owner: No, 'e's stunned!
>
> Customer: Stunned?
>
> Owner: Yeah! You stunned him, just as he was wakin' up! Norwegian Blues stun easily.

If history is everyman's memory, then there is no way to measure its reliability. As memory is fallible and given to invention, should history be as well? Becker dodged the question: "The history written by historians, like the history informally fashioned by Mr. Everyman, is thus a convenient blend of truth and fancy, of what we commonly distinguish as 'fact' and 'interpretation.'" Cultural historian Hayden White put the matter even more bluntly. For White, the entire enterprise of doing history is akin to the tricks that men of letters play on their audiences all the time. History is always propaganda or flight of fancy. All history was "figurative." How could it be anything else when knowing the past was itself a figure of speech?

We cannot conclude that doing history is the kind of folly that Erasmus warned against *In Praise of Folly*, a mischievous self-delusion that has always proven unreliable, because we need history—a **valid**, usable history—too much. This is the historians' paradox. I propose that we can fashion a philosophy of history that is both relevant and workable. In this book I'll combine historical anecdotes, examples of historians at work, a little popular philosophy, and some basic logical principles to lay out the plan for such a philosophy of history. Here are my specifications for that plan: a philosophy of history for our time must accommodate the imagination of ordinary people, while not abandoning the just requirements of analytical penetration and narrative depth. It must exhibit a willingness to entertain mystery, courage, and love. It must incorporate a due sense of humility, recognizing the legitimate place of paradox, irony, and uncertainty, and have a place for faith (though not necessarily in organized religion). A tall order—but see what you think when we are done.

If we are successful, our philosophy of history will enable us to do, read, and teach history with confidence, but that confidence will not rest upon any claim here to philosophical certitude. As one leading philosopher opened his recent essay on the subject: "Given the plurality of voices within the 'philosophy of history,' it is impossible to give one definition of the field that suits all these approaches. In fact, it is misleading to imagine that we refer to a single philosophical tradition when we invoke the phrase, 'philosophy of history,' because the strands of research characterized here rarely engage in dialogue with each other." Amen to that.

But if the philosophers cannot pinpoint the meaning of their own term, why should historians give philosophy of history—any philosophy of history (including the arguments in this present volume)—a second thought? Working historians are singularly indifferent to what philosophers have to say about history. As historian Richard J. Evans has lamented, "The subject [of philosophy of history] . . . is so theoretical, so far removed from actual problems experienced by working historians," that "we have what has often seemed to be a dialogue of the deaf" between the historians and the philosophers.

My answer is that philosophy of history is too important to working historians to be left to philosophers. Think about the term itself—*philosophy* means love of knowledge. *Philosophy of history* then must mean the love of historical knowledge. Who loves it more than historians? Indeed, as historian Charles Beard told his audience at the 1933 meeting of the American Historical Association, "The philosopher, possessing little or no acquaintance with history, sometimes pretends to expound the inner secret of history, but the historian turns upon him and expounds the secret of the philosopher, as far as it may be expounded at all, by placing him in relation to the movement of ideas and interests in which he stands or floats, by giving to his scheme of thought its appropriate relativity." And if philosophy belongs to the province of intellectual history, the philosophy of history cannot belong to philosophers.

Because we cannot know for certain about historical knowledge from philosophy and we cannot return to the self-satisfied era of scientific history, we have all the more need of a robust and realistic philosophy of history for our time. It must speak to everyone who joins in our enterprise—all of us who write and teach history. A definition of that philosophy here would be premature; this entire book is the definition. But a good starting place is the very last effort that Marc Bloch, a twentieth-century French historian, made to explain what he was doing and why.

No one was more skeptical of the old philosophies of scientific history than Bloch. Born in 1886 in the "Dreyfus generation," which warned educated Jews that they were only barely tolerated in France, Bloch nevertheless loved his country with the sincerest passion. A medievalist and a co-founder of the "Annales" school of social history, he was a consummate professional. But Bloch was no mere ink-stained scribbler. A much decorated veteran of the First World War and a resistance fighter in the second, he was captured by the Nazis in 1944 and executed. Even as he dodged the death squads he never laid down his pen, and in his briefcase when he was arrested by the Nazis was a fragment of a book later published as *The Historian's Craft* (1953).

Bloch conceded the inherent impossibility of history in *The Historian's Craft*. Time was "a continuum" that exhibited "perpetual change." The essence of the historian's craft was to leap over the changes, to reenter the past world. He needed no philosophy of history to do this. Bloch objected to the very idea of a science of history. "To me, the very idea that the past as such can be the object of science is ridiculous." *The Historian's Craft* offered instead a command to the working historian. History "requires us to join the study of the dead and of the living . . . [that is] the most comprehensive, the least exclusive, the most electric with stirring reminders of a more than age-old endeavor." History was the bridge we must build from the present to the past. Or as Edward Hallett Carr wrote in *What Is History?* (1962), history is "an unending dialogue between the present and the past."

Once more, why do we need a new philosophy of history? Or to be precise, why now? In 1974, when there was much turmoil within the historical profession, old-liners objecting to the borrowing of social science models and quantitative methods, and conservatives afraid that the "New Left" historians were about to tear down the house, mused aloud on what was wrong with history. Among these, and typical of them, Jacques Barzun worried that "empirical observation also suggests that History is sick, dying, dead. Whether one looks at the numbers enrolled in history courses or the tendency of history departments to make sheep's eyes at bold quantifiers, or the declining popularity of history among general readers . . . it is clear that the nineteenth-century pre-eminence of history in the sphere of intellect no longer obtains. The historical sense in modern populations is feeble or non-existent." A poor prognostication, as events proved. History today is a booming enterprise, with more and more students, more and more books, and greater popularity than ever.

But boom times have brought unique problems. It is no longer clear what history is and how we who write it and teach it fit into its exploitation. Is history to be a celebration of great men and their deeds, a patriotic inspiration to new generations? Is history to remind us of the promises we have made and broken, or never meant to keep, to the weakest among us? Is history to become the highly technical subject matter of a handful of experts, written in a language that only they can understand? Is history to be surrendered to popularizers who do not bother to consult the most recent scholarship and tell the same old stories in books with brand-new covers?

How then can we build a bridge to the past (conceding at the outset that the "bridge" is a metaphor for method) that combines sound methods and modern tastes in history? We begin the philosophy of history for our time with the thesis that history is always argument. Whatever our philosophy of knowing, whether we prefer narrative or analytical approaches, persuasive historical writing is always an argument. Any philosophy of history beginning with this premise must concern itself, at least in part, with logical matters—the requirement that historical argument be reasonable, free of **fallacy**, and supported by appropriate evidence that is itself tenable. It is thus with **logic** and its rhetorical kinsmen that we begin this book. We then explore how a philosophy of history-as-argument can reach out to include the loaded question, the imaginative fabrication, and the invisible linkages we call causation. We then test the philosophy in political discourse, in the marketplace, and in the realms of the literary and linguistic critics. Finally, perhaps most important, we weigh our philosophy of history against the claim that the highest purpose of any history is moral judgment.

Each of the following chapters is a self-contained essay on one topic, but all are way stations on a journey to recognizing how a philosophy of history for working historians can help us understand the most basic questions of human life. Each of the lessons is a little harder, as each builds on the previous ones. Each brings us a little closer to that far, mist-shrouded shore we call the past. Along the way, to pass the time, we will share stories and see what lessons we can draw from them. Erasmus taught us that humor is a great teacher. We will pause in our journey to learn from pun masters and pranksters.

1

It Would Be Logical to Assume . . .

Historians feel safe when dealing with the facts. We talk about "the
hard facts" and "the cold facts," about "not being able to get around
the facts," and about the necessity of basing our narrative on a
"sound foundation of fact." . . . But the simple fact turns out to be
not a simple fact at all [but] . . . a simple generalization of a thousand
and one facts . . . a statement . . . an affirmation . . . an argument.

—Carl Becker (1926)

"Just the facts," Los Angeles police detective sergeant Joe Fri-
day told witnesses. But witnesses left out key observations, mistook faces,
and gave fleeting impressions the weight of truth. The detectives had to
sort out the bits and pieces and assemble them into a viable case. *Dragnet*
was fiction, for in it the police always got the right man. Would that historians were as fortunate, for we too are detectives, but our clues have a way
of vanishing before our eyes.

For what is a historical fact? As Barbara J. Shapiro reveals in her *Culture of Fact: England, 1550–1720* (2003), the notion of "historical fact," a
true statement about the past worthy of belief, is itself a historical development. Only gradually did early modern historical writers denounce
romance, myth, antiquarianism, and rhetoric and champion impartiality,
the weighing of evidence, and scholarly expertise.

At the close of the nineteenth century, historians could be proud of
their discipline and their achievements because they were the master of
the irreducible fact. As James Ford Rhodes told the AHA in 1899: "Was
there ever so propitious a time for writing history as in the last forty years?
There has been a general acquisition of the historic sense. The methods of
teaching history have so improved that they may be called scientific. Even
as the chemist and physicist, we talk of practice in the laboratory." Men

like Rhodes regarded the facts in their accounts as the irreducible unquestionable truths with which any account of the past began. Documents, letters, diaries, artifacts, newspapers, and other survivals from the past were the source of these facts, and from their assembly historians built their narratives. Rhodes again: "The qualities necessary for an historian are diligence, accuracy, love of truth, impartiality, the thorough digestion of his materials by careful selection and long meditating." If there were such irrefutable facts, from them historians could construct perfect accounts. They would always get the culprit right. History would be not only possible but easy.

But even as this first generation founded its professional associations, sought funding to preserve documentary collections, and offered graduate instruction and Ph.D.s to a new generation of historians, the very notion of the irreducibility of historical facts was coming under fire. Younger scholars, enamored of the very social sciences that were emerging alongside the discipline of history, were asking: Could a mastery of individual facts fully explain the spirit of an age? Could the historian include enough facts to cover all the variety of actions and actors? They agreed that facts were not bricks or other ready-to-hand building materials, because one could always ask of the sources whether they were honest, truthful, and reliable.

James Harvey Robinson related this progress away from certainty to an audience at the AHA annual meeting in 1929: At the outset of the century, "We had made a very essential discovery, the distinction between the primary and secondary sources of historical knowledge. We inhaled the delicious odor of first hand accounts, of the 'original document,' of the 'official report.' We had at last got to the bottom of things. . . . [But] as we look back thirty years we find historians perhaps rather pedantic and defensive. They are humble enough now." Interpretation instead of narration became the major preoccupation of historians.

History itself played a role in spurring the historians' growing skepticism about facts. During the First World War, leading American historians joined forces in the Committee on Public Information to bend and shape the past to fit our participation in the war against Germany. The chairman of that committee, newspaperman George Creel recalled in 1920 that its purpose had been to instill "a passionate belief in the justice of America's cause that would weld the American people into one white hot mass instinct with fraternity, devotion, courage and deathless determination." After the war, disgruntled historians wondered if they had been duped by their own government into betraying their higher calling as scholars. Historical methods became even more self-critical. Even canonical documents were subjected to second and third looks. Did the drafters of these documents know what was going on? Did they have a bias that perverted their perception of events or a reason to lie?

The irreducible fact became a little argument built from pieces of evidence the historian selected and arranged. The selection and the arrangement, the emphasis and the argument, were the historian's, not the document's. Whether a story, an analysis, or a synthesis, history ceased to be "what actually was" and became what historians thought had happened. The historian's account became a big argument resting on a multitude of little arguments.

Reason to the Rescue?

Given that we can no longer contend that we are simply intellectual bricklayers, placing fact upon fact and mortaring up the cracks with quotations from primary sources that speak for themselves, can historians respond to the impossibility dilemma by claiming that their reasoning faculties link past to present? Or that history itself has its reasons that the rational historian can discover? Most historical scholars share the faith that **rationality** in argument is a good thing in itself. A philosophy of history with the reasoning prowess of the historian as its foundation seems eminently reasonable.

This faith in rationality is rooted in Western culture, beginning with Plato. For him, even the elusive mysteries of the soul could be—indeed only could be—revealed by reason. As Socrates tells Glaucon about the soul at the end of Plato's *Republic*: "Her immortality is demonstrated by the previous argument, and there are many other proofs; but to see her as she really is, not as we now behold her, marred by communion with the body and other miseries, you must contemplate her with the eye of reason, in her original purity; and then her beauty will be revealed, and justice and injustice and all the things which we have described will be manifested more clearly."

History is not always elevating. The real Socrates was a far less admirable fellow than the protagonist of the dialogues: nasty to his neighbors, indifferent to his domestic obligations, a philanderer, and a warmonger to boot. The more he harangued his fellow Athenians, the angrier they became. When he was tried for treason, he impudently told them that logic dictated they acquit him. Convicted and asked to leave the city, his logic directed suicide instead. Uncompromising ratiocination led to unmerited death.

But as Charles Beard would be the first to remind us, reason is not a universal element of history, like the forms in Plato's *Republic*. Instead, reason is a cultural construction, a by-product of human desire and literacy. It is not surprising, then, that our love of reason has a history, and that history is as much aspiration as experience. Worse, though not unexpected from the historian's perspective, the very notion of reason is full of contradictions.

Aristotle wrote the first formal treatise on reasoning, sometime around 350 BCE. Though he is better known as the author of works on politics and poetry, his six books of the *Organon* proposed a series of terms and laws of logic still used. He is the originator of the terms **deduction** and **induction** (another word for **inference**). His first law is the **law of identity**: A is always A. No wiggle room there, and no switching terms in the middle of the argument. Aristotle's second law is the **law of contradiction**: A is never not A.

This intuitively simple set of laws runs into trouble, however, when A becomes complex and value laden: in other words, when an abstract symbol becomes a living thing in the often contested world of real things. Historians must choose words to describe things. The choice is neither arbitrary nor dictated by any law of logic. When is a patriot a rebel? When is a terrorist a freedom fighter? On the eve of the American Revolution, the rebels (or patriots) called the loyalists Tories and referred to themselves as Whigs. These terms came into use at the end of the seventeenth century in England. A Tory was a defender of the absolute power of kings, according to the Whigs, and a Whig was a rebel, according to the Tories. When historians choose among these terms to describe the opposing sides in 1775, they are joining in the debate rather than standing above it. To repeat, historians know that words in statements they make, just like those in the statements made by people in the past, depend not on the logic of the statement itself for their meaning but on meanings that real people in real time ascribe to the words.

The third of Aristotle's laws was the **law of the excluded middle**. A was either true or false; you could not have it both ways. Except in *Fiddler on the Roof*—in this rich evocation of Jewish life in the shtetls of Russia, Tevye the milkman has occasion to agree with something one of his customers says. A second customer contradicts what the first customer said, and a compliant Tevye agrees with the second man. When a third man tells Tevye that he cannot agree with both of his customers, Tevye agrees with him too. Thus real life in a rural Jewish village circa 1905 confutes the last of Aristotle's famous laws.

Or does it? A twist inside the puzzle: Tevye, the creation of Shalom Aleichem, was a fictional character set in a fictional place that seemed to American audiences as real and as evocative as any Yiddish folk story could be. But the truth was a little different. *Shalom aleichem* is Hebrew for "peace be with you," the pen name of Shalom Rabinowitz, a Russian Jewish scholar and writer. When he published the short story "Tevye and His Daughters" he had already relocated to the United States. Literary conventions rather than folk memory guided his pen. The lesson? Reason is bent by the pull of culture just as light is bent as it passes through water.

Thus it is not surprising to learn that between the age of Aristotle and the modern era, reason and its handmaiden logic had their ups and downs. A history of logic reveals that it was included in the medieval university's required courses. Aristotle's writings were not lost in the Dark Ages of European history, unlike other classical authors' works, and philosophers relied on Aristotle's ideas to defend the life of the mind and the existence of God. At the same time, scholastic philosophers fruitlessly debated whether logic was artificial or corresponded exactly to reality.

For philosopher-theologians like the Dominican scholar St. Thomas Aquinas, the entire purpose of reason was to prove the existence of God. Aquinas had a simple deductive proof of the existence of God in his *Summa Theologica* (1273): "Although a perfect knowledge of the cause cannot be had from inadequate effects, yet . . . from any effect manifest to us it can be shown that a cause does exist, as has been said. And thus from the works of God His existence can be proved, although we cannot in this way know Him perfectly in accordance with His own essence." Aquinas's reasoning was that the world around him (and us) must be the effect of certain causes because all effects have causes. If we could trace the line back to the first cause, we would have proof of God, for what else could the first cause be.

Such "final causes," as they were called at the time, fit history into a very neat, linear pattern: creation, time on earth, final judgment. It was logical, rational, and compelling, though not for Thomas Paine. He concluded his *Age of Reason* (1795): "The most detestable wickedness, the most horrid cruelties, and the greatest miseries, that have afflicted the human race, have had their origin in this thing called revelation, or revealed religion. It has been the most dishonourable belief against the character

of the divinity, the most destructive to morality, and the peace and happiness of man, that ever was propagated since man began to exist." This
was a summary of history quite different from Aquinas's and very harsh
on Catholicism. But then, Paine believed in the universal rights and the
equality of men and women, a concept whose origin lay not in the history
of revealed religion but in the much more recent history of the English
and American revolutions.

Paine's depiction aside, later historians retrofit his title to describe the
somewhat antiseptic and ethereal praise of reason in the works of seven-
teenth- and eighteenth-century philosophers. Chief among these thinkers
was René Descartes, the French philosopher and mathematician whose
aphorism "I think, therefore I am" has become an anthem of the rational
person. Descartes wrote his *Discourse on Method* in 1637. His three rules
for clear thinking seem to speak directly to the historian:

> Never to accept anything as true when I did not recognize it clearly to
> be so, that is to say, to carefully avoid precipitation and prejudice, and to
> include in my opinions nothing beyond that which should present itself
> so clearly and so distinctly to my mind that I might have no occasion to
> doubt it. . . . Divide each of the difficulties which I should examine into
> as many parts as were possible, and as should be required for its better
> solution. . . . Conduct my thoughts in order, by beginning with the sim-
> plest objects, and those most easy to know, so as to mount little by little,
> as if by steps, to the most complex knowledge.

One could look a long time and not find a better introduction to historical argument as practical reasoning, but when Descartes himself applied his rules they paraded themselves in the garb of his time, not ours.
In other words, what reads in isolation as sound reasoning for historians
becomes in the context of the rest of his writing an apology for conventional religion. For example, the origin of thought had to be God: "When
we reflect on the idea of God which we were born with, we see that he is
eternal, omniscient, omnipotent, the source of all goodness and truth, the
creator of all things, and finally, that he possesses within him everything."
Because Descartes has reason, God must exist. A rationalistic notion of
mind had led almost directly back to Thomas Aquinas. Unfortunately for
modern historians wont to employ Descartes, a logic of history that relies
upon the innate idea of God seems a little far-fetched.

England's John Locke was not a historian, but like Descartes he provided what in the abstract appears to be a perfectly serviceable formula for historical reasoning. For him, experience and reason worked together. As he wrote in his *Essay Concerning Human Understanding* (1690):

> The greatest part of our knowledge depends upon deductions and intermediate ideas: and in those cases where we are fain to substitute assent instead of knowledge, and take propositions for true, without being certain they are so, we have need to find out, examine, and compare the grounds of their probability. In both these cases, the faculty which finds out the means, and rightly applies them, to discover certainty in the one, and probability in the other, is that which we call reason. For, as reason perceives the necessary and indubitable connection of all the ideas or proofs one to another, in each step of any demonstration that produces knowledge; so it likewise perceives the probable connection of all the ideas or proofs one to another.

Locke's theory of knowing was an interstitial one—we connect one idea to the next. Consistency and fit, measured by our reasoning faculties, reassure us that what we sense in the world around us is a true representation of that world. Historians use the same notion to move from one event or episode to the next in the narrative or one point to the next in an analysis. But nothing in Locke's assertion of the reasoning faculty in all of us proves that there is such a faculty.

Locke wrote in the first great age of science in western Europe, when England and France founded royal academies to foster scientific inquiry and experiment. A faith in the scientific method was tantamount to a faith in reason, and logical inferences from scientific experiments were to Locke "proofs one to another, in each step of any demonstration." Lockean-inspired historical studies could free themselves from the shackles of religious doctrine and emphasize the human element in events. The way was open for a new age of historical writing in which dispassionate scholars would find in human actions and motives immutable laws of history the same way that Isaac Newton had uncovered immutable laws of gravity and motion. But Locke's faith in reason was a faith in ghosts. For what was reason, apart from the functions of the human brain? Did it float in some etherlike substance within each mind? Who had ever seen it? Measured it? To tell historians to use their powers of reason in a Lockean fashion is simply to tell them to think about their work, a little vague to be a useful part of a philosophy of history.

Edward Gibbon's *Decline and Fall of the Roman Empire* (1776–88) was the epitome of the rationalist histories. Gibbon shared with Locke the belief that history was governed by reason and that human reason could discern the reasons that events transpired as they did. His explanation of religion in the fall of the Roman Empire is a classic:

> As the happiness of a future life is the great object of religion, we may hear without surprise or scandal that the introduction, or at least the abuse of Christianity, had some influence on the decline and fall of the Roman empire. The clergy successfully preached the doctrines of patience and pusillanimity; the active virtues of society were discouraged; and the last remains of military spirit were buried in the cloister. . . . Faith, zeal, curiosity, and more earthly passions of malice and ambition, kindled the flame of theological discord; the church, and even the state, were distracted by religious factions, whose conflicts were sometimes bloody and always implacable.

Gibbon thought this turn of events instructive for his own day. "It is the duty of a patriot to prefer and promote the exclusive interest and glory of his native country: but a philosopher may be permitted to enlarge his views," and "the same reflections will illustrate the fall of that mighty empire, and explain the probable causes of our actual security." In effect, Gibbon was applying the Lockean notion of the historian's reasoning powers to find and explain what had happened in the past. Reasonable men understood that history offered lessons open to reasonable inquiry.

But what if the lessons did not apply, or were applied entirely differently by different sets of historians? That is just what happened in 1776, the year Gibbon published his history. England had an empire that Gibbon celebrated, but the lessons Gibbon would carry from the decline of the Roman Empire to England's far-flung domain failed to avert and never explained American independence. Instead, American revolutionaries like David Ramsay, Mercy Otis Warren, and John Marshall saw in the history of Anglo-American relations before 1776 another kind of inevitability. As Marshall quoted George Washington, approvingly, "the certain and absolute loss of our liberties" would follow from supine obedience to parliamentary enactments. Only manly resistance, a heroic effort, would save American liberty. And it had. History proved that the new nation was unlike any that had come earlier—a proposition at the same time self-congratulatory and inherently contradictory. If the laws of history were everywhere the same and (according to Locke and Gibbon) open to human inspection, then every nation was subject to them, including the United States. How could it be unique?

At the same time as the American apologists for revolution wrote of the inevitability of independence and the propriety of heroic exertions in its fulfillment, loyalist historians of the American Revolution concluded that the rebellion was the result of a series of blunders on the British side and a conspiracy of unscrupulous rabble-rousers on the American side— hardly a proof that history dictated the victory of the revolutionaries. Peter Oliver, chief justice of the Massachusetts Superior Court of Judicature and loyalist refugee in England, wrote his own account, *Origin and Progress of the American Rebellion,* in 1781. His concluding passages were diametrically opposed to Marshall's. For the "effrontery" of the rebels "in publishing so many false facts to the world" had turned America, and its history, upside down. "A fine country . . . flowing with milk and honey, is turned into a dreary wilderness, enstamped with vestiges of war, famine, and pestilence." The same historical events led to wildly different historical accounts, an outcome hardly likely to reinforce a naive faith in the rationality of history, or historians for that matter.

The greatest treatise on logic in the early nineteenth century, Georg Hegel's *Science of Logic* (1812–16) tackled that problem. Hegel understood that contradictions were inherent in the nature of history. Finite being was inherently contradictory. "Being, the indeterminate immediate, is in fact nothing, and neither more nor less than nothing. . . . What is the truth is neither being nor nothing, but that being—does not pass over but has passed over—into nothing, and nothing into being." It may not seem that this somewhat opaque formulation would be much use for a philosophy of history, but that is exactly where Hegel took it.

Hegel believed that reason was not only a process open to us but a presence in the world. Thus history had its reasons, which the reasoning power of the historian could comprehend. As he wrote in his lectures on the philosophy of history:

> It is the aim of the investigator to gain a view of the entire history of a people or a country, or of the world, in short, what we call Universal History. In this case the working up of the historical material is the main point. The workman approaches his task with his own spirit; a spirit

distinct from that of the element he is to manipulate. Here a very important consideration will be the principles to which the author refers, the bearing and motives of the actions and events which he describes, and those which determine the form of his narrative.

Hegel anticipated Carl Becker—the actual writing of history would be **subjective**, dependent upon the aims and motives of the authors. Thus the patriots and the loyalists would differ, as German history written by German historians would be different from English and French history written by English and French historians.

What then of the universal history, the goal of which was the discovery of Reason? "A history which aspires to traverse long periods of time, or to be universal, must indeed forego the attempt to give individual representations of the past as it actually existed. It must foreshorten its pictures by abstractions; and this includes not merely the omission of events and deeds, but whatever is involved in the fact that Thought is, after all, the most trenchant epitomist." History must thus bow to philosophy, the particular to the abstract, and the lived to the imagined. For history itself had proven to Hegel that "that peoples and governments never have learned anything from history, or acted on principles deduced from it. Each period is involved in such peculiar circumstances, exhibits a condition of things so strictly idiosyncratic, that its conduct must be regulated by considerations connected with itself, and itself alone." On the verge of having a philosophy of history that gave to the historians the power to unite reason and experience, Hegel snatched it away and gave it to the philosophers.

The core concept of a universal history like Hegel's is convergence. All the differences in peoples' and nations' histories wear away over time, as each comes to the same final resting point. What that resting point may be—a liberal democratic, secular state, for example, as Francis Fukuyama optimistically wrote in his *End of History* (1992)—is a matter of speculation, to be sure. But even as Fukuyama posited this convergence, he recognized in it a contradiction. "For democracy to work, citizens need to develop an irrational pride in their own democratic institutions, and must also develop what Tocqueville called the 'art of associating,' which rests on prideful attachment to small communities." Thus the universal common direction of history required a very particularistic process. People had to find satisfaction in the unique and distinctive in order to arrive at the shared goal. Apart from Fukyama's own disclaimer, a skeptical observer might see strong similarities between his highly secular vision and the Judeo-Christian idea of a linear history ending with messianic days of judgment, when all people and nations will be weighed in the same scale according to the same measures.

Just as well, then, that the yearning for a universal history leads to another dead end in the search for a way out of impossibility. If the history of the twentieth century has taught us anything, it is that convergences like the inevitability of progress and the tie between technology and civilization are not based in some Platonic rationality at all. Nor do they conform to the Spirit of Reason Hegel called "the inward guiding soul of the occurrences and actions that occupy a nation's annals." Instead, they can lead to mass destruction, the ultimate irrationality.

But historians, working historians at least, will and should not be deterred by the discovery that reason cannot provide the foundation for a philosophy of history. For as the Chilean poet and essayist Pablo Neruda wrote in his Sonnet Number 17 of the *One Hundred Love Sonnets* (1959), historians love history "as certain dark things are to be loved / in secret, between the shadow and the soul / . . . as the plant that never blooms / but carries in itself the light of hidden flowers." We love the past, "without knowing how, or when, or from where." For us and for a philosophy of history for our times, reason is not a thing, either within us or out there, but a metaphor for the inquiring mind. Reason bids us look. Reason bids us not rest content with what others have concluded. Reason is a goad to search anew.

If reason does not shine through in history, if the study of history cannot supply sufficient reasons to resolve disputes vital to us, perhaps the handmaiden of Western reason, logic, can save history from its own impossibility. Logic is a way of analyzing arguments, a skill that has obvious value for historians, whose work involves argumentation.

A Logic for Historians

The *Oxford Unabridged Dictionary* reports that the word *logic* comes from the Greek word for "inference" and "formal argument." Inference is how we use evidence to make a point or prove a proposition, and **argument** is the construction of a set of connected statements. Logical arguments are a series of statements, **premises**, or **propositions** offered to support a conclusion. Historical analysis works in parallel fashion. We begin with evidence that we form into statements that together (hopefully) support a conclusion. The rules of logic that apply to all argument apply to historical scholarship.

But even the simplest of simple statements can be subject to logical fuzziness. This is because our language, unlike logic, is not a closed system. Take the command in the Florida Omnibus Education Act of 2006: "American history shall be viewed as factual, not as constructed, shall be viewed as knowable, teachable, and testable, and shall be defined as the creation of a new nation based largely on the universal principles stated in the Declaration of Independence." Very straightforward and completely bewildering. For the last part is not a fact but a construction, perhaps teachable and testable, but "knowable" only if true, and its truth is asserted, not proved, in the statement. So the statement that history is factual is controverted by the rest of the command.

Under the nineteenth-century guides for textual analysis, called "hermeneutics," devised to weigh the factual truth of statements in the Bible, to understand the meaning of the sentence in the ordinance we are supposed to figure out the intention of the people who wrote the rule. As the Oregon Supreme Court described this method in *Stranahan v. Meyer* (2000), the goal was "to understand the wording in the light of the way that the wording would have been understood and used by those who created the provision." According to the AHA Council resolution passed on January 7, 2007, however, "the language of the original draft suggests that the authors of the bill have little direct knowledge of history as it has been practiced in the modern world." The council concluded that legislators voting for the act wanted to remove the critical aspects of historical teaching in the secondary schools. Celebrate, memorize, but don't criticize. One should thus read the text of the act in the light of the knowledge that its purpose is to prohibit any effort at critical thinking.

Formal logic (or **propositional logic**) tells us how simple statements can go together into logically correct arguments. In the following list, *p* represents a statement, the premise of an argument, *q* represents another statement, and *r* represents a third statement. Together they form a proposition. *Then* means "implies the truth of."

If p then q, and p is true, then q is also true. If George Washington was elected president in 1788, then he was our first president under the federal Constitution. He was elected in 1788, which means that he was our first president. Note that we have to know that the Constitution was ratified by the time of his election. There are always background facts in history, what historians call "context," that have to be assumed before even a simple logical argument can be true.

If p then q, if q then r, and p is true, then r is true. If John Adams was elected immediately after Washington, then Adams was our second president. If Adams was beaten by Jefferson, then Jefferson was our third president. John Adams, Washington's vice president, was elected president in 1796. Then it follows that Jefferson was our third president.

If either p or q is true, but not both, and p is false, then q is true. Either Adams or Jefferson was our third president. Adams wasn't, which means that Jefferson was.

If "p and q" is true, then each is true. Washington and Adams were both Federalists. It follows that Adams was a Federalist and Washington was a Federalist.

The expressions "p or q" and "p and q" are the same as "q or p" and "q and p," respectively. In mathematics, this is the "commutative law" and is true of addition and multiplication. It does not matter what order a series of facts is given in, though in history we prefer chronological order. There are more rules of increasing complexity, and they can be made to fit together marvelously, for logic is what is called a closed or deductive type of system.

Many times, a formal logical argument is asserted in the midst of some longer piece of historical text—a scholarly historical journal article, a conference paper, a book, or an introduction to a collection. The argument knits together the primary sources—the evidence—into a persuasive whole. It teaches, reports, revises, counsels. The most common of these formal types of logical argument are reasoning from a general statement; reasoning from an incomplete body of evidence; reasoning from an **analogy**; and the **if-then** argument.

Deduction and Inference

Reasoning from a general rule to a particular event covered by that rule is one example of the logical process called deduction. In deduction, if the premise, the rule, is true, then examples of it must also be true. In history, there may be general rules from which particular statements are deduced. But as we have seen, in history all but the most obvious of general rules are open to question. Still, from the premise that all men die, a general rule, we can deduce that Napoleon died, and so did all of his Grand Armée.

Premises less general in their scope can still lead to deductions. For example, it may be proposed as a general rule that religious wars unleash terrible atrocities. If this is true, and a particular war is a religious one, then it will feature atrocities. This certainly seemed to be true in the Crusades by Christian forces to regain control of the Holy Land, and in the wars of religion in Europe during the Protestant Reformation.

One can find counterexamples, however. If we find a religious war that did not result in atrocities, then we may question the truth of the premise. If the English Civil Wars of 1642–47 are counted as religious wars, pitting the Church of England against an array of Puritan dissenters, the relatively few atrocity stories to come out of the fighting (except in Ireland) would suggest that the general rule is wrong. Of course, a historian who wished to defend the general rule would say that the English Civil Wars were really a conflict within the aristocracy, or some such rebuttal, rather than a true religious war.

The problem, then, is to first establish the truth of the general rule and then to prove that the particular fits that general rule. But history does not lend itself to such general rules, save those so general ("All men die," for example) that they are of no use in explaining anything. Nor do historians agree about particular descriptions of events, even when they concede that a general proposition has some **validity**.

If only history were a deductive science. Then a philosophy of history would be easy. John Aubrey, a seventeenth-century English biographer, wrote of the famous political philosopher, historian, and self-taught mathematician Thomas Hobbes, "He was forty years old before he looked on geometry; which happened accidentally. Being in a gentleman's library *Euclid's Elements* lay open, and 'twas the forty-seventh proposition in the first book. He read the proposition. 'By G ,' said he, 'this is impossible!' So he reads the demonstration of it, which referred him back to such a proof; which referred him back to another, which he also read . . . [so] that at last he was demonstratively convinced of that truth. This made him in love with geometry."

Hobbes's most famous work, *Leviathan* (1651), assayed to prove by deduction that absolute obedience to an absolute sovereign was the only logical outcome of any government based on the consent of the governed:

> From this institution of a Commonwealth are derived all the rights and faculties of him, or them, on whom the sovereign power is conferred by the consent of the people assembled. . . . And therefore, they that are subjects to a monarch cannot without his leave cast off monarchy and return to the confusion of a disunited multitude; nor transfer their person from him that beareth it to another man, other assembly of men: for they are

bound, every man to every man, to own and be reputed author of all that he that already is their sovereign shall do and judge fit to be done.

In short, once a people had agreed to a king, there was no going back, no room for dissent, and no way to curb the monarch's powers—a brave thing for Hobbes to write, and braver still to publish, in the midst of a revolution in which the winners had decapitated the reigning king. Hobbes's absolute faith in his powers of deduction gave him courage to argue about history as he did, but he was prudent to publish in Paris and not in England until his safety had been guaranteed.

"Historicism," the full-dress philosophy of history embodying the deductive nature of historical inquiry, offered at the beginning of the twentieth century the promise that history, like every science, could know, explain, and predict. As summarized by Karl Popper, in 1957, historicism was "the theory that society will necessarily change but along a predetermined path that cannot change, through stages predetermined by inexorable necessity."

Popper was a secular Viennese Jew who became one of the twentieth century's foremost philosophers. He had lived through (and survived) history in its rawest form. Yet he clung to the idea that liberal democracy and scientific inquiry came together in the quest for knowledge. It was the effort of solving problems that made us human, not absolute knowledge. So he rejected historicism. "There is no logical path" leading to objective and universal truths. "They can only be reached by intuition, based upon something like an intellectual love of the objects of experience."

Popper's *Poverty of Historicism* (1957) condemned those who thought that a single reason determined all historical change. "Historicism teaches the futility of any attempt to alter impending changes; a peculiar variety of fatalism, a fatalism in regard to the trends of history, as it were." For him, the end of such lockstep rationalism was inherently contradictory. "Since so much is done at a time [in the past], it is impossible to say which particular measure is responsible for any of the results; or rather, if we do attribute a certain result to a certain measure, then we can do so only on the basis of some theoretical knowledge gained previously, and not from the holistic experiment in question." In other words, only by supplying a general rule before we know the particulars can we insist that the particulars fit a general rule.

Though Popper was a philosopher, his demolition of deductive history has a familiar ring to working historians. Maybe this is because Charles Beard's famous 1933 presidential address to the AHA offered a very similar demolition of historicism: "Contemporary thought about history, therefore, repudiates the conception dominant among the schoolmen during the latter part of the nineteenth century and the opening years of the twentieth century—the conception that it is possible to describe the past as it actually was, somewhat as the engineer describes a single machine. The formula itself was a passing phase of thought about the past."

Deducing from history hard and fast rules is a good way to ignore histories' complexities. For example, when the United States Supreme Court heard the lawsuits the NAACP had brought against state-mandated segregation of elementary schools, joined them together, and decided them under the title *Brown v. Board of Education* (1954), it unanimously found that "in the field of public education the doctrine of 'separate but equal' has no place. Separate educational facilities are inherently unequal. Therefore, we hold that the plaintiffs and others similarly situated for whom the actions have been brought are, by reason of the segregation complained of, deprived of the equal protection of the laws guaranteed by the Fourteenth Amendment." How did the Court arrive at that decision? Critics said that the Court was moved by extralegal arguments: for example, evidence that black children thought that white dolls were good and black dolls were bad. But the Court did not rely upon the social psychological findings. Instead, it began with a rule derived from the history of the Fourteenth Amendment's Equal Protection Clause. That clause required that the states establishing public educational facilities provide to all their citizens "the opportunity of an education. Such an opportunity, where the state has undertaken to provide it, is a right which must be made available to all on equal terms."

The problem with this apparently airtight application of deductive reasoning to historical events is that the Court could just as easily have selected a different category of covering law, read the imperative of the category differently, or deduced a different outcome. In the case that *Brown v. Board of Education* implicitly overturned, *Plessy v. Ferguson* (1896), the U.S. Supreme Court found that "the object of the [Fourteenth] Amendment was undoubtedly to enforce the absolute equality of the two races before the law, but in the nature of things it could not have been intended to abolish distinctions based upon color, or to enforce social, as distinguished from political equality, or a commingling of the two races upon terms unsatisfactory to either." A law that limited where a person of one color could sit on a train passing through Louisiana did not so restrain a person of another color and did not disparage, harm, or make any assertion about the first person. "We think the enforced separation of the races, as applied to the internal commerce of the State, neither abridges the privileges or immunities of the colored man, deprives him of his property without due process of law, nor denies him the equal protection of the laws, within the meaning of the Fourteenth Amendment."

What moved the Supreme Court to deduce a different result from the same text was not the logical power of deduction itself but the fact that the times had changed from 1896 to 1954 and that by the latter year most Americans found state-mandated segregation in education no longer acceptable. Put in other terms, the power of deductive reasoning worked as rhetoric, not history.

Cues in writing or speech warn us that a deduction is on the way. When we hear or read words like *thus, hence, therefore, accordingly,* and *it follows that,* a deduction (or the claim of a deduction) will soon follow. Note that my conclusion about this is not a deduction at all but a different kind of logical argument, an inference from experience. Reasoning from a body of evidence to a conclusion about the evidence as a whole is called induction or inference. The bulk of the evidence points to the conclusion but does not guarantee that it is so. Historians rely upon inference to explain events.

Inference can supply motives. General James Longstreet delayed the Confederate charge up Cemetery Ridge on the third day of the Gettysburg battle until midafternoon, by which time Union forces had reinforced the position. We cannot deduce his reasons, but we can infer them from what we know about him and the setting in which he had to make his decision. He was not in favor of the frontal assault, quite rightly recognizing that the massed infantry attack over open ground of approximately a mile against a fortified position would likely lead to slaughter of the attackers. He had seen it firsthand when federal troops assaulted Confederate positions at Fredericksburg. He hoped that the artillery barrage he had ordered would clear the path, and it was not completed until nearly 2:00 p.m. He also hoped, perhaps, that his commanding general, Robert E. Lee, would relent and allow Longstreet to maneuver around the Union position. His hopes were dashed, and the defeat of his army corps marked the end of Confederate offensive operations in the eastern theater of the Civil War. After the war, Longstreet and defenders of Lee engaged in a war of words, each side writing histories blaming the other for the defeat, inferring the worst about the other's motives.

Sometimes historians have to infer the tendency or trend in a set of events from an incomplete set of data. If the data the historian examines are intentionally selected from a larger data set—for example, every tenth case from a census record—the historian is sampling. By sound statistical methods, the **sample** should be either representative (selected so that its characteristics are in direct proportion to the characteristics of the entire data set) or truly random (selected so that it is free of both statistical bias and content bias). The trends or tendencies the historian then identifies in the sample should reflect the trends or tendencies in the whole.

Sampling can be the foundation of sound inferences, but there are many historical examples of **sampling fallacies**, or sampling gone awry. When pollsters infer from very small or skewed samples the distributions of opinions in the whole country, they must have entirely representative samples. The most hilarious blooper in sampling design came in polls predicting the victory of Republican presidential candidate Alf Landon over Democratic incumbent Franklin Delano Roosevelt in 1936. FDR won in a landslide. The pollsters had chosen to send their queries before the election to people who had registered their autos—little realizing that this was not a truly representative sample of Americans during our worst depression.

Sampling can be repeated to increase its reliability, but historians face a special problem of inference that other social scientists do not. The best kind of inferences are based on experiments that can be repeated and whose results are clear to all observers. But historical events and personages are not available for repeated experiments. We can write as many books about the coming of the American Civil War as we wish, but we cannot recreate in the real world the world of 1860. That is why explanations of the coming of the war differ so greatly. The more evidence we have, the greater the detail in our account, but increasing the amount of surviving evidence does not of itself increase the accuracy of our inferences. We know a great deal more about events surrounding President Harry S. Truman's decision to drop the atomic bomb on Japan than we do about Lincoln's decision to resupply Fort Sumter, but there is more controversy about the former decision than the latter.

People who rely on inference from bodies of evidence are sometimes called **empiricists**. Historians are empiricists. We cannot be otherwise. We are always trying to infer motive and causation from the evidence of human action and thought. The sources for the study of the past—surviving documents, for example—do not talk to us. We must make educated inferences from bits and pieces. To do this, we often reason from analogy. Is this event like another we have studied? Is this law case similar to a previous one?

In thinking by analogy, we engage in a logical exercise, comparing an event, person, or object we do not know to another we do know on the basis of certain common characteristics. All analogies are comparisons (though all comparisons are not analogies). An analogy is a good comparison. A weak analogy is not really an analogy at all, though it has the same outward appearance.

Though perilous at times, reasoning by analogy, like all forms of comparison, is a psychological necessity. How are we to proceed when we face a new situation? The answer is that we try to match it with similar events we have already encountered. We think, "This reminds me of . . ." The more we know about both the new and the previous events, in other words, the better we understand them, the more accurately we can draw parallels, and the more successful we will be in dealing with the novelty.

But some analogies, like some generalizations, have a hidden motive and rest, not on the desire to simplify what needs to be done, but on what the person making the analogy is trying to defend. In a 1902 treatise championing European imperialism in Africa, John Hobson argued that "there can be no inherent natural right in a nation to refuse that measure of compulsory education which shall raise it from childhood to manhood in the order of nationalities." The maturation analogy was not only illustrative but offered as a proof that European colonizers' African subjects should not object to their subjection. "The analogy furnished by the education of a child is prima facie a sound one." Children had no voice in their education, just as the ignorant peoples who did not inhabit the "white Western nations" should have no voice in the imposition of civilization upon them, according to Hobson. Knowing when the historical analogy is strong and when it is weak requires more than logic. The commitment to wait until one knows more and can weigh evidence, which in turn helps us know when a comparison is justified, is one of the qualities of a good historian.

If-Then

We are familiar with the if-then form of reasoning from our brief tour through propositional logic—"If p then q." The logical if-then is very common but sometimes sneaks up in disguise. Take "A square has four sides." That sounds like a definition and as a definition is true. But the statement we get in the real world often takes the form, "If this geometric figure is a square, it has four sides." That is the if-then (or "conditional") statement. It can mutate into its **converse**: "If this figure has four sides, it must be a square." Or it can go negative, changing into its **inverse**: "If it is not a square, then it doesn't have four sides." Finally, it can do another flip and become its own **contrapositive**: "If it doesn't have four sides, then it is not a square." (In propositional logic notation, "If p then q" is equivalent to "If not q then not p.")

Note that the converse and the inverse of a true proposition may not be true. A figure may have four sides and not be a square, and a figure that is not a square may still have four sides. That does not stop people—including people who should know better—from arguing from the converse or the inverse. During World War II some historians were convinced that President Franklin D. Roosevelt had deliberately ignored warning signals that Japan was preparing a sneak attack on Pearl Harbor. According to this thesis, he wanted us to enter the war and needed a dramatic way to overcome popular preferences for neutrality. Pearl Harbor's "day in infamy" did lead Congress to agree to a declaration of war, but arguing that without Pearl Harbor we would not have entered the war is arguing from an inverse.

Historians employ a faux version of the if-then all the time. In a book on historical writing entitled *Past Imperfect,* I opined, "If those mistakes [the author made in not revealing his sources] include plagiarism, the author is responsible, because the author's name is on the published work." This is not an if-then logical proof but a stylistic convention I used to assign moral responsibility. Another form of this convention is the definitional if-then: "If the author borrowed words from another writer without quoting or citing, then he was guilty of plagiarizing."

In the if-then, the premise may be true but the conclusion may not follow from it. This common error in logic is called the **non sequitur**. In Laurence Sterne's novel *Tristram Shandy,* whose subtheme is the illogic of life, the non sequitur makes an early appearance. It is "an unhappy association of ideas which have no connection in nature." A contemporary version of this is "They are Middle Eastern terrorists. They must belong to Al Qaeda." The premise and the conclusion may be true, but the conclusion cannot be proved from the premise. There is a missing middle whose truth must be asserted for the truth of the argument to stand, namely "All Middle Eastern terrorists belong to Al Qaeda."

Historical Reasoning's Rivals

The mastery of formal logic, a closed system, has a reassuring feel to it, much like mastery of any mental discipline. But mastery of a closed system does not enclose the world within a system. Similarly, a mastery of logic will help the historian frame arguments, but logic itself cannot establish the truth or falsity of premises. As fine and satisfying as our categorizations of objects and relationships in history through logic may be, logic itself does not touch the past except insofar as we allow the real world to inform our logical reasoning.

Because logical argument can be retained in the service of other masters than history, and because historical memory is malleable, historical reasoning has faced two potent rivals in the Western tradition: **magic** and **dogma**. Both are, in their way, just as rigorous, just as compelling (to their adherents), and just as satisfying as historical thinking, and each has its own logic.

Magic claims the power to reach absolute truths through unquestionable means. Those means—spells, secret knowledge, invocation of unseen forces—are of course rooted in history. The wizard learned them sometime from someone who learned them from another, and so on back into a mystical past. Historians have found that magical thinking is part of every recorded culture, because magic performed a vital cultural function. Once upon a time, not only did magic explain the world's mysteries, but spells cast by wizards and priests made the world go around. A magician could be the most important person in the entire village, healing the sick, helping the crops grow, and making the hunt succeed.

Recent studies reported by Benedict Carey in the *New York Times* on January 24, 2007, revealed that people accept their hundreds of daily "little rituals" as "irrational" but persist in them. Modern science, they know, has dispelled the mystical powers of the magi and replaced them with sound physical, biological, and chemical explanations. Still, people persist in touching, saying, and imagining magical powers. The reason, biologists and psychologists suggest, is that magical thinking is hardwired into our psyches. "The sense of having special powers buoys people in threatening situations and helps soothe everyday fears and ward off mental distress."

Historians know that naming is a kind of magic bringing together our psychological and social needs. While writing a book about fire in America entitled *Seven Fires,* I learned that "we give names to particularly vicious fires, as if by naming we could mitigate the horror they wrecked. . . . We acknowledge the power of the big conflagration by calling it great— the 'Great Chicago Fire' of 1871, for example." What does naming fires do? It turns a frightening natural phenomenon into a manageable human event. For the same reason, the renaming of history as "herstory" in the

1970s satisfied the need of many in and out of the profession to claim for women their rightful place in the annals.

The magic of naming can fold into political history. When Christopher Columbus wanted to claim all of the Antilles islands in the Caribbean for Spain, he started giving the islands Spanish names. That is how they now appear on maps. He called the inhabitants Indios, the Spanish for "inhabitants of the Indies" (he thought he had reached the edge of the East Indian spice islands), another term that endured. The Taíno names, along with the bulk of the Taíno peoples, disappeared. History records the Spanish Empire, the Spanish Main, and New Spain. Mexico, the name that the Mexica peoples gave to their land, was adopted by the Spanish conquistadors and retained. So, too, Hernán Cortés arranged for his officers to marry into the Aztec elite, perpetuating Spanish rule through the renaming of the Aztec princesses with Spanish names.

The second system of thought that poses a challenge to history's logic with its own logic is dogma. The word comes from the Greek for an opinion or belief so strongly held as to admit no dissent. Dogma is a kind of reasoning whose assertions take form within the closed box of orthodoxy. Advocates of particular dogmatic belief systems liberally incorporate readings of history. Certain canonical works associated with dogmatic faiths are in fact part history, part cosmology, part ritual guide. The Bible is one, historians have argued: written in historical time, by actual historical actors, and incorporating previous historical incidents. But the Bible can be interpreted wholly outside historical time and place, as a closed system of precepts and applications.

The refusal to countenance dissent or to admit error is **dogmatism**, and enlightened liberal thought condemns dogmatism. **Zealotry**, from which we derive the word *zealous*, is extreme dogmatism in action. The original **zealots** were a sect of ultraorthodox Jews who refused to accept Roman presence in Israel, hated other Jews who were not as orthodox as they, and began a rebellion in the first century against the Roman rulers of Judea. When they were trapped on the mountaintop fortress of Masada, they killed themselves, women and children included, rather than surrender.

Dogma often garbs itself in moral clothing. That is, its logic applies to actual moral situations. Abolitionists before the Civil War denounced slavery as an unconditional moral evil. In turn, southern intellectuals denounced the abolitionists as zealots and antislavery as a species of dogmatism. Both sides claimed reason as their ally as they came to regard one another as mortal enemies. The Civil War resolved the issue when dueling logical poses did not.

The disputants in the debate over slavery relied upon fundamentally different premises. For the abolitionists, denial of basic human rights, including the fruits of one's labor, was wrong. That was not a logical position per se but one rooted in a set of values. Nor was their stance wholly consistent, for some abolitionists opposed giving freed slaves other basic human rights like the right to choose marriage partners of different races, the right to vote, and the right to hold office. For the defenders of slavery, all human rights were relative to one's "state in society," and slaves were not in a state of society. Whether by a biological inferiority they could not change or by social degradation they would not change, slaves were not entitled to basic human rights. This was a stance based not on logic but on the social and psychological facts of the "peculiar institution" as white southerners read it.

History reveals that dogma and dogmatism have a staying power that even their critics must confess. The comforts of being a true believer derive not from the logic of the beliefs but from their psychological benefits. Dogmatic belief reduces cognitive dissonance, the mental unease introduced when we encounter sense impressions, information, and ideas that do not fit our existing cognitive framework. According to social psychologist Leon Festinger, "The presence of dissonance gives rise to pressures to reduce or eliminate the dissonance."

Festinger introduced this term to students of cognitive psychology in 1957, in the course of one of the most fascinating experiments in that field. He had asked, among other questions, how an antebellum millenarian sect in upstate New York handled the fact that the world did not end when they had predicted its end. Did they disband? Cast off their leaders? Denounce their beliefs? None of these—they simply returned to their calculations and found an error—the world was supposed to end later in that year. Only when repeated predictions failed did they begin to question their basic assumptions. Festinger's *Theory of Cognitive Dissonance* was an instant classic.

A philosophy of history for modern times must skirt the many shoals of magical or wishful thinking and the whirlpools of dogma. They are the counterfeit of logical reasoning and the antithesis of fact gathering. That is not as easy as it sounds. Certain organizations and self-styled "institutes" embedding themselves within the campus setting (though often separate from the college) or portraying themselves as independent minded think tanks employ historians as resident fellows or underwrite historical projects for partisan ends. A typical such institute promoted its purposes as the study of "freedom, democracy, and capitalism," and others hold conferences on "the principles of America's founding." In a March 16, 2007, interview with a *Chronicle of Higher Education* reporter, Robert P. Kraynak, the director of the Center for Freedom and Western Civilization at Colgate University, explained its aims: "There's this general problem of lack of ideological balance on campus. You have a debate about the war in Iraq, and everyone is against it, and no one on the faculty will take the pro-war position. How can you educate students if they've never talked to a Christian evangelical, someone in the military, someone who's against abortion? All these people are completely missing from college faculty."

The notion, I suppose, is that good history is the product of an adversarial debate, something like the two sides in a lawsuit, and thus the two sides must both be in court to present their case. What if no historian can be found to present one of the sides? Logically, one might conclude that such a position had no scholarly credibility—but not if one was a partisan of that point of view. Then magical or dogmatic readings of current events and slanted or highly selective application of historical anecdotes to support particular policies supplant reasoned historical discourse.

History's impossibility is not relieved by associating history with reason or logic, but historians cannot function without reason and logic. To be able to argue from inference, selecting appropriate pieces of evidence, may not itself bridge the impossible gulf between present and past, but it provides a firm approach abutment (to continue the bridge analogy), the foundation on which the initial span of the bridge to the past is attached to the shore. We need to assume that reasoned logic will provide that first stage of the bridge, or we cannot begin to imagine the entire span.

2

What's Wrong with This Argument?

Historical problems never present themselves as neat logical
exercises. Almost every historical puzzle has to be solved in part,
and often wholly, by methods peculiar to itself. In determining
antecedence and consequence, most historians proceed by plain
common sense, not by the rules of logic.

—Allan Nevins (1938)

If a commitment to reason and a knowledge of logical rules
do no more than begin constructing the span from present to past, they
still reassure us that we can make sense of what has survived from the
past. In 1938 Allan Nevins recommended that we trust our common sense
to make our historical arguments, but that common sense is prey to common logical mistakes.

I am not the first to see that logical fallacies and history-as-argument
are related. In 1970, historian David Hackett Fischer published *Historians'
Fallacies*. It was a relentless and somewhat humorless exposé of the illogical arguments famous historians made. Fischer worried that "the work of
too many professional historians is diminished by an antirational obses-
sion—by an intense prejudice against method, logic, and science. . . . In
fact historians . . . go blundering about their business without a sufficient
sense of purpose or procedure."

Fischer regarded all fallacies as "wrong turnings." They misled; they
misrepresented; they were wrong. Avoiding them, his challenge to us,
would make historical scholarship—and the lessons of history—more
trustworthy. But Fischer's remarkable catalog of slips and slides into fallacy by the foremost historians—he even indicted "a great and gifted
historian" named Allan Nevins in the section on "fallacies of irrelevant
proof"—never explained why such fine scholars were guilty of such

elementary mistakes. Turning Fischer's argument on its back, one can ask: If elite members of the profession were guilty of a variety of fallacies, might there be some legitimate or, in the alternative, necessary role for certain types of fallacies in historical narration and analysis?

Historians concede the role that fallacious thinking has played in the past. According to diplomatic historian Ernest May, a weak analogy to appeasement at Munich before World War II led Harry S. Truman to misunderstand the civil war dimension of the Korean conflict and make its ultimate resolution considerably harder. As he told Congress on July 19, 1950, "The fateful events of the 1930s, when aggression unopposed bred more aggression and eventually war, were fresh in our minds." Another fallacy, that of assuming that all conflicts involving communist forces must be part of the Cold War, a sweeping generalization that turned a nationalistic war into one of communist aggression, led Presidents John F. Kennedy and Lyndon B. Johnson to broaden American commitment to a corrupt and unpopular administration in South Vietnam. Johnson reported to Congress on August 5, 1964, "This is not just a jungle war, but a struggle for freedom on every front of human activity. Our military and economic assistance to South Vietnam and Laos in particular has the purpose of helping these countries to repel aggression and strengthen their independence."

Can a fallacy ever be right? Our rationalist instinct tells us no, but fallacies may be instructive, particularly when they are honest attempts to summarize masses of information. The boundary between the necessary compression of thinking and the fallacy is not a high wall but a semipermeable membrane. Some arguments come close to fallacy but turn out to be helpful and even necessary aids to clear thinking. Historians cannot do without these **near-fallacies**.

Near-Fallacies

We need to make a distinction between **informal logical fallacies**, or what I have called near-fallacies, and **formal logical fallacies**. The former are types of argument that straddle the line between acceptable and unacceptable in historical writing. The near-fallacies include the **hasty generalization**, **stereotyping**, the **argument from authority**, the **all-or-nothing fallacy**, arguments based on weak or mistaken analogies, the **sweeping generalization**, and **begging the question**.

We begin with the hasty generalization. At what point in time does the hasty generalization become the educated surmise? Were historians to wait until all the evidence was in before making a generalization, they would never write a word. As Edward Hallett Carr wrote in his *What Is History?* historians who want to publish anything have to start writing before they have finished the research. "For myself," he confided, "as soon as I have got going on a few of what I take to be the capital sources, the itch becomes too strong and I begin to write." All the evidence will never be in because all the evidence can never be in. Too much is lost forever, and even that small portion that has survived is flawed. I have known academic historians who will not write a word until all the evidence is in. The result: they find it almost impossible to finish and submit a piece of research. Failing to publish, they perish.

Professional historians have developed methods to improve upon the largely unsupported surmise, but if they want to publish in their lifetimes, they have to make some generalizations that are, simply put, hasty. We pride ourselves on the thoroughness of our research. But the fact is that we jump to conclusions all the time. Sometimes they are inadequate, while on other occasions they are acceptable. Two examples will demonstrate what I mean. In the first, famous historian Daniel Boorstin was too hasty. In his Bancroft Prize–winning *The Americans: The National Experience* (1965), slaves made a fleeting appearance as helpless victims. Boorstin argued that slavery "tended to destroy [the slave's] African culture and to denude him of his traditions as he was deposited in the new world." Worse, in America "the African immigrant was a man without a family. . . . Among the dehumanizing effects of slavery, none were deeper than the obstruction and diversion of maternal affection." Boorstin had generalized too hastily, for slaves did bring African ways to America, and slaves did reconstitute families here, though often the law did not recognize them. These hasty generalizations do not pass muster.

The second example comes from a Pulitzer Prize–winning history of the United States from 1929 to 1945. David M. Kennedy's *Freedom from Fear* (1999) concludes its chapter on the New Deal: "In the last analysis, Franklin Roosevelt faithfully discharged his duties. . . . He did mend the evils of the Depression by reasoned experiment within the framework of the existing social system. He did prevent a naked confrontation between orthodoxy and revolution." One might dissent that unemployment and underemployment, a depressed standard of living, particularly in the rural South, the lack of full equality for people of color, and the yawning gap in wealth and power between the haves and the have-nots were largely untouched by the New Deal, and some historians have argued this. But in the main, Kennedy's apparently hasty generalization is tenable.

If the hasty generalization runs risks, **stereotypical thinking** is a daredevil act. Knee-jerk categorization of others different from ourselves, in which we see not an individual but a hasty stereotype of a poorly defined and sketchily perceived group, leaves us prey to our own prejudices. While some stereotypes are defensible shortcuts, too often we conclude that "they" are inferior, dangerous, and alien. A comment by U.S. Supreme Court Justice Hugo Black after World War II that during the war "people were rightly fearful of the Japanese. . . . They all look alike to a person not a Jap" reflected his racial attitude. Sharing this view of the potential disloyalty of every Japanese American who lived on the West Coast, Congress and President Franklin D. Roosevelt ordered removal of patriotic Japanese Americans from the West Coast, "relocating" them to "internment camps." Had the authorities looked more carefully at the nearly one hundred years of Japanese American experience, they would have found a deeply patriotic people.

Historians fall into this trap. The classic example is the famous nineteenth-century American historian Francis Parkman's caricature of the Indians. In *The Jesuits in North America* (1867), Parkman married a sweeping generalization to pure stereotype, describing "that well known self control, which, originating in a form of pride, covered the savage nature of the man with a veil, opaque, though thin. . . . Though vain, arrogant, boastful, and vindictive, the Indian bore abuse and sarcasm with an astonishing patience." All Indians were the same, not changed by the arrival of the Europeans, a culture frozen in time. This is an unfair stereotype.

Parkman's stereotype had its roots in class and cultural prejudices. As another Boston Brahmin of the late nineteenth century, Henry Cabot Lodge, put it in an 1896 speech, "The men of each race possess an indestructible stock of ideas, traditions, sentiments, modes of thought, an unconscious inheritance from their ancestors, upon which argument has no effect." Behind every sharply etched stereotype is a far less distinct mosaic of assumptions about people and their ways. Historians today shiver at Parkman's easy lumping of all Indians into the sneaky savage category and Lodge's barely concealed ethnocentrism, but truth to tell, we have our own cognitive maps formed by experience, traditions, and aspirations that influence how we characterize others.

Our stereotyping can be pretty sophisticated. In his defense of the spread of Western capitalism, historian David Landes took a shot at the "losers" in the race for wealth by celebrating the skills of the winners: "From working with modest if ingenious tools and techniques, we [the Western masters of the universe] have become masters of great machines and invisible forces. Putting aside magic and superstition, we have passed from tinkering and intelligent observation to a huge and growing corpus of scientific knowledge that generates a continuing flow of useful applications." Modern individuals less committed to the idols of science and material improvement were fooling themselves. "Those who secede from the rich material world to find spiritual renewal in nature may leave their watches behind, but . . . they usually know enough to get medical help when they need it." In a footnote, Landes spoke directly to the reader: "I am reminded that superstition and magic are not dead, and some would argue that religious faith is part of this package. No doubt, because weak mortals that we are, we look for comfort where it is to be found"—a very sophisticated stereotyping of all those mortals who did not see the world through Landes's glasses.

Malicious stereotyping is pretty easy to spot and condemn in a work of history today, if not so easily in years past. Not so why and when (or if) an argument from authority is false. The argument from authority has two prongs, which, unlike the ends of a pitchfork, overlap one another. The first is that I am right because I am an authority on the subject. The second is that I am right because I have authority over the subject. Take, for example, the argument from authority in academia. Despite what any colleges and universities in the United States today may say about faculty self-government, authority in schools is top down. The regents tell the president what to do; the president tells the deans; they tell the department heads or chairs. Now, on any given subject, a member of the faculty may reply that he or she should be listened to and followed because of being an authority on the subject. That is when the two prongs cross. Another example: when faculty members vote to promote and tenure a colleague, the full professors vote on the associate professors, and both full and associate vote on the assistant professors. Authority and rank coincide. But anyone who is familiar with departmental meetings or faculty senate sessions knows that authority comes from expertise, not formal rank. A third example: scholars looking for a publisher for a manuscript know that there is a hierarchy of presses. Publish with one of the top university presses, and the book, along with its author, gains authority. Publish with a lower-ranked press, and the book has less authority. The author suffers accordingly.

For those outside academe (and some inside as well), authority may rest upon rankings of institutions. *U.S. News and World Report*, the *Chronicle of Higher Education*, and other publications rank-order schools. Faculty members within the top-tier schools speak with more authority than faculty members in the lower-ranking schools, or at least the media prefer to quote faculty from the top schools. Young scholars looking for jobs report that the degree-granting institution is the most important initial advantage—or disadvantage—that a job applicant has when seeking interviews. Rankings of the top graduate training programs appear every year in *U.S. News and World Report*, a source of anxiety to all and agony to those graduate programs that slip in the rankings. In protest, a loose alliance of top colleges and universities has called for an embargo on information to the magazine.

Expertise and official standing together make an argument from authority credible. But Americans are sometimes reluctant to concede the authority of experts when it comes to history. If everyman is his own historian, and the measure of history is memory, then the dentist and the deliveryman have as much to say about history as the professional historian. In the controversy over the National History Standards for public schools, both varieties of argument from authority played a critical role. In 1988, the National Endowment for the Humanities funded an institute at the University of California, Los Angeles to write model curricula for teaching history in school from fifth to twelfth grades. The institute assembled a blue-ribbon panel of expert teachers and scholars to prepare National History Standards. Led by historian Gary Nash, they made, in effect, an argument from authority: we are the experts, and we know what is the most accurate and useful version of history for students.

Nash explained what he thought the direction of the standards should be: "The view that history is with the people is not only more fitting for a democratic society, in which it is assumed that an active citizenry is essential to the maintenance of liberty, it is more accurate." The AHA chipped in as well, arguing that standards for world history had to abandon the Europe-centered model and give equal time to the other culture centers of the world. When, some six years and lots of committee meetings, drafts, revisions, and reviews later, the National Center for History in the Schools published the standards and model lesson plans, the sky fell on them.

It was the heyday of the "culture wars," when liberals and conservatives were hacking away at one another over who should be teaching what in our schools and colleges. Instead of celebrating what great men had achieved, the National History Standards consistently took a critical-thinking view of America's past, a mainstay of the "new history" of the 1960s and 1970s and the view that many leading historians share. On January 18, 1995, the U.S. Senate voted 99 to 1 that the standards were unacceptable because, in part, the senators decided that the expertise of the panelists had steered them wrong. As Republican Senator Slade Gorton of Washington put it, "If the department of Education, the National Endowment for the Humanities, or any other federal agency provides funds for the development of the standards . . . the recipient of such funds should have a decent respect for the contributions of western civilization, and United States history, ideas, and institutions, to the increase of freedom and prosperity around the world." Outside Congress, the assault on the Standards and the expertise of their authors was even ruder. Popular radio commentator and political conservative Rush Limbaugh, for example, boasted that he was no expert and that for this very reason he knew more than all the professors put together. Any bus driver or dentist could have done better than they, he opined.

Ironically, some of the severest media critics of the National History Standards see history as its own authority. "History tells us," "history teaches," "the lesson of history is," these self-appointed pundits report, and only the foolish or willfully obstinate refuse to listen. Charitably, one may term this version of the argument from authority a naive form of historical objectivism, but too often claims of this sort are rooted in a political objective. For example, Newt Gingrich plugged his novel about Pearl Harbor by saying, "As a former history teacher, I prepare for the future by studying the past. So we made sure that we conveyed through the stories told in *Pearl Harbor* some important lessons for America today." That lesson was political: "The most enduring fact about that fateful morning in Hawaii in 1941 is something that . . . seems to exist—untaught and untutored—in the American spirit. There are many tales of heroism that emerged that morning and no tales of cowardice." The lesson was still good: "Come to think of it, we witnessed the exact same thing on 9/11." Gingrich evoked Lodge's "indestructible stock of ideas," the innate spirit of a people, peculiar to it, able to surmount any challenge. History itself gave Gingrich the authority to celebrate American heroism.

The critics of the proposed National History Standards roused public opinion by accusing the experts of making a fallacious argument from authority. But the history of the historical profession shows the opposite development—the shift from talented amateurs in the nineteenth century to credentialed professionals in our time. Most history is now written by Ph.D.s trained at the very best universities. The training is rigorous, and not everyone makes it through. Even the best of the lot find getting a university or college job difficult, so competitive is the job market. Then, having found a slot, the assistant professors have to run the gauntlet of tenure review. Outside referees read the candidates' publications. Internal committees weigh the candidates' scholarly achievements. At most colleges and universities, the candidate needs to publish a book with a reputable press, get good reviews, and have a major new project under way to gain tenure. It is all very frightening, but when these first hurdles are surmounted, the young historian has begun to learn the craft. Expertise, from beginning to end, makes all the difference.

Another version of arguments based on expertise is the **appeal to authority**. The Latin for this is *argument ad verecundiam*. The problem for historians is the same as the problem for everyman. Authorities do not always agree. The U.S. Supreme Court is one such authority. After an agonized two years of oral argument, conference meetings, drafts and revisions, the Court issued *Roe v. Wade* (1973). Justice Harry Blackmun wrote for himself and six of his brethren that women had a due process right "of privacy" and that this included the termination of a pregnancy in its early stages. Justice William O. Douglas joined in the Blackmun opinion and added, in a concurrence, "Freedom of choice in the basic decisions of one's life respecting marriage, divorce, procreation, conception, and the education and upbringing of children" was protected by the ultimate source of authority in America, the Constitution. "A woman is free to make the basic decision whether to bear an unwanted child." Every state that had a law making abortion a crime henceforth had to junk those laws.

But Justices Byron White and William Rehnquist strongly dissented. Justice Rehnquist explained why he demurred: "I have difficulty in concluding, as the Court does, that the right of 'privacy' is involved in this case. Texas, by the statute here challenged, bars the performance of a medical abortion by a licensed physician on a plaintiff such as Roe. A transaction resulting in an operation such as this is not 'private' in the ordinary usage of that word." Justice White's comments demonstrated a more personal antipathy to abortion. "At the heart of the controversy in these cases are those recurring pregnancies that pose no danger whatsoever to the life or health of the mother but are, nevertheless, unwanted for any one or more of a variety of reasons—convenience, family planning, economics, dislike of children, the embarrassment of illegitimacy, etc. The common claim before us is that for any one of such reasons, or for no reason at all, and without asserting or claiming any threat to life or health, any woman is entitled to an abortion at her request if she is able to find a medical advisor willing to undertake the procedure."

When the decision was announced, the National Conference of Catholic Bishops issued a formal statement that "there can be no moral acceptance of the recent U.S. Supreme Court decision which professes to legalize abortion. . . . Catholics must oppose abortion as an immoral act." Catholics were to follow, not the authority of the Court, but a higher authority, as interpreted by the Church fathers. It was authority against authority, and the dispute continues because the authorities cannot agree.

One can find less passionate examples in every "letters to the editor" section of learned historical journals. A scholar whose book has received an unflattering review will argue that he knows a lot more than the reviewer and should have been treated more respectfully. "Should not a responsible reviewer provide readers with an overview of the book's contents?" is a refrain of angry letters to book review editors. The outraged author or righteous reviewer might also decry his opponent's lack of experience or absence of qualifications. "A fiercely combative yet befuddled individual," one reviewer called an author, who replied that his adversary had "stigmatized" him and failed to corroborate the attack.

Web sites of some scholars are dedicated to authoritarian put-downs of opponents. On one of these, a senior law professor who writes history condemns the "outright lies that [Professor X] has told or written." Professor X, an assistant professor of political science who also writes history, has replied in kind: "[Professor Y] has spearheaded a multipronged campaign of slander and vilification" against Professor X. Professor's Y's campaign included letters to the publisher of Professor X's book and to the governor of the state in which the publisher does business, demanding changes in the book, and then, a year later, letters to the assistant professor's university denouncing him and calling for his colleagues to deny him tenure. Although it hotly denied that the attacker's letters had any influence on its decision, the university terminated the younger man's employment. The battle goes on in the adversaries' respective Web sites. What makes these accusations and replies rise above the level of schoolyard finger-pointing is that both professors claim to be experts in their common subject matter: the history of the state of Israel. In this contest of authority versus authority, they have even written books to reply explicitly to one another.

In another version of this near-fallacy, two or more individuals are having a dispute about whether some statement is true, so they appeal to authority to settle it. In the scholarly seminar, arguments about other scholars' works often take a similar form, with individuals praising or damning research on the basis of the appeal to the authority of the authors. Two of these history seminars, both at leading universities, became infamous for the vehemence of the verbal combat. In one, the dispute overlay a political divide between two leading scholars of nineteenth-century American history. In the other, the convener of the seminar, an English expert on seventeenth-century England, brought the English academic style of sharp criticism and one-upmanship to the seminar. But appeal to authority is only a near-fallacy. In any particular case, if the authority is good, the argument from authority should have weight, though an authority can be wrong.

In the **all-or-nothing (either-or) fallacy**, everything is black or white, good or bad, true or false. The all-or-nothing fallacy asserts that if one premise is not true, then its opposite must be so. In formal logical notation, it is "either p is true or q is true. P is not true, therefore q must be true." But in the real world, both p and q may be false, or both may be true, or p may have no relation to q at all. The complexities of history do not readily lend themselves to such exacting judgments.

When historians agreed to prepare a "friend of the court" brief in *Webster v. Reproductive Health Services* (1989) in support of the right of women to end a pregnancy, the historians thought that a nuanced account of abortion law in our past would help resolve the dispute. The lawyers told the lead author of the brief that complexity was not wanted. Instead, the brief should provide clear and one-sided evidence that women in nineteenth-century America had the right to end pregnancies. The resulting brief did not mute the controversy, and the confrontation between prochoice and prolife forces over the right to an abortion goes on. If such a black-and-white opposition on this issue is real enough today, it is only because the advocates on both sides bring to the subject a set of rigid moral categories. Historians should be wary of such global appositions, and so should a philosophy of history.

There is a psychological dimension to the all-or-nothing fallacy that nevertheless appeals to historians in untoward ways. This is particularly true of biographers. Robert Caro's biography of city planner Robert Moses is a scorching portrait of a megalomaniac. The closing passages of *The Power Broker: Robert Moses and the Fall of New York* (1974) are hard to forget. "Once he had battalions to boss and on which to demonstrate his administrative ability; now he had only his secretaries and his chauffeur, so he did so on them. He was harsh and abrupt and arrogant in talking to them, and about them. . . . His name had faded from the headlines in New York City long before. . . . He was forgotten—to live out his years in bitterness and rage. . . . In private, his conversation dwelt more and more on a single theme—the ingratitude of the public toward great men. . . . Why weren't they grateful."

Caro's *Moses* was relentlessly negative. But Caro is the exception. Most biographers fall in love with their subjects. David McCullough has written Pulitzer Prize–winning biographies of Harry S. Truman and John Adams, and both men shine in his estimation. Of Adams, he told an interviewer, "To find someone who's held our highest political office and did what he thinks is right, irrespective of what it might mean to his political hide—to me, [that is] an appealing subject. . . . The privation, the sheer breadth of his travels and the risks he took to his life and comforts. The fact that this fellow never failed to answer the call to serve, no matter his own private interests or the wherewithal of the security of his family."

All-or-nothing thinking was behind some of the worst mistakes our leaders have made in our history. General Philip Sheridan's aside that the only good Indians he knew were dead, for example, reflected the systematic dispossession of the native peoples, even those who were allies, were friendly, or had accepted a European way of life. Signs saying that "No Irish Need Apply" for jobs in pre–Civil War America not only ostracized Irish immigrants but pitted neighbor against neighbor and community against community. "You are either a patriot or a Communist sympathizer," the mantra of the cold warriors during the Red Scare of the 1950s, cost many good people their careers and their reputations.

All-or-nothing judgments lean on another near-fallacy for support. This is the fallacy of the sweeping generalization, or, in Latin, *dicto simpliciter.* In his classic, sweeping history entitled *Modern Times* (1983), Paul Johnson opens his chapter "The Collectivist Seventies" with a sweeping generalization: "Economic disorder precedes the military disorder of war." One cannot argue with this, for wars do follow period of economic disarray. They also follow periods of economic expansion (for example, the economic expansion of Europe led directly to the colonial wars in the seventeenth and eighteenth centuries). It also happens that economic distress may not lead to war, for no war followed the economic doldrums of the 1980s in America. In the late David Halberstam's wonderfully evocative *The Fifties* (1993), a chapter on suburbanization begins, "As more and more people were moving to the suburbs, a need was created for new places and ways in which to shop—and also for new things to buy to fill these thousands of new houses. . . . Shopping and buying were to become major American pastimes." True, but the sweeping generalization hides the fact that from the moment European traders brought their iron pots and glass beads to America, shopping and trading became American pastimes. The suburban mall is the successor to the village crossroads market, and the adman is the descendant of the backwoods peddler. In short, there is nothing really new in the 1950s about consumerism. A sweeping generalization has misled us.

But before we decide not to trust any book that tackles a big topic (and must therefore have some sweeping generalizations) we need to understand how necessary they are, and how popular. If a sweeping generalization tends to ignore particular context, including precedents, in its effort to tie together lots of bits and pieces, it can also bring together the many threads of a story into a compelling whole. As Bernard Bailyn, one of America's foremost historians, told the yearly conference of the AHA in 1981: "The great proliferation of historical writing has served not to illuminate the central themes of Western history but to obscure them. . . . To write such essential narratives—dominated by a sense of movement through time, incorporating the technical studies, and devoted to showing how the present world was shaped by its emergence from a very different past and hence concentrated on critical transitions from the past toward the present— seems to me to be the great challenge of modern historical scholarship."

In a less grand way we often rely on **rules of thumb (reasoning by default)** to reach decisions. A rule of thumb is not a proof. In fact, it is only an estimated measurement of length that carpenters used. Because some of us may have big thumbs and others small thumbs, the length of our thumb may be an inaccurate measurement. So may any conclusion based on approximations and estimates. But, as in the hasty generalization, we need rules of thumb. In academia we call them standards, and sometimes, as when grading an essay exam, it is hard to do more than generalize about them. When Justice Potter Stewart of the United States Supreme Court had to define pornography in *Jacobellis v. Ohio* (1964), he could not give a rule but offered a rule of thumb: "I know it when I see it." Using this rule of thumb, the High Court found that the French film *The Lovers* was not obscene.

Just as the historian needs to generalize, the historian needs rules of thumb. The danger lies not in the rule of thumb itself but in how we form the rule of thumb. "Trust no one over thirty" was one rule of thumb for counterculture gurus in the 1960s. The rule became moot when its promulgators passed the age of no return. Good rules of thumb are not made in haste or anger. All of the September 11, 2001, terrorists were Arabs who had spent some time in the United States. Many Americans leaped to the conclusion that all Arabs in America were potential terrorists. There may have been other "sleeper" cells of terrorists in the Arab American community, and some Arab Americans may have given aid to or sympathized with the terrorists, but that cannot logically lead to suspicion of all Arab Americans, any more than the fact that the Oklahoma City bomber Timothy McVeigh and his allies in the militia movement were all Anglos means that all Anglos are members of domestic terror organizations.

Good historical rules of thumb derive from the historian's mastery of the material. For example, when historian Willson H. Coates had to decide how many men had participated in a seventeenth-century English riot, he accepted the account with the smallest number. His rule of thumb was that on such occasions accounts tend to be hysterical or to exaggerate. This rule of thumb can be applied to other violent events—for example, to estimate the number of dead in a battle.

Take, for example, the terrible losses of the Army of the Potomac at the battle of Cold Harbor, on June 3, 1864. General U. S. Grant later reported, "On the 3d of June we again assaulted the enemy's works in the hope of driving him from his position. In this attempt our loss was heavy, while that of the enemy, I have reason to believe, was comparatively light. It was the only general attack made from the Rapidan to the James which did not inflict upon the enemy losses to compensate for our own losses. I would not be understood as saying that all previous attacks resulted in victories to our arms, or accomplished as much as I had hoped from them, but they inflicted upon the enemy severe losses, which tended in the end to the complete overthrow of the rebellion."

Grant did not report an exact number of dead, wounded, and missing. How many were they? The leading historian of the Civil War, James McPherson, repeated the number customarily given: "Grant and Meade attacked on June 3. In a series of frontal assaults, the Federals were slaughtered, sustaining approximately 7,000 casualties compared to Confederate losses of 1,500. Grant always regretted ordering the assault at Cold Harbor." Gordon Rhea's *Cold Harbor* (2002) lowers that estimate to about three to four thousand men dead, wounded, or missing on June 3 at Cold Harbor and perhaps another two thousand lost in battle nearby. Because of conditions during the battle, the exact number can never be known. Which estimate is likely to be more accurate? Using Coates's rule of thumb, one would select the most conservative estimate, for men counted as dead or missing would be returning to their units for many days after the battle.

But rules of thumb, and estimates based on them, can be badly misleading if the estimator has a bias or a vested interest in the outcome. In one of the most notorious misuses of a rule of thumb, Vietnam War commander General William C. Westmoreland ordered his subordinates to report "body counts" of dead Vietcong and North Vietnamese after every encounter. Victory in battle came to be measured by the body count. But because the Vietnamese enemy removed their dead and wounded from the field, such counts had to be estimates. Because field commanders who wanted to please their boss, and a boss who wanted to show Americans at home that the war was winnable, had an ulterior motive in inflating the count, their rule of thumb seemed to many critics of the war to be evidence of the untrustworthiness of the military.

In her obituary for Westmoreland, *Washington Post* reporter Patricia Sullivan recalled the upshot of the controversy: "In 1982, enraged by a CBS news documentary 'The Uncounted Enemy: A Vietnam Deception,' he filed a $120 million libel lawsuit. The 90-minute program charged that Westmoreland directed a 'conspiracy' to 'suppress and alter critical intelligence on the enemy' by understating enemy strength in 1967 and 1968 in order to deceive Americans into believing the war was being won." Westmoreland and CBS settled the suit, and the network admitted that there had been some errors in its reporting. But *body count* has become a synonym for a bad rule of thumb.

Analogies are a form of comparisons, and historians must make comparisons. Without comparisons, history would be mindless recitation of names, dates, and places. The analogy enables the historian to compare and contrast. The problem historians face in avoiding weak analogies is not reasoning from analogy itself but ignoring relevant facts. Tipoffs to weak analogies include excessive language (watch for the superlatives *best, worst, most,* and *least*), leaps of time and space, and strange bedfellows (a perfectly normal person compared unfavorably to Hitler, Stalin, Attila the Hun, or the Antichrist).

Still, the weak analogy can make a strong impression. Consider antigay activist Paul Cameron's striking analogy: "Homosexuality is an infectious appetite with personal and social consequences. It is like a dog that gets a taste for blood after killing its first victim and desires to get more victims thereafter with a ravenous hunger." This analogy is unfair to both homosexuals and dogs. Percentagewise, fewer gays and lesbians are sexual predators than heterosexuals in the same age group. Most domesticated dogs do not get a taste for blood from their first kill, nor do they seek out victims of any kind. Wild dogs have such appetites from birth.

The key words in the analogy are *is to* and *as.* Old versions of the Scholastic Aptitude Test (now called by its initials the SAT) featured analogies with the *is to* represented by a colon and the *as* by a double colon: for example, "man : skin :: beaver: pelt." Some historians reject the very idea of such analogies in history, for no two events are alike. History does not repeat itself. Bloggers love to point out that public figures are sometimes inept or, worse, deceitful in their use of weak or preposterous historical analogies. Nevertheless, useful historical analogy does not require exact duplication. It simply seeks and identifies resemblances.

Some events and movements in history do resemble one another enough to make comparison useful. Some do not. The historian's job is to distinguish one from the other. Thomas Paine and other radicals compared the French and the American revolutions. The comparisons were faulty—there were too many variations between the two to make any but the most superficial comparison. True, there was a "general revolutionary disturbance," as the late R. R. Palmer noted of the final thirty years of the eighteenth century, and "certain old ideas, or old words and phrases, took on a new application and a wider and more urgent meaning."

The industrial revolution came to the United States a half-century after it had begun to profoundly change capital and labor in Great Britain. But certain analogies between the two events exist, and by engaging in them one can tease out connections hard to see otherwise. For example, in both a kind of "moral economy" emerged, in which craftsmen and artisans left behind in status and influence by the introduction of factory labor protested against injustices of the owning classes. These protests informed the founding of the first labor organizations. Without the analogy between England and America, deepening our understanding of the moral underpinnings of the labor movement, it is hard to explain why the Knights of Labor and other late nineteenth-century American unions saw the working world in such moralistic terms.

Not so useful is **circular reasoning**, also known as begging the question. In this fallacy, one either states as proven what one is trying to prove or assumes the truth of the conclusion before proving it. If one is simply trying to define a term or idea, then one cannot use the term itself in the definition. One cannot logically say that "a circle is a circular figure." In the same fashion, one should not assume the truth of what one is supposed to be proving. Antebellum southern defenders of slavery claimed that African Americans were especially suited for heavy agricultural labor. They produced little actual evidence for this sweeping generalization other than the fact that African American slaves already labored from sunup to sundown in the tobacco, cotton, sugar, and rice fields. They must be suited for the labor, else they would not be doing it. In this example, as in many others of circular reasoning, the person guilty of the fallacy has an ulterior motive. Here it was to justify slavery.

Begging the question can reduce contested and complex questions to simpleminded equations. Even our High Court has fallen into this trap. In *Plessy v. Ferguson* (1896), the Court decided that Louisiana could mandate segregation on trains running through the state. While this seemed a direct violation of the Thirteenth and Fourteenth Amendments to John Marshall Harlan, the only dissenter, the rest of the justices were convinced that separate but equal accommodations fulfilled the mandate of the Reconstruction amendments to the Constitution. But what if the black people forced to ride in segregated train cars objected that such discrimination was a mark of inferiority? Justice Henry Brown found a logical way to answer the victims' plaint: "[The state] is at liberty to act with reference to the established usages, customs and traditions of the people, and with a view to the promotion of their comfort, and the preservation of the public peace and good order. Gauged by this standard, we cannot say that a law which authorizes or even requires the separation of the two races in public conveyances is unreasonable." Indeed, such invidious discrimination was odious "solely because the colored race chooses to put that construction upon it." Circular reasoning gave the imprimatur of the Supreme Court to over fifty years of state-mandated segregation.

Mistakes of Formal Logic

We come next to formal logical fallacies or mistakes in formal logic, forms of statement that violate the rules of propositional reasoning. I want to distinguish these from the near-fallacies. They are errors in logic that have no useful purpose in historical works. The twins in this menagerie of fallacies are **denying the antecedent** and **affirming the consequent**. Other formal logical errors are the **false identification fallacy** and the **skeptics' fallacy**.

In denying the antecedent, we reason like this: "If it is snowing, there is snow on the ground. It is not snowing. Therefore, there is no snow on the ground." I taught history one year at the lovely, very snowy campus of the University of Notre Dame, in Notre Dame, Indiana. The students, the faculty, and the fathers were wonderful, but the weather was awful. That year, we had 192 inches of snow. Some days it snowed. Some days it did not. But snow was on the ground from November to April. You simply cannot determine whether snow is on the ground (the consequent) from the whether it is snowing at the moment (the antecedent statement).

In affirming the consequent, we simply reverse the polarities of the fallacy. "If it is snowing, there will be snow on the ground. There is snow on the ground, therefore it must be snowing." Not if it snowed yesterday and the snow has not melted yet. Not in Notre Dame, Indiana. All that is necessary to make the evil twins into a valid deductive argument is the rearrangement of the statements. "When it snows, there is snow on the ground. It is snowing, therefore there is snow on the ground." Note that in this as in all formal logic, it is the claimed relationship among the statements, not their truth per se, that matters.

Sometimes affirming the consequent leads to bad public policy. In "profiling," a police agency stops and searches certain groups because, according to the preestablished profile, they are more likely to commit crimes. When federal appeals court judge Richard Posner, one of the most brilliant members of the federal bench, a prolific author, adjunct professor of law, and public intellectual, spoke of profiling that "might take the form of disproportionately frequent searches of vehicles driven by Hispanics because Hispanics are disproportionately represented in illegal drug trafficking," he made the logical error of affirming the consequent. He ignored the very real possibility that "Hispanics are disproportionately represented in illegal drug trafficking" precisely because they are disproportionately stopped and searched. Stopping another easily profiled group might result in the very same disproportionality. The result is hostility between police forces and Hispanic communities based on faulty logic.

The false identification fallacy goes like this: if the famous English novelist George Eliot was really Mary Ann Evans, and George Eliot wrote *The Mill on the Floss* and *Silas Marner,* then Mary Ann Evans wrote the two novels (true by **syllogism**). In fact, "George Eliot" was the pen name for Mary Ann Evans. You can always logically substitute things that are identical for one another. But if you tried this with things or names or people that were not identical, then you would be making a logical mistake. So if you said that the author of *Tom Sawyer* was Mark Twain, and the reader believed that the book was well written, you could not logically continue that the reader believed that Mark Twain was a good writer. Mark Twain and the book are not the same. The reader's opinion would be about the book, not about the author. He might have liked the book until he found out that the rascal Twain had written it!

The last of the formal logical pitfalls is a nice twist on all the others. It is a fallacy to argue that something cannot be true if the argument for it is fallacious—the skeptics' fallacy. A conclusion may be true despite the illogic of its proponent. The best-known case of this is the (in)famous last theorem of Pierre de Fermat, a seventeenth-century French lawyer and mathematics whiz. He scribbled in the margin of his copy of an ancient Greek text on arithmetic that he had found an elegant proof that the equation $x^n + y^n = z^n$ had no integer solutions if n was greater than 2 and x, y, and z were not 0. But he wrote that the margin of the book was too narrow for him to insert the proof. He died, the book was lost, but his son reported the marginal note. For the next 350 years mathematicians labored over a solution, coming up with many false starts (and more than a few false finishes).

Just because their proofs turned out to be incomplete or wrong did not mean that Fermat was wrong. In 1994, Andrew Wiles finally found a solution. As with all great puzzles, there is a denouement to this one. Wiles had to use a lot of very sophisticated mathematics, most of which did not exist when Fermat scribbled his marginal note. It is entirely possible that Fermat's elegant solution was nothing but the first of the very many dead ends that preceded Wiles's work.

There is so much that we do not know about ourselves and our world, so much that we are learning each day, that we should not let false starts and erroneous premises deflect our yearning to know more. Take the case of catastrophe theory, the theory that the history of the earth was marked by a series of short-lived but terrible events in prehistorical times. As proposed by Immanuel Velikovksy in the 1950s, the notion that fallout from a celestial war was the prime force in geological and biological change on earth was pooh-poohed by scientists and even banned from college reading lists. Instead, geological and biological evolution was supposed to be a gradual process—that is the very meaning of the word *evolution*.

In an example of the skeptics' fallacy, the outrageousness of Velikovsky's version of the thesis undermined scientists' willingness to accept the possibility that objects from space might have collided with our planet and had tremendous consequences. More recent studies have proven that there were at least three very short, abrupt, and massive catastrophic events in our past, each causing the dying out of nearly all living things. One of these may well have been a meteoroid or comet impact some sixty-five million years ago. That collision ended the long reign of the dinosaurs, opened space for the evolution of mammals, and ultimately led to *Homo sapiens sapiens*—us.

Formal logical fallacies have no place in historical reasoning. They are the shifting sands underneath the piers or foundations of a bridge we need to take us back to the past. Arguments built on them will be swept away by wind and tide. But near-fallacies are part of historical depiction and description. We can identify them and denounce them, if we choose, with ease, but we cannot seem to rid ourselves of them. Their persistence in our writing and our thinking may be ascribed to some flaw in us, or more accurately, to their utility for us.

What possible use can near-fallacy have for reasoned discourse? What use is near-fallacy in an argument based on evidence and logic? Well, remember that the act of doing history is based on the impossible claim of being able to know what we cannot know. All the shortcuts, all the leaps, all the twists of the near-fallacy may, if we know what we are doing, get us closer to a place we can never reach by strictly logical means. They are the sand we pour into the piers that will support the span.

Groucho Marx told a joke that perfectly illustrates how the near-fallacy becomes a common practice in history and may help in framing a philosophy of history for our time. A man goes into a psychiatrist's office and says, "Doc, you've got to help my brother-in-law. He thinks he's a chicken." The doctor replies, "Why don't you have him hospitalized?" The man recoils at the suggestion: "Doc, we can't. We need the eggs." Because we can only proximally approach our object, we must be able to circle it, to fill in blanks with estimates, surmise, and even well-calculated invention. Historians need the eggs.

3

Historians and the Loaded Question

> What is the West? What has it been in American life? To have the
> answers to these questions, is to understand the most significant
> features of the United States of to-day. . . . The problem of the
> West is nothing less than the problem of American development.
> A glance at the map of the United States reveals the truth.
> —Frederick Jackson Turner (1935)

One of the near-fallacies that so intrigue, and seem so to
plague, historians deserves its own chapter. This is the **loaded question**.
The loaded question is a misnomer because it is not really a question at
all. It is a statement hiding in question form, answered at one's peril, unless one is, like Frederick Jackson Turner, the author of the question. Then
its answer makes history come alive. Could such a dodgy device be a legitimate part of a philosophy of history for our time? Yes.

Loaded questions have changed our history. When Abraham Lincoln
gained the presidency in 1860, South Carolina hard-liners called a secession convention. They asked themselves the loaded question, What if
the newly triumphant Republican Party "announced that the South shall
be excluded from the common territory, that the judicial tribunals shall
be made sectional, and that a war must be waged against slavery until
it shall cease throughout the United States"? Well then, South Carolina
would have to leave the Union. At which point, the delegates chorused
their unanimous assent for secession, even though their question had not
been answered except by their own precipitous action.

Historians have asked themselves loaded questions, questions to which
they knew (or thought they knew) the answers. In a famous 1940 article
for the *Mississippi Valley Historical Review*, J. G. Randall proposed that
the men who had brought on the Civil War were a blundering generation,

driven by their own ambition, greed, and passion. He asked, What if the romance of the Civil War were replaced with terms like *human slaughterhouse* and *organized murder*—would historians think the same of the war? "If it were a 'needless war,' a 'repressible conflict,' was the generation of 1850 misled in its unctuous fury?" A powerfully loaded question, to which Randall knew the answer—the Civil War was a needless waste of life and property, hence the men who stumbled into it had lost their way.

But not every loaded question that historians ask is questionable. If some loaded questions are aimed with malicious intent at us, and we cannot answer them without wounding ourselves, others are designed to motivate us to act, and still others are benign instructional tools. Some even reveal to us the limits of our ability to know, a useful tool in fashioning a philosophy of history. Cousins of the loaded question—the humorous quip, the shaggy-dog story, and wordplay—turn illogic into irony. And irony is perhaps the single most important theme in history. Indeed, irony ties historical events to the study of history in a vital way.

Loading the Question

The classic loaded question has a built-in answer, an answer that the questioner already knows. The South Carolina secessionist and the Civil War historian knew the answers to their loaded questions, or thought they did. Asked such a question, you may know that no answer is right, but to avoid it you must put yourself in an awkward position.

In the hands of a clever interviewer, loaded questions can be devastating. Hurled at a political candidate, they can determine the outcome of an election. Historical examples abound. At the start of the second presidential debate in 1988 between then–vice president George H. W. Bush and Massachusetts governor Michael Dukakis, the moderator asked Dukakis, "Governor, if Kitty Dukakis [the candidate's wife] were raped and murdered, would you favor an irrevocable death penalty for the killer?" That was a loaded question, in part because it was so personal and in part because Dukakis was on record as opposing the death penalty. In fact, at the time he was under attack for being soft on crime. He honestly replied, "No, I don't . . . and I think you know that I've opposed the death penalty during all of my life. I don't see any evidence that it's a deterrent, and I think there are better and more effective ways to deal with violent crime." Dukakis lost the election, with his stance on crime, according to pollsters, playing a key role.

The questions the U.S. Immigration Service asks prospective citizens are pretty straightforward—how many branches of the federal government are there, how many stars are on the flag, who is the president, and the like. Not so other nations that don't want to give citizenship to certain groups. Take the questions required of Muslim applicants for German citizenship in the state of Baden-Württemberg, as reported in the *New York Times* on January 23, 2006: "What is your position on the statement that a wife should belong to her husband and that he can beat her if she isn't obedient?" "What do you think about parents forcibly marrying off their children? Do you think that such marriages are compatible with human dignity?" When you learn that such questions are asked only of Muslims, and that some observant Muslims do not share the ideals of the German or the European Constitution on the liberation of women, the loading of the questions becomes evident. The right answers—answers that demonstrate the applicant is not a conservative Muslim—were the ones that the officials of Baden-Württemberg wanted to hear.

Loaded questions like these may **poison the well** or imply **guilt by association**. In poisoning the well, the loaded question implies that the other side or other person is morally or intellectually defective and so his or her position cannot be taken at face value. But the questions themselves are not illogical. Instead, their very puissance derives from their mixture of logic and illogic.

The origin of the term *poisoning the well* may be one of the so-called blood libels made against Jews during the Middle Ages in Europe. Jews were accused of poisoning the wells of the cities where they lived with the blood of Christian children. As it is used today, the poisoned-well loaded question creates mistrust and fosters ill will, so that when its victims try to explain themselves minds have already closed against them. For example, if one wanted to poison the well against liberals in the course of ongoing national debate on politics, one might ask, along with the conservative writer Ann Coulter, "Don't all Liberals hate America?" Or, with columnist Michelle Malkin, if one wanted to bash the liberal media, one might write, "These TV news directors and newspaper editors act like they're lethally allergic to red, white and blue. Do they plan on boycotting the Fourth of July, too?" These loaded questions poison the well.

As in the previous example, poisoning the well may verge on slander or libel. Asking poisonous loaded questions, as Philip Roth has written in his *Operation Shylock,* begins "the whispering campaign that cannot be stopped, rumors it's impossible to quash, the besmirchment from which you will be never cleansed, slanderous stories to belittle your professional qualifications, derisive reports of your business deceptions and/or your perverse aberrations, outraged polemics denouncing your moral failings, misdeeds, faulty character traits."

Guilt by association is a deliberate attempt to demean or defame someone by saying that he or she is like some hideous moral reprobate. It loads questions with false identifications, flimsy analogies, or unproven assertions. Historians have been guilty of this kind of argument. In the war of words among historians about the history of the modern state of Israel, guilt by association is a staple of all sides. Does one condemn Israel for its treatment of the Palestinians? Then one must be a Nazi, or at least an anti-Semite. Does one defend Israel for its conduct? Then one must be a Nazi, or at least a racist. Certain red flags signal an argument based on guilt by association with a historical event. "This is a witch-hunt" associates an accusation with the discredited Salem witchcraft trials, for example. In a newer version of this, if one takes a position that is "thesis driven," then one must be wrong because the thesis is similar to one that has been discredited—guilt by association, not with a person or a movement, but with a collection of words.

If you want to blast radical professors in American colleges, for example, don't compare them to other radicals in American history like Thomas Paine, Margaret Fuller, William Lloyd Garrison, Susan B. Anthony, Eugene V. Debs, W. E. B. DuBois, and Rita Mae Brown (to name a few), the obvious comparisons, or locate them in the long history of radicalism on campus; try guilt by association built into a series of loaded questions. David Horowitz, formerly a radical student activist but now, according to his own account, come to his senses, is a master of this kind of guilt by association.

To nail Columbia University history professor Manning Marable, Horowitz offered a two-step version of guilt by association. Marable was damned by the company he kept, and the company he kept was denounced through guilt by association. It was a masterpiece of denunciation by loaded question showcased on Horowitz's own frontpagemag. com. Among Marable's allegedly sinister crew were "an embittered faculty racist," Derrick Bell; an unrepentant 1960s gangster now on the staff of Emory Law School, Kathleen Cleaver; "a world class bloviator" Michael Eric Dyson, whose upper-division seminar "Great Religious Thinkers" devoted an entire semester to the religious prose of gansta rapper Tupac Shakur; "Marxist political hack and 'University Professor'" Angela Davis, who was a member of the same "Central Committee of the same Communist Party" as Marable himself; and, last but not least, the "Jew-hating" sometime poet laureate of New Jersey, Professor Amiri Baraka. Then the loaded question: "How could the university have hired and then raised to such heights an individual of such questionable character and preposterous views as . . . [fill in the blank]?"

Note that Horowitz did not linger over the achievements of the dangerous five or sit and talk with them about their opinions. He did not do historical homework on their ideas. Instead, he loaded the deck with associations—for example Dyson with Tupac Shakur. The illogic of the association is that Dyson is a fraud because he teaches about a criminal and that Marable is a fraud because he is Dyson's friend. While the point of Horowitz's exaggerations and denunciations may be entirely logical in commercial terms—to sell his own *The 101 Most Dangerous Academics in America*—Horowitz's blast is a perfect example of guilt by association riding on the back of the loaded question "How pervasive was the conflation of political interests and academic pursuits on university campuses or in college classrooms?"

Law professor Geoffrey R. Stone, an expert on the history of the First Amendment, reported an example of loaded questions on recent historical events. In the *Chicago Tribune* on December 24, 2004, the law scholar wrote: "I was invited to appear on the TV show 'The O'Reilly Factor' to debate the question: 'Is dissent disloyal?' After the producer and I discussed the issue, host Bill O'Reilly (according to the producer) decided to redefine the question: "Can an American who wants the United States to lose the war in Iraq be patriotic?" One loaded question had been replaced with another.

As in Horowitz's mauling of the professors and O'Reilly's hardly less subtle assault on the opponents of the war in Iraq, guilt by association with an obnoxious or feared group works the same way as association with a hated individual. During the so-called McCarthy era of American history at the start of the 1950s, guilt by association hit its high-water mark. Wisconsin Republican Senator Joseph McCarthy opened his crusade against the Red enemy in a speech in Wheeling, West Virginia, on February 9, 1950. The crucial rhetorical moment came with a fully loaded question: "Ladies and gentlemen, can there be anyone tonight who is so blind as to say that the war is not on . . . between Communism and Christianity"? Anyone who criticized the Wisconsin senator's search for communists in government, education, and the arts he accused of being a communist sympathizer or a "pinko" (tainted with red) in the service of the Soviet Union.

Although unfair to many who were simply defending the concept of free speech and intellectual liberty and had no connection with or sympathy for the Soviet Union, McCarthy's effective use of guilt by association drove many of his opponents to cover and some to suicide—for example, Philip Loeb, whose left-leaning sympathies and association with the Communist Party in the 1930s made him a target of the Red Scare. It cost him his role as Jake Goldberg in the popular TV program *The Goldbergs.* When in 1955 he could not get another acting job because he was "blacklisted," he committed suicide.

On June 9, 1954, lawyer Joseph Welch turned the tables on McCarthy in a famous televised hearing on supposed communist influences in the U.S. Army. In defense of one of the junior lawyers in Welch's firm whom McCarthy smeared and Welch defended, the advocate asked, "You've done enough. Have you no sense of decency, sir, at long last? Have you left no sense of decency?" McCarthy was not left speechless; he rambled on, unaware that two loaded questions had blown up in his face.

Useful Loaded Questions

Welch's loaded question to McCarthy had a beneficial outcome—a bully was put in his place. Not every loaded question is a viper waiting to strike. A loaded question can be friendly, in effect a compliment or offer of support in the form of a question. One finds these at scripted political rallies, where preselected questioners ask friendly loaded questions. According to an Associated Press report on January 23, 2006, "'It's always good to have a plant in every audience,' [President George W.] Bush joked last week in Sterling, Va., after a woman rose and said she was proud of him." Even a news conference that is supposed to be spontaneous may have some "ringers" who ask supportive loaded questions. At one of President George W. Bush's press conferences, conservative blogger James D. Guckert asked the president how he could deal with Democrats "who seem to have divorced themselves from reality." It was not the first time that Guckert had offered a show of support by loading a friendly question.

The **rhetorical question** is a loaded question that has the virtue of being honest about itself. When you ask a rhetorical question, you signal in some way that no answer is needed or wanted. It can be an accusation: "Why am I such a dummy?" It can be an extended form of exclamation or emotional response: "Why does this happen to me all the time?" It can be an appeal to a jury or an audience ("How can you convict someone with such an innocent face?") or a literary device ("Shall I compare thee to a Summer's day?"). It can and often does express or imply its own answer, sometimes ironically, and sometimes mortally. In the movie *Bugsy*, gangster Benjamin Siegel, before assassinating an employee who had cheated him, asked, "Did you think you could fool me?" The rhetorical question may begin inquiry into a subject one had not thought interesting previously. For example, *New York Times* architecture critic Nicolai Ouroussoff opened a piece in February 2006 with the rhetorical question, "Is there any show more overdue than a major one about contemporary Spanish architecture?" Who knew?

From its inception rhetoric was a teaching device. Rhetoric combined logical argument and literary imagination. Boethius had more in mind than philosophy when he wrote the foundational early medieval text on rhetoric, the sixth-century *Consolation of Philosophy*. The Roman world in Europe had collapsed, leaving Roman learning tottering. The man of letters found in philosophy a refuge against the violence of the day. "Our leader, Reason, gathers her forces into her citadel, while the enemy are busied in plundering useless baggage. As they seize the most worthless things, we laugh at them from above, untroubled by the whole band of mad marauders, and we are defended by that rampart to which riotous folly may not hope to attain." History lay too heavily on the shoulders of educated men of Boethius's time for them to ask rhetorical questions about the past. But even the most cloistered observer could not do without rhetorical questions: "How, too, would God's Providence be better than man's opinion, if, as men do, He only sees to be uncertain such things as have an uncertain result?" All must be certain to God, a belief that reduced the course of history to the answer to the rhetorical question. "The order of the universe, advancing with its inevitable sequences, brings about this coincidence of causes. This order itself emanates from its source, which is Providence, and disposes all things in their proper time and place."

In 399 BCE, Socrates of Athens was tried and convicted of offenses against the gods and the state and sentenced to death or exile, in part for his use of rhetorical techniques like the rhetorical question. At his trial, according to Plato's *Apologia* (the Greek for explanation), Socrates relied upon the same dialectical methods as he had throughout his career as a philosopher. Philosophical exchanges that Socrates supposedly had with students, scoffers, and even bystanders began with Socrates asking a series of questions that led his respondent toward the correct answer or embarrassment. At his trial, he asked himself these questions. "I dare say, Athenians, that someone among you will reply, 'Why is this, Socrates, and what is the origin of these accusations of you: for there must have been something strange which you have been doing? All this great fame and talk about you would never have arisen if you had been like other men: tell us, then, why this is, as we should be sorry to judge hastily of you.'" The rhetorical question was Socrates's invitation to himself to offer his version of history. "I found that the men most in repute were all but the most foolish; and that some inferior men were really wiser and better. I will tell you the tale of my wanderings and of the 'Herculean' labors, as I may call them." But the rhetorical question and Socrates' answers were not enough to deflect the enmity that a lifetime of pulling down the idols of the crowd had earned him.

The rhetorical question in a historical account may make us aware of our moral failings. Thomas Jefferson told this true story: on the Virginia frontier, in 1774, two Shawnee Indians got into a fight with two white men and killed them. A gang of Virginia vigilantes, inflamed with anger at all Indians, decided to gain revenge on any they saw. At a bend in a stream, they ambushed a small group of women and children traveling in a canoe. They had not been involved in the earlier incident; indeed, they were the family of the Indian Chief Logan, a friend and ally to the whites who had helped keep the peace on the frontier. Logan, a great orator in the Native American tradition that honored public speaking highly, fashioned a series of loaded questions to express his grief. "I appeal to any white man to say, if ever he entered Logan's cabin hungry, and he gave him not meat; if ever he came cold and naked, and he clothed him not? . . . Who is there to mourn for Logan? Not one."

The tearful oration that Logan made to a representative of the Virginia royal lieutenant governor Lord Dunmore in 1774 became an instant classic of oratory. Jefferson heard it from Dunmore, copied it into a notebook, and later transcribed it into his *Notes on the State of Virginia* (1785). Jefferson, like many of his comrades in the founding generation, was an avid reader of history. History, they believed, taught vital lessons in statecraft. Jefferson worried that the true history of his generation would never be written. "What is to become of our past?" he queried his friends after he retired from politics, a rhetorical question. Asked by a doubter in 1797 whether Logan had spoken truth, Jefferson replied that "if I find that Logan was right in his charge, I will vindicate . . . a chief, whose talent and misfortunes have attached him to the respect and commiserations of the world." Jefferson's brooding concern for revolutionary history and his reply to the critic of his account of Logan were both phrased as rhetorical questions.

A variety of the rhetorical question is the **hypothetical** or hypothetical question. The hypothetical is a loaded question that opens an inquiry. To be sure, the hypothetical may be pretty heavily loaded, particularly when someone who is not a trained historian indulges in a historical hypothetical. In a January 29, 2006, op-ed piece in the *Philadelphia Inquirer,* famous geneticist and atheism advocate Richard Dawkins asked, "Is religion the root of all evil?" It was a loaded hypothetical that, presumably, could be answered only by history. As he wrote in 2003, "My point is not that religion itself is the motivation for wars, murders and terrorist attacks, but that religion is the principal label, and the most dangerous one, by which a 'they' as opposed to a 'we' can be identified at all."

Other, less fraught hypothetical questions instruct us, even if they are plainly contrary to fact. For example, how is the historian to evaluate the proposition that without in-migration from the countryside early modern cities would have declined? The loaded question is "What other conclusion can we reach?" In fact, cities like seventeenth-century London were sinkholes of disease; in fact, there was migration from the countryside; and in fact, the early modern city prospered. Only a hypothetical can help us answer the question. A contrary-to-fact model of population growth, taking out the effect of in-migration, shows that the migrants actually increased the death rate for children in the city but did not increase the birth rate—a startling analytical finding. The cities would have gained in population without the in-migrants.

Other kinds of contrary-to-fact historical studies change the narrative story line to help answer questions about what did in fact happen. We can call this the **what if** question. It is a contrary-to-fact statement in question form. "What if the British under William Howe had pursued George Washington and the Continentals into New Jersey after Washington had lost the battle for Manhattan in September 1776?" They did not, and he was able to regroup and score the startling victories at Trenton and Princeton at the end of the year, but had they forced the Continental army to disband and flee, might the British have won the Revolutionary War? That hypothetical question helps us understand why the British lost the war—for Washington and the Continentals could always trade space for time, but the British supply lines were tied to the sea. "What if Robert E. Lee and the Army of Northern Virginia had defeated the Union forces at Gettysburg and marched on Washington, D.C.?" Would the Confederacy have won the war? No, for Lee's losses were almost as great as those of George Meade and the Army of the Potomac. The lesson of the hypothetical is that battles did not determine the course of the war. A combination of will and manufacturing capacity, multiplied in some way by the size of the forces, dictated a Union victory even though Union forces won few battles outright.

As Robert Cowley has written in the introduction to *What Ifs? of American History: Eminent Historians Imagine What Might Have Been* (2003), "Counterfactual history . . . casts a reflective light on what did [happen]. Why did certain events (and the trends and trajectories that grew out of them) dominate, and not others? At what point did possibilities become impossibilities?" Thinking about the hypothetical question leads to a clearer understanding of the nature of both war and peace. What if Lincoln had dodged John Wilkes Booth's bullet? Would the whole project of full equality for the freed men and women of 1865 have been achieved? What role might a Lincoln have played in the stark drama of Reconstruction? The contrary-to-fact question allows us to explore actual events more closely by posing alternatives. The hypothetical allows inquiry to proceed in the absence of facts, taking logical thinking into the realm of the imaginary.

A critic of such speculation might cry out that historians have no business guessing what would follow from events that did not occur. Figuring out why things happened as they did is hard enough. What is more, every contrary-to-fact assumption that we make opens the door to many more "second-order" hypotheticals that arise from the initial contrary-to-fact proposition. Like a chess game, each move has many countermoves that in turn have many more countermoves. The number soon becomes astronomical. The rules of chess constrain the number of responses to any move, but our historical imagination, once freed from the constraints of facts, is not as limited as the pieces on the chessboard.

Humoring the Loaded Question

The loaded question provides a vital clue to how to do the impossible—know about the past. To get closer to this clue, we will have to deal with a special variant of the loaded question—humor. In the movie *My Favorite Year,* Peter O'Toole utters a universal truth: "Dying is easy; comedy is hard." Still, a sense of humor seems to be one of the most well-developed and unique characteristics of our species. Jokes have histories of their own, evolving with changing times; only the names are changed to insult the innocent. Ancient Roman comedy plotlines from the playwright Plautus, reworked, made *A Funny Thing Happened on the Way to the Forum* into a modern movie and theater rib-tickler. The eighteenth-century English stand-up comedian Joe Miller gave his name to two hundred years of joke books, some of whose themes Plautus must have known. Plainly humor is not only topical but historical.

Recent research suggests that some historians are allergic to humor. In a study reported in the American Association of University Professors journal *Academe* (January–February 2006), University of Texas anthropologist Karl Petruso found that at least one major university's history faculty was singularly devoid of a sense of humor. "The primary objective of this study is to determine the relative levels of zaniness and seriousness of faculty in various liberal arts disciplines," a whimsical riff on a lot of social science research. Petruso "developed a research design based on tabulation of the number of humorous versus serious postings on office doors." After all, the office door of a professor was a mirror of his or her worldview!

After gathering and weighing the data, Petruso found that "history [office doors] requires special comment." If one excluded an "outlying, anomalously zany professor" whose door displayed "forty-seven cartoons and absolutely nothing of a serious pedagogical nature," the history faculty's index of humorousness, the ratio of humorous to strictly pedagogical postings, would be "a dismal 0.433, which would consign the department—and, by association, the discipline—to the depths of humorlessness." To Petruso's admittedly satirical study I can add my own impressions. As someone who has attended nearly one hundred conferences of historians and sat through countless panels of scholars reading detailed and dry papers followed by commentators reading equally detailed and dry comments, I can say that many historians do not seem fond of humor. Our textbook editors tell us not to write wryly in textbooks; the students will not understand the humor. Apparently there is nothing humorous in what we study and humor has no place in how we do our studies. To paraphrase Georges Clemenceau's remark that war is too serious to be left to generals, perhaps history is too serious to be left to people with a sense of humor.

Nevertheless, when one considers a kind of humor known as the shaggy-dog story, one will see the connection between the loaded question and a philosophy of history for our time. No one is quite certain of the origin of the term, though it first widely circulated in the 1940s. The shaggy dog is a historical vignette whose ending does not quite measure up to our expectations, flying off at a tangent. Here is one of my favorites:

A young man decides to discover the secret of life. He wanders all over the world, asking its most revered holy men and women to explain the secret of life to him. Dissatisfied with their answers, he travels to Tibet to seek the wisdom of the holiest man there. From the holy man's disciples, the seeker learns what he must do to purify his soul and prepare his mind for the answer. For years he practices the most rigorous exercises, and finally he is permitted to approach the holy teacher. "Holy man," the now older and frailer seeker asks, "What is the secret of life?" The holy man replies, "Life is like a bending branch." Still perplexed, the seeker asks, "How is life like a bending branch?" The holy man thinks for a moment and then answers, "You mean life is not like a bending branch?"

The shaggy-dog story's ending, a loaded question, depends upon irony. Irony is a vital component of all history. There are a thousand little ironies in our everyday teaching, researching, and writing of history. "If something can go wrong, it will," a version of "Murphy's Law," applies to us. We lose reference notes, forget that we are paraphrasing, borrow too freely from others, occasionally fail to acknowledge our debts fully. We are also subject to a variant of the "Peter Principle" that people will be promoted at work until they reach a position they are unqualified to fill. For us the Peter Principle works in similar fashion. We will write book chapters that go beyond where they should stop. In our delight at finding evidence that fits our notions (called source mining) we will overstate our conclusions. "Parkinson's Law" that "work will expand to fill the time allotted to it" surely applies to the historian who cannot stop doing research and start to write, or the historian who insists on putting all the note cards into the text, ballooning a concise two-hundred-page essay into a bloated five-hundred-page book.

In history itself, irony abounds. The impact of chance, contingency, the unexpected development, and the accident on events can change the entire course of history in an unanticipated direction. The theory is called "Cleopatra's nose" because, had her nose been a little longer or shorter, she might not have been so attractive to both Julius Caesar and Mark Anthony, and the Roman Republic might still be with us. As Daniel Boorstin wrote in *Cleopatra's Nose: Essays on the Unexpected in History,* "When we focus on turning points in history we recognize the crucial role of the accidental and the trivial." History, in this sense, is one long shaggy-dog story. (As it happens, history and the shaggy-dog story share another characteristic. A good shaggy-dog storyteller can spin out the tale by adding details. So can a good historian.)

But there are larger ironies in the tales we tell about our past, as in the quest for the understanding of our Civil War. Edward Ayers, in his deeply moving tale of the coming of the war in two Shenandoah Valley counties, Pennsylvania's Franklin and Virginia's Augusta, notes that "the North went to war to keep people in a Union based on the consent of the governed, to maintain connection with a slaveholding society it despised. . . . The South, for its part, went to war under the flag of freedom to maintain a massive and growing human slavery."

A less catastrophic irony applies to the unexpected and unplanned for development of ideas. American protests against the English Parliament's Stamp Act in 1765 were based on what the protesters saw as the constitution the colonies shared with Britain. As the protests grew and Parliament rejected them, the protesters began to explore some of the hitherto hidden implications of their own arguments. They discovered a vast conspiracy against liberty with its headquarters in the imperial government. In the end, the intellectual basis of their resistance became an idea of natural law outside and above the English constitution, a body of precepts that once again would lead in entirely unexpected directions: independence, the end of slavery in many of the new states, and republican governments based on written constitutions, bills of rights, separation of powers, and the sovereignty of the people.

Doing history is like explaining the holy man's bending branch. One has to make certain assumptions to do it, and these, like the humor of the shaggy-dog story, reveal the ironic springs of human life. Indeed, pressed by an adversary who denies the possibility of anything more than history-as-rhetoric, the working historian can reply only with the ironically loaded question, "Are there any skeptics in the archives?"

Translated, that means that we who do history have to have a certain humility amounting to a sense of humor about ourselves and the outcome of our labors. That is not easy, not after a career of tracking down hints and clues in obscure places. But the loaded question "How did you know your story is the right one?" is a question we simply cannot answer. The willingness to press ahead with our inquiries, to make the necessary leaps without a safety net, as it were, is essential if we are to lay the bridge spans from pier to pier. But our consideration of the loaded question has led us to understand ourselves a little better and appreciate the perilousness of our task, even if we don't have an answer to it.

4

Cause for Alarm

Who has ever heard of Ebenezer Chaplin? . . . The effort to
comprehend, to communicate, and to fulfill this [American revolu-
tionary] destiny was continuous through the entire Revolutionary
generation. . . . It was then that the premises were defined and the
assumptions set. It was then that explorations were made in new
territories of thought. . . . It was the most creative period in the
history of American political thought. Everything that followed
assumed and built upon its results.

—Bernard Bailyn (1967)

Part of the value of certain kinds of loaded questions is their
analytical force. Who was Ebenezer Chaplin? He was a minor figure in a
major event, the intellectual origin of the American Revolution. He wrote
a sermon, reprinted as a pamphlet. The pamphlet writings of the future
revolutionaries revealed to them a conspiracy against American liberty.
That revelation powered a "transforming debate." The debate let loose the
tide of rebellion and at the same time channeled it. The result was a republic of laws and liberty. By making us ask and answer "why?" through
loaded questions like "Who has ever heard of Ebenezer Chaplin," the author turns history from one damn fact after another into an explanation of
the facts. Just as no one wants a diagnosis of their illness as "idiopathic,"
so no one wants a history without causation.

After 9/11, Americans asked a great many "why" questions. Why had we
been unprepared for a terrorist attack? Why had the Twin Towers fallen?
Why had so many first responders to the fires been trapped in the buildings when they collapsed? A blue-ribbon commission sifted evidence,
took testimony, and finally published its report. The conclusion makes
sober reading: "In composing this narrative, we have tried to remember

that we write with the benefit and the handicap of hindsight. . . . But the path of what happened is so brightly lit that it places everything else more deeply in shadow. . . . As time passes, and more documents become available . . . the bare facts of what happened become clearer. Yet the picture of *how* those things happened becomes harder to reimagine." Cause? Multiple failures in "imagination, policy, capabilities, and management": in short, mistakes that cascaded, each leading to the next.

While the multiple mistake is a common form of answer to the why question, the more closely we focus the camera of history on individual events, the more clearly the causes come into view. Alas, clarity does not bring agreement about causation. For example, no one doubts that the buildings in the World Trade Center collapsed because of a combination of their design and the fiery impact of the two collisions. But investigations differed on the precise cause.

As I wrote in *Seven Fires,* engineers and design consultants asked to determine the reasons for the towers' collapse came to opposing conclusions. They clinically examined the burned trusses and outer wall "curtain" panels, built computer simulations, reviewed the videos of the accordion collapse, went back to their computers, and still disagreed.

At their inception, skyscrapers were giant heavy-limbed cages—lattice works of steel, concrete, and tile many feet thick. Influenced by the terrible 1904 fire that reduced the high-rises in Baltimore to burned-out skeletons, builders put larger cages of steel around smaller cages of steel until the shell of a high-rise looked like an impenetrable maze of columns and girders. The columns placed every twenty feet or so anchored the floors. Redundancy provided strength. If there was a local collapse, the rest of the building could support the fallen floors. To prevent fires from spreading, offices and apartments were sealed compartments, and building members were encased in concrete and fireproof ceramics. Fire stairwells were distributed throughout the building and "hardened" with fireproof doors and walls.

Not so in the Twin Towers. The architect and the builders found a way to replace the multiples of interior columns with load-bearing external panels and heavy core supports. To reduce weight on the outside walls and interior core columns, thin steel was used for the floor trusses, and a spray-on fire retardant replaced the conventional concrete and tile fireproofing. The result was more open, rentable space—and the chance for fire to spread rapidly across entire floors. The entirely inadequate number (three) of too-narrow internal fire escapes were clustered in the core space instead of distributed throughout the towers.

In 2002, the Federal Emergency Management Administration (FEMA) released the preliminary findings of its World Trade Center Building Performance Study. It concluded that the external panels on both buildings had withstood the shock of the collision. The fireball from the airplane fuel was hot enough to start structural fires, which ultimately softened and weakened the floors. The culprit in the avalanche or pancake type of collapse was not the walls but the floors. In the final minutes of each of the towers, victims on the upper floors called down to the lobbies saying that the floors were buckling. The explosion blew away much of the sprayed-on fireproofing on those trusses. What the explosion did not blow away was from its inception inadequately protected against fire.

On August 22, 2002, the federal government inaugurated another investigation of the collapse of the towers and WTC Seven, across Vesey Street. The National Institute of Science and Technology (NIST) completed this study in February 2005 and announced its findings on April 5, 2005. The FEMA study was wrong—the design was not at fault. "These fires, in combination with the dislodged fireproofing, were responsible for a chain of events in which the building core weakened and began losing its ability to carry loads. The floors weakened and sagged from the fires, pulling inward on the perimeter columns" and causing the columns to buckle and bow inward. "Collapse then ensued."

Not so hidden was the message that the Port Authority and the designers wanted to hear—the towers were not "doomed" by design flaws. The impact of the planes, the heat of the fuel, and the fire itself had led to the collapse. The director of the NIST study insisted that "the buildings performed as they should have," neatly avoiding the question of whether more traditional design and construction methods would have stood longer in the face of the same impact and fires or even survived them.

The cause of the collapse, so vital for us to understand and so thoroughly studied, seemed almost impossible to pin down. Yet we continued to ask "why." It is in some respects the most important question that historians can ask, even though we rarely come to incontrovertible conclusions about causes.

Now How Did That Happen?

Are certain outcomes inevitable? Or is it a waste of time arguing about such questions because we can always hypothesize a perfectly reasonable alternative outcome? Is human agency—and human choice—the fundamental cause of all human events, or are there forces beyond human control that dictate the outcome of history?

In the eighteenth century, with scientific experiment replacing divination as the most favored way to explain natural events, Scottish philosopher and historian David Hume proposed that causation was simply the constant conjunction of certain sequences of events in our experience. We think that A causes B because in our experience A always immediately precedes B. If the historian were to simply apply Hume's formula, there would be no need for causal analysis at all. Cause would be presumed. One detail would follow another, a mindless recitation of the pieces of evidence. Facts would be their own causes, for they would be all the historian had. Everything else would be the historian's surmise.

In the alternative, we might adopt the **scientific method** that every school child learns. It is based on a theory of causation. First we observe an event. Then we try to explain it by posing an answer, called a **hypothesis**, to a question or series of questions that can be tested and whose results can be examined. Then we perform these tests, called **experiments**, and see if our hypothesis works. Sounds simple. But it is not that simple, for history is different from science. It does not repeat itself and certainly does not lend itself to laboratory experiment. Ivan Pavlov, a Russian scientist, found that ringing a bell before feeding his dog conditioned his dog to believe that the bell would always be followed by food. Anticipating the food, the dog salivated when the bell rang. Imagine the drooling dog's chagrin when the bell rang and the bowl was empty. He thought that the bell caused the food to appear. But this time was different. It always is, in history.

Misleading operant conditioning to one side, we assume causes all the time. Walking during a blustery day, I saw a tree limb on the road and wondered how it had gotten there. The best empirical explanation seemed that the wind had blown it off. I did not see the wind do this, for who actually sees the wind, but I had seen previous occasions on which the trees seemed to be bowing, branches flew about, and something was pushing me to one side. Must be the wind.

Why did the limb land on the road? It fell down because of gravity. Gravity is the name we give to a force exerted by all objects having mass. Why? Because Isaac Newton identified gravity as one of the basic forces affecting matter. The earth is a big mass and has a strong field of gravity. But what is gravity? Have I ever seen it (as opposed to its operation)? No more than the wind. I believe that gravity exists because objects always go to ground (especially in my kitchen), but this is really little more than what Hume taught us. Cause lies in the habits of our experience, but our reading of that experience, and our treatment of historical causation, have to be a little more complex.

Refining Hume's concept, we insist that if we are to assert that A causes B, A has to precede B, and that without A happening, B would not happen. In short, the idea of cause forces us to accept a certain notion of time. Time is a difficult concept for astrophysics, cognitive psychology, and, apparently, the students in my early morning classes. If time is, as Steven Pinker proposes in his wise and witty *The Stuff of Thought* (2007), "a moving window on life" allowing most of us "a now and a little bit of then," historians' "then" is a lot bigger and more pliable. If I am writing about the American Civil War, my "now" extends back to a "then" 150 years ago. By making claims about causation in the past I have to bend time to bring the past and the present together. I am not advocating a kind of time travel, for the past time we historians inhabit is not lived but remembered. We do not take readers back in time; we use causal language to denote the passage of time.

Sometimes we can have A and B does not follow. We would say then that A was necessary for B to occur but not sufficient. For the American Revolution to occur, Americans would have to become restive at British rule. Those actions were necessary causes but were not sufficient because the colonists might have just swallowed hard and done nothing, or they might have done what they always did—violate the law by smuggling, paying off the customs officials, and getting juries to look the other way when culprits like John Hancock were caught in the act.

If A always leads to B, then A is a sufficient cause. If a particular strain of influenza always results in joint pain, then that flu bug is a sufficient cause of the pain. Note that other ailments and debilities (arthritis, neuropathy, and a vicious elbow from an opposing player during a pickup game of basketball) may also cause joint pain. A sufficient cause is not necessarily the only cause of an event. The Civil War was caused by Lincoln's decision not to let the Confederacy sunder the Union, a sufficient cause. But absent their fear that Lincoln's Republican Party, victorious in the 1860 elections, would deprive them of their slaves, the southern states' leaders would never have wanted secession or formed the Confederacy.

False Causes

As clear and simple as this formal understanding of causation may be, historians have tripped and stumbled into errors of explanation. These include **predeterminism**; the fallacy of **concomitance** and the closely related *post hoc ergo propter hoc*; the fallacy of **hindsight**; the **clustering illusion**; the **self-fulfilling prophecy**; and the **false cause**.

In predeterminism, the historian knows how everything turned out because he or she knew how it had to turn out, and knew how it had to turn out because one *big* cause trumps all others. That cause is so big that everything fits under it and nothing can escape it, like the "black holes" in the universe whose gravity is so great that even light cannot escape. Predeterminism reduces all explanations to one, and its adherents are sometimes called **reductionists** for that reason.

How do they know that the big cause is behind everything? For many, the appeal of the one big cause is almost religious—it explains and comforts. Behind many of the reductionist causal arguments, thus, is a moral or an ideological commitment. This sort of reasoning is ahistorical because it begins, not with a study of the past, but with the ideology itself, to fit which evidence is bent and twisted.

The best known of these predeterministic theories of history is Marxism. According to Karl Marx, the key to the development of human society was the advance of the means of production. It was the foundation on which all societies rested, and it gave shape to how people thought and acted. The struggle for control of the means of production was the engine driving historical events. At the center of this all-encompassing ideology was the notion that history passed through certain fixed stages, that these always followed and led to one another, and that nothing an individual or group could do would alter the sequence or its outcome. In the capitalist stage of the struggle, the proletariat, the workers, battled the owning classes, and the resulting revolution would bring the final stage of history, true communism. Although the outcome of the struggle for control of the means of production was as inevitable as the outcome of any natural event under laws like gravity, at the same time all right-thinking men must act to speed the arrival of the final stage of history.

Marxism's attraction for scholars, whether they admired or disliked communism, was that it was scientific. History evolved, much as the species evolved. In Marx's *Poverty of Philosophy* (1847), one finds the simple formula, scientifically elegant and universally valid:

In changing the modes of production, mankind changes all its social relations. The hand mill creates a society with the feudal lord; the steam mill a society with the industrial capitalist. . . . Under the patriarchal system, under the caste system, under the feudal and corporative system, there was division of labor in the whole of society according to fixed rules. Were these rules established by a legislator? No. Originally born of the conditions of material production, they were raised to the status of laws only much later. In this way, these different forms of the division of labor became so many bases of social organization.

There is no contingency here; there are no surprises, no twists and turns. Everything happens the way it is supposed to happen because history, like science, is a matter of natural laws.

Predeterminism has a psychological advantage for its adherents. Not only does it explain everything that has happened, it predicts the future. Thus Hitler's racial theories of history led to the promise that the Aryans would inherit the earth: "No more than Nature desires the mating of weaker with stronger individuals, even less does she desire the blending of a higher with a lower race, since, if she did, her whole work of higher breeding, over perhaps hundreds of thousands of years, night be ruined with one blow. Historical experience offers countless proofs of this. It shows with terrifying clarity that in every mingling of Aryan blood with that of lower peoples the result was the end of the cultured people." History's predetermining causation gave Hitler confidence to predict a thousand-year reign of Nazi Germany, so long as the Germanic blood remained untainted.

Historians in a democratic republic of ideas like our own are not above falling into the trap of presuming a predetermined link between past and future. For example, it is a seductive assumption that our rise to international economic and political power was based on our particular system of government or our particular economic system and thus that democracy and capitalism are the "end of history." Francis Fukuyama, who published *The End of History and the Last Man* in 1992, explained how this notion of causation worked:

> I argued that a remarkable consensus concerning the legitimacy of liberal democracy as a system of government had emerged throughout the world over the past few years, as it conquered rival ideologies like hereditary monarchy, fascism, and most recently communism. More than that, however, I argued that liberal democracy may constitute the "end point of mankind's ideological evolution" and the "final form of human government," and as such constituted the "end of history." That is, while earlier

forms of government were characterized by grave defects and irrationali-
ties that led to their eventual collapse, liberal democracy was arguably
free from such fundamental internal contradictions.

Hegel was back—in far easier-to-understand prose. Fukuyama: "What
I suggested had come to an end was not the occurrence of events, even
large and grave events, but History: that is, history understood as a single,
coherent, evolutionary process, when taking into account the experience
of all peoples in all times."

In a remarkably different version of the predetermined course of a
democratic republic's history, Niall Ferguson, a historian at Harvard University, saw the rise and fall of empire, not liberal democracy, as the predetermining theme in our history. In the September 2006 edition of *Foreign
Policy,* he wrote "Empires with Expiration Dates": "The American empire
is young by historical standards. Its continental expansion in the 19th century was unabashedly imperialistic. Yet the comparative ease with which
sparsely settled territory was absorbed into the original federal structure
militated against the development of an authentically imperial mentality
and put minimal strain on the political institutions of the republic. By
contrast, America's era of overseas expansion, which can be marked from
the Spanish-American War of 1898, has been a good deal more difficult
and, precisely for this reason, has repeatedly conjured up the specter of an
imperial presidency."

But rest easy, Ferguson continued, for our empire, like all modern empires, was not destined to last long. Or at least that was history's verdict. A
simple calculus explained why: "An empire, then, will come into existence
and endure so long as the benefits of exerting power over foreign peoples
exceed the costs of doing so in the eyes of the imperialists; and so long as
the benefits of accepting dominance by a foreign people exceed the costs
of resistance in the eyes of the subjects. Such calculations implicitly take
into account the potential costs of relinquishing power to another empire." Here Hegel was replaced by a cost analysis version of the old Stoic
theory of cyclical history.

In the fallacy of concomitance, we mistake coincidence for causality.
Two things happen together, so one must have caused the other. Defending the George W. Bush administration's policy of lax enforcement of
mine safety legislation on March 2, 2006, as reported in a *New York Times*
piece, Dirk Fillpot of the Federal Mine Safety and Health Administration
reported that under the permissive policy there had only been twenty-

two deaths in coal mines in 2005, well below the yearly average. To him, that meant that "safety is definitely improving." In fact, there may be no relation between the absence of regulation and the low numbers of accidents. That is why they are called accidents. Moreover, Fillpot implied or expressed no reason why a hands-off policy should reduce accidents. He presumed a causal relationship where only concomitance could be shown. In 2006 the number of mine deaths skyrocketed because the owners were permitted to ignore safety inspectors' recommendations the year before— an actual causal relationship.

A first cousin of the fallacy of concomitance is the fallacy of assuming that anything that comes just before an event is the cause of the event (*post hoc, ergo propter hoc,* literally "after this, therefore because of this"). The most obvious example: the cock crows just before dawn. The sun comes up after the cock crows. Thus the cock crowing must be the cause of the sunrise. Another version: "I've been having a really good day. It must be the lucky rabbit's foot I bought yesterday." Or my own experience with the stock exchange: "Every time I sell a stock, it zooms up in value. My sale must cause a sudden spurt in buyer interest."

This kind of argument is used all the time to warp statistics to fit an argument. If the state of Massachusetts passed strict gun control laws and the number of homicides fell dramatically the next year, advocates of gun control would claim that the law caused the decline in homicides. If the state of Florida passed a law allowing people to carry concealed firearms and the number of homicides diminished, advocates of the right to bear arms would claim that the law caused the lower homicide rate. In fact, the two states did pass such laws, the rate of homicides in both did decline, and advocates of the two positions did attribute the decline in homicide to categorically opposite causes.

There is no fancy Latin term for mixing up cause and effect. An event occurring later cannot be the cause of an event occurring earlier. Take, for example, the Salem witchcraft episode of 1692. What caused neighbor to turn on neighbor and not only accuse the neighbor of being a witch (mere slander) but insist on trials and capital punishment for those convicted of the accusation? In a prize-winning book, Paul Boyer and Stephen Nissenbaum proposed that a long-simmering feud between two powerful Salem Village clans, the Porters and the Putnams, divided the farming community and opened the door to the fatal accusations. "For Salem Village . . . the critical stage [of social disintegration] came in the 1690s, and the Villagers lashed out with accusations." What was at stake?—the loss of future prospects, bound with land, timber, and status. "But there is guilt as well as rage in all of this: for when the family of Thomas Putnam was deprived of its birthright" in a series of disputed wills, "it was forced to openly and perhaps even consciously to confront the fact that it cared, and cared profoundly, about money and status." And the accusations came.

The problem with this brilliant and beautifully demonstrated causal chain is that "the final blow to the rest of the family came, as it happened, in that same month of April 1695, with the death of Mary Veren Putnam." The matron had rewarded the Porters but not the Putnams. Why had she not left more to her blood kin? "More would have come to them, the will pointedly noted, had they not 'brought upon me inconvenient and unnecessary charges and disbursements at several times.'" But the accusations began in the terrible winter of 1692, three years before the "final blow" that pitted Putnam against Porter. Indeed, the crisis and scandal that followed matched the two factions against one another in the way that earlier quarrels had not. A powerful and moving explanation of the local causes of a major event, an explanation that has found its way into every textbook survey of early American history, is an example of the consequent causing the antecedent.

In the fallacy of hindsight, we all have twenty-twenty vision after the fact. We could see what was going to happen. "I told you so" is the operative phrase for this fallacy. Ancient oracles who spoke in riddles that were almost impossible to understand and modern newspaper astrologers whose predictions, like the little papers in fortune cookies, are so general and vague that they could mean anything profit from the fallacy of hindsight. In Greek mythology the prophetess Cassandra told the Trojans what would happen to them in the war with the Greeks, but no one listened. If we go around warning everyone about everything that is going to happen, I guarantee that we will be right some of the time and people will avoid us all of the time.

Hindsight is not causal explanation. It is just a recitation of what actually happened on top of which we place our own judgments on who was at fault, what might have been, and why we should not let it happen again. The 9/11 Commission report on the attacks on the World Trade Center and the Pentagon is filled with hindsight. The authors even warn against hindsight as they apply it. In hindsight, it was possible to see the threat. In hindsight, the intelligence community did not perform adequately. In hindsight, the administration made mistakes. By selecting from the multitude of bits of information and assessments available at the time and putting these selected pieces together to become a warning of what did in fact occur, the commission created a causal narrative that is, incontestably, correct. But to look back at those days from the perspective of 2003 and 2004 and lift out those gossamer threats of causation from all the other forces at work is hardly a model historical method.

That said, hindsight can yield useful results for a historian. In *The Tipping Point,* popular sociologist and reporter Malcolm Gladwell explains how "change so often happens as quickly and as unexpectedly as it does." Relating a series of case studies of epidemics and similar events, Gladwell suggests that "things can happen all at once, and little changes can make a huge difference." The tipping point—the big change—comes when enough little changes have occurred to tip the balance and trigger a big change. "It's the boiling point. It's the moment on the graph when the line starts to shoot straight upwards."

In fact, no one at the time knows when or how many of these little changes are necessary for the big change. Nor does Gladwell actually provide causal explanations in the conventional sense. He simply tells stories about a series of big changes and notes the accumulation of little changes that came earlier. Hindsight, not causal analysis, connects the two. Although it is an example of hindsight, the "tipping point" is a heuristic, a teaching device of some novelty and validity, because it shows that big events can come upon us unawares.

Another useful version of hindsight for historians is the "paradigm shift" thesis. For a time, this was the hottest catchphrase in historical writing. In 1960, historian of science Thomas Kuhn proposed to explain how the Copernican model of the solar system (with the sun at the center) replaced the Ptolemaic model (with the earth at the center) by arguing that Copernicus had taken part in a paradigm shift. More and more astronomical observations had piled up that did not fit the Ptolemaic system. Astronomers clung to it, making it more and more complex to fit the data. By the time Copernicus began thinking about the solar system, the weight of the observations was too great for the older model to bear. The time was now ripe for a new model that fit the new observations. But did this piling up of contrary evidence cause the Copernican model of the planets orbiting the sun to sweep away its rival at the time that it did? Might Copernicus's theory have been brushed aside? The paradigm shift describes what happened but does not explain it. The weight of new evidence did not cause the old system to fold—Copernicus's insight did that. The value of the "paradigm shift" is that it reminds historians to give due weight to past thinkers' unwillingness to abandon long-held ideas, even in the face of lots of new, contradictory evidence.

The clustering illusion is similar to hindsight. In the real world, any data set or even a single data point may or may not be part of a pattern. People who study disease outbreaks run the risk of misrepresenting their cause when there is a cluster of cases near a suspicious environmental concern. The proximity of the two does not prove that the latter caused the diseases. During one of the terrible yellow fever epidemics that hit Philadelphia in the 1790s, doctors moved people out of the low-lying parts of the city and treated them with emetics (drugs that caused vomiting). The people did not catch the disease, and the doctors claimed that the emetics were an effective treatment. In fact, the disease is a virus transmitted through the bite of a mosquito. Moving the people away from the marshy, mosquito-filled areas on the edge of the Delaware and Schuylkill rivers saved the people, not the emetics. We cannot just assume that the data prove anything until we find out, independent of the cluster, how it got there. Correlation is not causation.

The self-fulfilling prophecy is rarely given credit for what it is—an argument about causation. The term was coined in 1949 by the sociologist Robert K. Merton, but the phenomenon is as old as human psychology. Merton was one of the giants of sociology in his time but is largely forgotten today. History sometimes does not give great minds their due. He introduced the concepts of role models and role theory, focus groups and opinion leaders. His imprint can be found all over modern sociological and social-psychological practice.

In the self-fulfilling prophecy we are told what will happen, and it does happen, not because the causal argument linking the initial and the subsequent event was sound, but because the prediction intervenes as its own cause. Various kinds of homeopathic remedies may work in this manner. They are supposed to relieve symptoms, and trusting in their efficacy, we do improve. The same process underlies the "placebo effect," where patients in a controlled experiment are told they are getting an experimental drug that is, in fact, nothing more than a sugar pill. For no other apparent reason than the self-fulfilling prophecy, the patients mend. Voodoo and other curses may work in the same way. Because the victim believes in the efficacy of the curse, anxiety and self-induced or "psycho-somatic" symptoms appear, and the promised evils come to pass.

The psychology is plain—we live up or down to others' expectations— but the self-fulfilling prophecy itself is poor historical argument because an effect is caused by its prediction. "You'll grow up just as bad as your brother," an angry teacher tells you, and lo! you do. The prediction, supposedly based on a sound comparison, is actually a cause of the later event. With our feelings of self-worth dashed, we decide that we are no better than our brother and let temptation overcome our sense of right and wrong. A self-fulfilling prophecy can work the other way. In a series of experiments, school teachers told average students in a class that they had been selected for that class because they had a special talent or ability. Their grades improved markedly as they lived up to their advance billing. The same kind of prophecy can improve the performance of teachers. Told by their supervisors that they had been selected to lead a class of especially talented students, the teachers enjoyed teaching the class more than their other classes and upgraded their classroom performance. (I should add that other studies have called these findings into question.)

In the fallacy of the false cause, we mistake an excuse for a cause or a motive for a cause. "My friend made me go to the movies instead doing my homework" may be an excuse rather than a cause. "I didn't have any choice" often conceals motive, purpose, or design behind the false cause. Motive is a form of causation but has to be proven. Too often, historians simply assume that the interest groups they saw at work in an event dictated or reflected the aims of the individual historical characters. The real person becomes a rational caricature of a human being, acting with uncanny insight and logic. In fact, the historians' hindsight has supplied this logic, for we often know far more about what was happening than the people on the scene.

False cause may arise from errors of "animistic language." Historians may assign motive to nations, armies, cultures, and other general things or inanimate objects. People have motives; nations do not. The Great Awakening was a religious revival that spread through the American colonies, especially New England, in the eighteenth century. The many preachers and their converts shared certain motives that caused them to act as they did. But to speak of a "New England mind" at work is to supply a single motive cause where many existed.

When we simply cannot fathom what made our subjects act as they did, we often supply motive from our own store of reasons. Behind this is the potent but unproved (and I think unprovable) thesis that human motivation has never really changed, for human nature is a constant. David Hume tackled this question in his *Treatise of Human Nature* (1739): "We must . . . glean up our experiments in this science from a cautious observation of human life, and take them as they appear in the common course of the world, by men's behaviour in company, in affairs, and in their pleasures." Hume found (I think no surprise to him, nor should it be to us) that human nature was really custom and values and that it varied from time to time and place to place. Our ideas, including those about ourselves, are "always deriv'd from a succession of changeable objects, and can never be convey'd to the mind by any thing stedfast and unchangeable."

Statistics and Causation

Some historians, often called quantifiers by those who would dismiss their work, rely upon numbers to prove their arguments. A statistical argument is merely another form of a causal statement. The historian knows, or should know, that numbers do not speak for themselves any more than a document speaks for itself. The tables and charts and other summaries of the numbers are assembled, assayed, and displayed according to the historian's choices.

Numbers and statistical analysis of numbers are like the facts in a narrative, evidence selected and offered to persuade us. As economists Robert Fogel and Stanley Engerman wrote in the technical second volume of their two-volume study of American slavery, "Where hard evidence was lacking on issues vital to the interpretation of slavery, we, like the historians who preceded us, were forced into speculation." But "by taking advantage of the extensive quantitative work of the cliometricians [quantitative methods historians] we have been able to reduce significantly the number of issues on which speculation was the only option." Their *Time on the Cross* (1974) won a prestigious Bancroft Prize even though Fogel and Engerman had found that slaves were, on the whole, better fed and housed than the urban working poor, that slavery was both profitable and expanding, that southern slave plantations were more economically efficient than northern family farms, and that most slaveholders neither bred slaves nor wanted to break up slave families by sale or gift.

I should add that the outcry of both economic historians and social historians of slavery against their findings—and their use of numbers in particular—rocked the profession for years. The contestants met in panels and gave talks at professional meetings. Paul David, Peter Temin, Richard Sutch, and Herbert Gutman published a collection of essays, *Reckoning with Slavery*, to rebut every substantive claim, along with many of the statistical conclusions, that Fogel and Engerman had reached. Gutman and Sutch concluded that Fogel and Engerman's most important contribution was a proof of "the failure of quantitative methods to provide historical evidence when divorced from the qualitative methods of history." In the collection, and in a separate work, Gutman, a student of the slave family, raised both moral and psychological questions. For example, even if whipping was not so common, what was the impact on the slave of the master's untrammeled power to use corporal punishment?

In the end, the interpretation of the statistics, not the statistics themselves, was what mattered. Was a small increase in the number of births of slaves on some plantations a proof of the intent to breed slaves? How many families broken as a result of the slave trade, or the migration of slavery from east to west, were enough to conclude that slavery tore apart families? Were samples unrepresentative? Were inferences warranted? Fogel and Engerman responded, in an exchange of views in the 1979–80 issues of the *American Economic Review*, that it was "now clear" that the antebellum South was not "economically stagnant" and that "free agriculture" was less profitable and less efficient than slave agriculture.

In a later book, Fogel continued his defense of method and substance: "The discovery that slaves were effective workers who had developed a much stronger family life, a more varied set of occupational skills, and a richer more distinct culture than previously recognized created an agonizing dilemma. . . . Did the findings [his and Engerman's] rob blacks of a history of resistance to slavery and cast them instead in the role of collaborators in their own oppression?" Loaded questions, all of them, and none susceptible to definitive statistical answers. The real problem of slavery was not that it was wasteful or unprofitable but that it "permitted one group of people to exercise unrestrained personal dominion over another group of people."

Even if one concludes that Fogel and Engerman's methods have withstood the assault of their critics, there are traps and snares for everyone who thinks that numbers speak for themselves. Three such perils are the **Atlantic City fallacy** (a.k.a. the **"gambler's hope" fallacy**), the **statistical fallacy** or **regression fallacy**, and the **unrepresentative sample**.

A gambler has spent the day playing games of chance in Atlantic City. His luck, he thinks, had been running bad. He has been losing steadily. But he keeps on playing because he is convinced that his luck must change. After all, it has to change—that is statistically certain, isn't it?

Nonsense. Take a coin and flip it. It comes up heads ten times in a row. Very unlikely statistically (.5 x .5 . . . ten times). What is the probability that it will come up tails the eleventh toss? The answer is one out of two. So long as each toss is independent of its predecessors, the odds on a single flip don't change. Now the gambler's luck may seem to shift, but like his losses, his winnings have no logical pattern save that of pure probability, and the longer he plays, whoever those probabilities favor (the house) will come out ahead.

Sounds like a problem for compulsive gamblers, but this kind of thinking about past and future events can have a devastating impact on all our lives. Desperate acts are more often bred by a faith that one's luck must change than by hopelessness and despair. We "throw the dice" hoping that the odds will favor us because we have not yet won. The buildup of troops in Vietnam during 1964–66 was such a throw of the dice. Each massive addition of men produced no improvement in the situation there, but President Johnson and his military advisors, falling into the gambler's fallacy, gambled that another increase in troops would change our luck. The "surge" in troop deployment to Iraq during the spring and summer of 2007 was another such gamble. Surely luck would favor American forces this time.

To be fair, defenders of the Vietnam War then and now would argue that it was or would have been won in the field, in part because of the troop concentrations, but that it was lost at home because of a lack of political will. If this were true, then the case above might be condemned as an example of the fallacy of hindsight. But if the premise is correct— that is, if there was no real improvement in the political situation in Vietnam—pouring in more troops was an example of the gambler's fallacy. As the adage goes, one should not throw good money after bad. Or, to quote Kenny Rogers, "You got to know when to fold 'em, know when to walk away and know when to run." Of course, that song is all about gambling too.

The contrapositive of a false statement is just as false. You are on a winning streak. You plunge in deeper and deeper. You cannot lose because your luck is running. That was how the American economy overheated in the late 1990s—everyone investing in the e-stocks, disregarding voices that said the multiplicity of new e-company start-ups were all selling the same items. They could not all be profitable. But no one was listening because everyone was on a winning streak that could not end. And the more investors sunk into the market, naturally, the more the stock prices of inherently valueless companies rose—until they went into reverse. Then pension plans crashed and life savings vanished into a bottomless pit.

Sometimes historians are victims of traps that illogic sets for gamblers. I know historians who have spent a career pursuing the one document that always seems to disappear around the next corner or who have pushed a thesis far beyond its limits. They are sure that all their hard work must bring a result—the prize-winning book, the chair at a top school, the long-sought fellowship—if only they persevere. Persistence in a scholar is a virtue; gambling a lifetime's labors on a daydream is a tragedy.

The regression fallacy is more complex than the gambler's fallacy but proceeds from the same kind of error. It applies to the distribution of characteristics within populations of people or things. It assumes that what is true of the mean (the average) or the mode (the most common type found) is true of everyone or everything thing else in the population or sample. In a now-legendary clash of historians serving as expert witnesses for the two sides in a lawsuit, Sears and Roebuck Company had to defend its policy of denying its female employees access to higher-paying commission jobs against the Equal Employment Opportunity Commission (EEOC). Statistics, causation, and history all came together in the courtroom.

The district court judge wanted to know whether women wanted the commission jobs. His opinion was as much a judgment on the use of statistics (which he found wanting) as on the liability of the defendant company. "An important concept to bear in mind in evaluating any statistical analysis is that no statistical analysis can prove causation per se." The expert witness for the company, historian Rosalind Rosenberg, had reported that women in the retail workforce generally preferred shorter hours so that they could spend more time with their families. The judge summarized Rosenberg's findings: "Differences between men and women have diminished in the past two decades, [but] these differences still exist and may account for different proportions of men and women in various jobs. . . . Differences in the number of men and women in a job could exist without discrimination by an employer." Historian Alice Kessler-Harris had, without success, argued for the EEOC that the wide disparity in numbers of men and women in commission sales at Sears "can only be explained by sex discrimination by employers." Judgment was given for the defendant company.

Expert witnesses testifying about statistics are an everyday occurrence in our courts. But this exchange between historians was different. In a surprise move, Rosenberg replied to Kessler-Harris's testimony by citing Kessler-Harris's own earlier work. Allegedly, it found that women wanted the regularity that noncommissioned jobs offered. In technical legal terms, Rosenberg had impeached Kessler-Harris's testimony in *Sears* by showing how it contradicted her previous scholarship.

There are two lessons in this tale. The first is that the federal district court judge, in following Rosenberg rather than Kessler-Harris, had committed the regression fallacy. Even if most women did not want the sales commission jobs, it did not mean that all women felt that way. A policy that denies to any what the majority may not want is still discriminatory. And if Sears denied all women the chance to move up, then it should have lost the suit.

The second lesson concerns the history profession. Like the authors of *Time on the Cross* and their critics, Rosenberg and Kessler Harris took their act on the road. They appeared singly and together on programs of conferences. The case caused waves in the profession as well. According to Kessler-Harris, Rosenberg had not played fair. "I did in fact write those words, and they are correctly quoted. But they describe the ideology of womanhood that emerged in the United States in the years before the Civil War. Why then use them as if they illustrated my perspectives on women in the 1970s?" Fair play in the arena of courtroom advocacy was not fair play in academe. Or was it?

The collateral damage for Rosenberg was a drumfire of criticism of her and her tactics by some feminist scholars. Others came to her defense. As Thomas Haskell and Sanford Levinson reported in a *Texas Law Review* article in 1988, the fallout from the Sears case led to "an unusually bitter academic controversy that has divided the field of women's history for almost three years." Haskell and Levinson asserted that "the vehemence of the criticism directed against Rosenberg raises troubling questions about academic freedom in terms of the consequences of political dissent within the scholarly community." Viewed a little more dispassionately, the issue should have been the conclusions one could draw from the statistics, as the EEOC case was purely statistical. Instead, the issue among the historians at least became one of ideology and interest group affiliation.

Without taking sides in this matter, it should be clear to all parties that a display of statistics of who wins and who loses (the experts on discrimination law would call this a "disparate impact" study) does not of itself substitute for sound causal argument. Quantitative methods merely allow, if done properly, the historian (or the judge) to see patterns in the evidence that may require causal explanations.

The regression fallacy overlaps other causal fallacies when we mistake the distribution of an event or characteristic over the entire group for a cause of relationships within it. In medicine, doctors may find that most patients on a particular treatment regimen are improving. To assume that the regimen was helping everyone is an example of the regression fallacy. Some people will have been improving on their own without the specific medical intervention, and others may be getting better in spite of the medication. Only by establishing the causal relationship between the medication and the illness can the medical researcher conclude that the medication itself is helping.

The fallacy of the unrepresentative sample is similar to the regression fallacy but applies to a sample portion of the population. Sampling design is a highly complex process. Experts use it to pick out a jury from a jury panel that will favor their client at trial. Police use it when "profiling" suspects. The "exit poll" after an election is based on a sampling design. The sample population's tested characteristics are supposed to match the same characteristics in the larger population, so that findings based on the sample will explain or predict the behavior of the larger group.

An unrepresentative sample can lead to some pretty misleading findings. The Alfred Kinsey reports on male sexual habits are an example. Although he did not employ a sampling design, he interviewed only a small sample of Americans. Hence his results were a sample of the whole, and from them he reached some pretty striking conclusions. Kinsey found that one in ten men were homosexual, one in two had committed adultery, and one in six had been victimized by or had victimized another family member sexually. Recent research into his data has discovered that his sample (the men and women he asked) included prisoners and hospital patients in considerably larger numbers than their proportion of the actual population. In fact, they were more likely to have been homosexual, violated their marriage vows, and been victims of sexual abuse by other family members than the population at large.

Fallacies that misuse numbers often come in combinations. Sometimes the multiple fallacies overlap one another, particularly in the hands of someone doing history who has a predetermined agenda. In a recent student law review note on the *Roe v. Wade* abortion decision, two statements illustrate how one statistical fallacy can lead to or support another. The author proposed two statistical arguments, both persuasive when taken at face value, for why abortion should be made harder to obtain. First, he cited a lawsuit in which one thousand women joined in a "friend of the court" brief reporting that their abortions left them with physical and emotional scars. While the women's statements were deeply moving, the logic linking them to the author's argument combined statistical fallacies with *post hoc, ergo propter hoc.*

With over one million abortions a year in the United States, were the one thousand women a sufficiently large sample? Perhaps, if they were representative of the female adult population as a whole or, in the alternative, a purely random group of women. In fact, they were a self-selected group who opposed abortion. Were these women, all of whom had come forward to join the brief because they felt that they had been given poor advice or poor care, representative or random? Hardly.

To this statistical boner, the author added a causal error. It was reasoning backward to argue that the right to choose an abortion (the precedent) should be curtailed because some of those choices had turned out to be poor ones (the consequent). The same argument could be made about any choice that turned out badly—for example, sexual intercourse itself. Would anyone argue to criminalize lovemaking because some relationships later turn sour?

The student author's second argument once again combined statistical and logical errors of causation. He suggested that legalized abortion would lead to increased rates of abuse of women by men. His basis for this argument was the fact that more men than women favored legalized abortion. While this was a numerical fact, it did not of itself imply a logical connection. Instead, it exhibited the regression fallacy. Did all or even most men who favored legalized abortion wish to force women to have abortions? The numbers themselves do not provide the answer. Was it possible that at least some of the men who favored legalized abortion did so because they were generally in favor of women's rights, or because they were liberals, or because they were influenced by women who favored legal abortion, or in spite of their personal opposition to abortion? If the author's argument was valid, was not the contrapositive just as valid—that men who opposed the right to abortion were unlikely to abuse women by forcing them to carry their pregnancies to term? Evidence presented to the Supreme Court in the course of *Casey v. Planned Parenthood* (1992) demonstrated the contrary proposition—that women seeking abortions were sometimes threatened by husbands demanding that the women bear and birth the child.

Mistakes in causal arguments may result from simple negligence or from ideological intent. An appreciation of the strengths and weaknesses of causal thinking enables us to pierce the veil of a spokesman's self-proclaimed neutrality. As the Civil War approached, southern intellectuals like Virginia's George Fitzhugh became more extreme in their praise for slavery and more determined to defend it against those who would end it. Fitzhugh's proslavery essays purported to explain why slavery was good. This reasoning bears examination:

> We would remind those who deprecate and sympathize with negro slavery, that his slavery here relieves him from a far more cruel slavery in Africa, or from idolatry and cannibalism, and every brutal vice and crime that can disgrace humanity; and that it Christianizes, protects, supports and civilizes him; that it governs him far better than free laborers at the North are governed. . . . Our negroes are not only better off as to physical comfort than free laborers, but their moral condition is better.

How exactly did slavery perform this benevolent transformation of the barbarous African into a moral and docile worker? One might supply the answer that the master—benevolent in general, stern when required, always having the best interest of his servants at heart—was the missing link in the causal chain. Thus the very men that the abolitionists excoriated as whoremongers and thieves were in fact the cause of slavery's benefits. But Fitzhugh left out all causal analysis. There remains the bald comparison.

When an account omits cause, the historian—and all the rest of us—should become especially wary. If slavery was the centerpiece of the southern economy, if slave labor was essential to the staple crops that benefited every white southerner, if those same white southerners feared the consequences of freeing the people of color in their own midst, if there was no way out of the dilemma, then the most reasonable thing to do was to defend slavery as good for the master class and for the slaves. Surely northern factory owners did the same thing when they extolled the virtues of free labor and paid their immigrant workforce a pittance? Surely western land speculators did the same when they boasted of the glories of westward expansion as they gouged the would-be farmer on the plains? Thus the cause of slavery's spread through the South and the cause of Fitzhugh's defense of it converge, though he never hinted at the economic basis of either.

Good history requires causal analysis. But it is not always easy to identify causes. There are also minefields of fallacies and mistakes, shortcuts that led to deadfalls and barely hidden booby traps. A philosophy of history for our time must be rigorously self-conscious about causation. Events do not explain themselves. At the same time, we should be chary of too-easy and too-uniform assertions of causation. Finally, we need to be charitable with one another's causal reasoning, recognizing that the trusses that support the roadway of our bridge to the past are no more visible than the causal links we describe in our histories.

5

One of Us Is Lying

Many historians who shy away from any suggestion of fictional
. . . history welcome the invitation to be "imaginative," "inventive,"
"creative"—words bandied about so frequently in the profession
today that one almost does not notice them or consider their
implications.

—Gertrude Himmelfarb (1994)

History is a lie we tell about the dead, the old saying goes, and the saying has some truth, for some histories are out-and-out propaganda. Given this lurking peril, Himmelfarb's warning about the thin line between imaginative reconstruction and simple invention should trouble us. The history in the many editions of the *Great Soviet Encyclopedia* changed as successive leaders of the Communist Party needed a particular version of history to sustain their policies. Post–World War II German and Japanese history textbooks had convenient memory lapses when it came to describing wartime atrocities. American history textbooks either omitted mention of slavery and Jim Crow or minimized the pervasiveness of racism until the civil rights movement changed the way we taught history in our schools.

Truth and lying are at the center of some of the most often quoted stories and reputations from our early republic—for example, the account by the preacher, author, and itinerant bookseller Mason Weems concerning young George Washington and the cherry tree. "I cannot tell a lie, I chopped down the cherry tree," Washington supposedly tells his father. In fact, the incident never happened. Weems invented it for his biography of Washington to make a point for the young reader (and sell copies of his book). Weems knew that he was lying about Washington but thought that the fabrication would teach children not to lie—a perfect example of the theme of this chapter. Lying may be rational or illogical or both, but it is a subject that cannot be avoided in any philosophy of history for our time.

History itself is replete with lies and lying. The best and worst example is the **big lie**. The big lie is a simple message of allegedly great importance. Repeated over and over, despite the piling up of counterevidence, it has a power that truth cannot deflect and evidence to the contrary cannot undo. One master of the big lie was Nazi German dictator Adolph Hitler, not least because he used the big lie himself while accusing his enemies of using it. In his memoir, *Mein Kampf,* Hitler accused the Jews of costing Germany victory in World War I. (Actually, some German Jews did not support the war, but others did, and some died in the trenches.) Allegedly, Jews convinced the masses of Germans to accept defeat.

> All this was inspired by the principle—which is quite true in itself—that in the big lie there is always a certain force of credibility; because the broad masses of a nation are always more easily corrupted in the deeper strata of their emotional nature than consciously or voluntarily; and thus in the primitive simplicity of their minds they more readily fall victims to the big lie than the small lie, since they themselves often tell small lies in little matters but would be ashamed to resort to large-scale falsehoods. It would never come into their heads to fabricate colossal untruths, and they would not believe that others could have the impudence to distort the truth so infamously.

This was, as Hitler knew, a perfect description of the technique that he and his minister of propaganda, Joseph Goebbels, mastered. They told the big lie as they insisted that the Jews were guilty of that very offense. A clever lie, told enough times, became a perfect counterfeit of truth.

A lie does not have to be all that big to make a difference in history. Peter Sagal's *The Book of Vice* (2007) tells the story of a lie that may have determined the outcome of the 2004 presidential election. "In the 2004 election season John Kerry spent a lot of time shaking his long face slowly back and forth, wondering how in the world anybody could ever question the fact that he was a war hero [in Vietnam]. He was there, it had happened, there were witnesses." But "the people lying about him wore ties and looked calm on TV. They had theories, and spoke of dates and names, and pointed out inconsistencies." All this while Kerry and his witnesses "were handicapped by their own incredulity: how could this be happening." The denunciation of Kerry's wartime activities was a collection of little lies, opinions masquerading as facts, and misrepresentations that now take their place in the history of lies under the rubric of "swiftboating." Sometimes a lot of small lies can do as much damage as the one big lie.

Lies about the Dead

Despite infamous examples of lying in histories and lying in history, lying is part of history. I do not mean this ironically. Insofar as the lie is part of human behavior, indeed perhaps an essential part of human behavior, it is a proper subject for history. History teaches us that lies and truths are related to one another in complex ways. To reason your way out of a possible lie, you must know something of the truth already. At the same time, for a lie to work—for it to fool us—it must wear the mask of truth. In everyday life, the answers we get and give are not binary but complicated. Lying and truth telling are not the opposites they appear to be.

The building blocks of historians' accounts are the facts we present to our readers. What if those facts are wrong? Is that lying? I traced some of these questions in my *Past Imperfect*. The *Journal of American History* is the journal of record for historians in that field, and every submission goes through many hoops before it is published. The "refereeing" process is stringent, with up to six experts in the particular subject matter of an essay submitted to the *Journal* writing careful assessments of the submission's originality and accuracy. The editor of the journal selects the readers and weighs in himself or herself, acting as a preliminary screener of submissions. All in all, only one in ten submissions makes it into the journal. One would suppose, then, that one could trust the authority of any article in the journal. The very best article each year wins a prize. In 1996, it went to Michael Bellesiles for a stunning piece of detective work that overturned much conventional wisdom on gun ownership in early America.

Bellesiles's essay was a sketch for a full-dress book to come. It was striking in its clarity of argument: "Before we accept an individual right to gun ownership in the Second Amendment, we must establish who were 'the people' who were allowed to 'keep and bear arms.' Did they in fact own guns? What was the popular attitude toward firearms? Did such perceptions change over time? We will find that gun ownership was exceptional in the eighteenth and early nineteenth centuries, even on the frontier, and that guns became a common commodity only with industrialization, with ownership concentrated in urban areas. The gun culture grew with the gun industry." To support this conclusion, Bellesiles presented both quantitative and qualitative evidence. The former came in the shape of a table of gun ownership in a variety of places based on guns in estate inventories. The conventional count was around 50 percent. Bellesiles found that it was less than 15 percent.

Many historians are chary of numbers, fearing that numbers can be manipulated. The debates over *Time on the Cross* and *Sears v. EEOC* sustained those fears. Bellesiles was confident of the story his numbers told. He concluded that if "there are problems attached to the use of statistics in history . . . the most thoughtful critics of quantitative methods agree that there is no real alternative to employing these records, with the proper caveats inserted. Without such efforts at quantification, we are left to repeat the unverifiable assertions of other historians, or to descend into a pointless game of dueling quotations—matching one literary allusion against another. Far better to match an entire collection of documents with other primary materials; for instance, probate and militia records. . . . In other words, the aggregate matters."

The book that followed, *Arming America* (2000), won the prestigious Bancroft Prize and was hailed by leading scholars in trade reviews. It was, for a time, the new authority on gun ownership in early America and was widely cited as authority for gun control laws and a narrow reading of the Second Amendment's "right to keep and bear arms."

The only problem was that Bellesiles either had not found what he claimed—indeed had not even looked—or had looked and falsified his findings. He could not duplicate them when challenged or replicate them when invited to do so by other scholars in the field and a special panel his own university created to revisit his work. He resigned in disgrace from his post, and his publisher removed his book from its list. Columbia University rescinded the Bancroft Prize awarded the book.

Long before Bellesiles took up his yellow legal pads and began to make tick marks on them representing, he said, guns in estate inventories, another American historian wrote what most scholars today would dismiss as untruths. One of the first graduates of the Johns Hopkins Ph.D. program was a stern-faced and sober-thinking southerner named Woodrow Wilson. He would go on to a career as a scholar and teacher at Princeton University, becoming its president, then governor of the state of New Jersey, and finally president of the United States in 1912. He was a moralist and a Progressive reformer. One might expect that he would bring to his historical explanations the scientific, impartial objectivity of the professional historian.

In 1901, he edited a ten-volume collection of documents on American history. Its introduction surveyed the broad landscape of the American saga. When the English came to America, according to Wilson, they found "that the interior was one vast wilderness, grown thick with tangled forests." Now this was a factual error. The English found Indian gardens and palisaded towns as well as woods and swamps, and the primary sources available to him at the time said so. Wilson continued that North America exhibited a wildness that baffled some of the Europeans, but not for long. Those Anglo-Saxons were a "whole race of venturesome and hardy" men, whose "sober mind" and "steady business sagacity" combined with "high imaginative hope" had led them to sea and then "towards new ports and new homes in America." Actually, the first of these Anglo-Saxon entrepreneurs were terrible businessmen. Their ventures uniformly went bust, leaving investors back home to pick up the pieces.

Wilson continued that the "wild savagery" of the tribesmen did not deter the English, for the Indian "feared the white man with an overmastering dread." Actually, the first English accounts found the Indians admirable in many ways and gave no evidence that the Indians dreaded the English—came to despise, perhaps, but did not dread. Wilson: "Steadily, relentlessly, and by a masterful advance from settlement to settlement which they [the Indians] could in no wise withstand, they were pushed back into the forests." In fact, the Indians held their own until European epidemic diseases, to which the natives had no immunities, reduced the natives' numbers by 90 percent. Were Wilson's "facts" actually lies? A lie requires intent; did Wilson's introduction have the purpose of justifying the dispossession of the natives and the triumph of the ruling races, and if so, was this sufficient intent to misread his own primary sources?

For the historian trying to tell a larger story, for example in a textbook, selection and arrangement of evidence are necessary and inevitable. We simply cannot get it all in, and if we did no one would be able to understand what we were saying—the dense foliage preventing us from seeing the whole forest. No synthesis, no matter how informed, no matter how comprehensive, represents more than a small fraction of the whole story. Now if lying includes saying nothing about something, when is the decision to omit facts tantamount to lying?

In the Cold War era, textbooks' selection of facts all pointed in the same direction. As Columbia University's Allan Nevins and Williams College's Henry Steele Commager explained in their *Pocket History of the United States,* "it was inevitable from the beginning" that settlement would sweep over the continent from east to west; that the savages would be overcome; that the progress of civilization would pass "through several marked stages" in which toleration of religion would gain ground and the power of European institutions like state churches recede; and that the "common heritage" of English language and political ideas would direct the nation on its upward course. Such facts had an immediate utility in the Cold War of words. American history was proof that dialectical materialism was bad history. The end of history was not the Soviet Union's dictatorship of the proletariat. Were the obvious omissions—the dispossession of the Indians, for example, or the persistent violation of Indian treaties by the settlers and their government—lies?

For the historian trying to make sense of a story, the problem is one of explaining. If lying is slanting an account against the evidence, then historians have some answering to do. There is no better example of this than the way leading southern historians made the slaves and the freedmen into the scapegoats for southern problems. Thus Claude Bowers, in 1929, called Reconstruction a "tragic era" and believed that blacks participating in public life presented an "astonishing" and hideous spectacle. Black people were responsible for the South's troubles.

Bowers's book was hugely popular, but as scholarship it paled in comparison to Paul Buck's deeply sentimental *Road to Reunion, 1865–1900* (1937), a Pulitzer Prize winner. Buck lamented that the end of the Civil War and the advent of "Negro rule" by an "inferior race" had brought to the South a "disorder worse than war, and oppression unequaled in American annals." In the meantime, the "nobility of sacrifices" of the Confederacy's bold warriors had been overwhelmed by force of numbers alone. He opined that only when the Negro and his Republican puppeteers were driven from their roosts could "peace and brotherhood" among the whites of North and South be achieved. Over time, with the eventual consent of the whites of the North, "the South" (by which term Buck invariably meant the white South) would be allowed to deal with the "Negro problem" on its own. Then the "stability of race relations" would give "the Negro a chance . . . to take the first steps of progress." Wrong, surely, and hatefully so, but lies?

Liars All!

Why did men as honored and honorable as those I have quoted write as they did? Perhaps they simply believed what they were saying. Perhaps they believed that the lie saved them from facing an unpalatable truth. Or could it be that they regarded history as mere rhetoric—shades of Hayden White's warning? Before we begin to discourse on the prejudices of past historians, we need to take a closer look at lying and human nature.

In his best-selling work of political satire, *Lies and the Lying Liars Who Tell Them,* humorist and political commentator Al Franken offers a list of his favorite liars. While the evidence he presents may or may not be convincing, his list is surely too short. Who are the lying liars? We all are. In police interrogations even the innocent lie about some things. In our everyday relationships, we lie because it is easier than telling the truth, or because the lie will make us look better than the truth, or because the lie will make our listener feel better. In the cartoonist Scott Adams's *Dilbert and the Way of the Weasel,* the "weasel-zone" at work is where everyone "is aware that you're a manipulative, scheming, misleading sociopath." Our leaders lie to us regularly, so much so that politicians rank very low on public opinion polls of occupations because we do not trust them to tell the truth.

There are lies that signal their own arrival, so commonplace that everyone knows what they are. "We have great confidence in coach," the general manager says, a sure sign that coach is on his way out. "No matter what, I'll always love you" forewarns the end of an affair, the speaker having already forgotten why he or she became infatuated in the first place. "The check is in the mail" as soon as I find my checkbook, put some money in my bank account, buy stamps, and sit down with your bill. Lawyers' prevarications seem so commonplace that it has become a joke to ask, "How do you know when lawyers are lying?" (Answer: when their lips are moving.)

When we resort to **rationalization,** we lie to ourselves and others. Psychologist Albert Bandura's "social learning theory" has identified the myriad forms of this kind of lying when it explains away an act we know is evil. Often the lie involves a logical or semantic fallacy as well. We say that we have acted in the greater good—the end justified the means. We use euphemisms to conceal the enormity of our misconduct. We say that it was "ethnic cleansing" instead of mass murder. We compare the victim to an evil person, relying on guilt by association, a weak analogy, or loaded words to excuse our own conduct. We shift the blame: "I was just following orders." We share the blame: "Everyone was doing it." We deny the effects of our actions: "Nobody really minded." We deny our victims their humanity: "They're all criminals anyhow," a form of stereotyping. Finally, we blame the victim: "She had it coming."

Philosopher Harry Frankfurt's clever *On Bullshit* explains that "after all, every use of language without exception has some, but not all, of the characteristics of lies." And make no mistake, clever lying can work wonders. The lie we tell ourselves lets us sleep at night. Psychologists tell us that one way we cope with tragedy and anger is through make-believe. They call it fantasizing. In other words, lying works because we want to be told lies. Lies can comfort us. For example, the doctor who tells a patient dying from inoperable cancer that she does not want to invade the patient's body with the surgery is lying with the patient's willing compliance. The lie we tell others can gain ends otherwise unattainable. Our lies may keep us safe from prying eyes.

Artful Artifice

I am not defending lying. But I do believe that the historian may find that the lie serves artistic goals. *Artful* and *artifice,* like so many English words, have two very different meanings. *Artful* means learned and wise, as well as clever and deceitful. *Artifice* is skill at construction and also trickery. Today, from special effects in movies to plagiarism in prize-winning works of music, a mixture of truth and lie infuses the fine and lively arts. Deception in them holds the eye and captures the heart. The vanishing point in the Romantic landscape paintings of John Constable in England and Thomas Cole in America gives the illusion of depth to a flat canvas surface. When Iago lies to Othello, a costume drama turns into one of the world's great tragedies. The plot twist in the most famous of all "film noir" movies, *The Third Man,* is a lie about a hit-and-run death that makes all the pieces of the puzzle fit. The mystery story that made Agatha Christie a household word, and still one of the grandest detective novels ever penned, *The Murder of Roger Ackroyd* (1926), revolves around two lies and an apparently unsolvable logical puzzle so ingenious that the reader is held captive to the final page.

Like the fictional detective, historians have to deal with lying in the documentary record. Even the most important of our leaders lie. As Arthur Schlesinger Jr. wrote in his journals (recalling what he had said to the congressional committee during the impeachment hearings for President Bill Clinton), "Most people have lied about their sex lives at one time or another. . . . Gentlemen always lie about their sex lives." Schlesinger had meant to be flip and came away chastened from the storm of criticism his remark stirred: "I guess flippancy is a great mistake." It may have been the wrong occasion for the comment in the investigation of a president's sexual conduct, but every historian who writes biography knows that Schlesinger was right.

Historians can be reticent about such lying—Schlesinger never mentioned John F. Kennedy's or Robert F. Kennedy's extramarital sexual adventures in his books about them—or they can make the lying a central feature of a biography, as some biographers of Benjamin Franklin, Thomas Jefferson, Franklin and Eleanor Roosevelt, both Kennedys, Lyndon Johnson, and Bill Clinton have. Whether to reveal the lie or let it lie is up to the historian. Does the historian lie when he or she decides not to reveal the truth? If a lie requires the intention to deceive, is omitting the truth lying? "It wasn't important, so I left it out" is the most common reason that historians offer for not telling the reader, but concealing a lie is another form of lying.

Perhaps equally important for us to understand is that historians can invoke the artful/artifice formula in their work. They fool the eye and add to the plot to gain legitimate ends. A superb example is John Demos's multiple-prize-winning book *The Unredeemed Captive* (1994). In it, Demos imaginatively recaptured conversations that must have taken place in some form or another but were not recorded. In the dramatic centerpiece of the book, a New England family is attempting to ransom a child back from the Indians who captured her. In one passage, the girl's brother and she speak to one another through interpreters, she having forgotten her English, in a smoke-filled Canadian longhouse. "Perhaps it went something like this. . . . Smoke from the firepit stings their eyes. Voices float indistinctly toward them from the far walls. Human forms, a dozen or more, loom in the murk: squatting, lounging, bent to one or another little task. Slowly, one of the forms—no, two—move forward: a woman, slightly ahead, then a man. The woman draws very near, her eyes searching the three strange faces in front of her."

We know from historical records that the meeting did take place, but its details are lost to us. Using the techniques of the novelist, Demos filled in the empty spaces in the canvas. He admitted that he had taken liberties with the records—inventing dialogue, for example—but surely the historian, borrowing from the historical novelist, could fill in the missing evidence with educated guesses. From novels, as he reported in an 1998 essay for the *American Historical Review*, he learned the "strategies, the techniques, the 'moves'" to recreate a full-bodied past from fragments that survived. These enabled the historian to peer over if not cross the "boundary" between fact-based scholarship and fiction. The trick was to combine an almost excessive concern with those details that could be verified with a sense of the human condition—the ties that bound us to people in the past.

Demos's attempt to use novelistic techniques to fill in gaps is necessary when historians want to write about ordinary people. Most people do not leave much of a paper trail behind. In the past, when literacy was hardly universal and writing took time, effort, and the money to pay for paper, pen, and ink, ordinary people simply passed from view without a documented record of their lives other than birth, marriage, and death. Historians have found ways, artificial but effective, to bring these men and women back to life.

Novelistic history (to coin a term) has an answer to the puzzle that history is impossible. Appropriately, it is drawn from a tried-and-true novelistic technique. In *Tristram Shandy* Lawrence Sterne recounts the fictional life story of the title character, beginning with the events leading up to his conception. Periodically, he addresses the reader directly, commenting upon his own tale. Novelistic historians deploy the same literary device, pausing their histories to tell us how they were constructed. In his tale of the many histories of East Hampton, Long Island, Timothy Breen reveals, "I observe myself going about the business of interpreting the past out of a concern to let the reader know where I stand. . . . Historians have a responsibility to converse openly with their readers." Breen was more than a chronicler in this story, he was a participant of sorts in the town's attempt to rediscover a lost past, but his reflections apply to all of us. In his remarkable survey of life among the woodlands Indians, *Facing East from Indian Country*, Daniel Richter did not cite Breen, but he assayed the same answer to history's impossibility. "So the chapters that follow are as much about *how* we might develop eastward-facing stories of the [Native American] past as about the stories themselves." He opened his book with three vignettes of encounters between Indians and European explorers, all from the now irretrievably lost Indian point of view. Hence "these scenes are imagined." The more liberties novelistic historians take with the existing sources, the greater their need to "converse openly" with the reader. Unfortunately for anyone who expects to find definitude—and an answer to the impossibility of history—these methodological asides almost always confess that the author cannot really know what happened.

Another of these methods is called "experimental history." Historian Martha Hodes described this "unconventional" and highly imaginative method in "Experimental History in the Classroom," a piece in the May

2007 issue of the AHA journal *Perspectives*. Experimental history "offered scholars new ways to develop argument and to convey complexity." It expanded the boundaries by empowering historians to tell a story from different perspectives at the same time, much as a novelist would. The attention to small details to make a scene come alive and engage the reader is not new, or even experimental, but the idea that history is a "conversation" that the historian, and the reader, overhear is also a borrowing from the novel. At the edge of experimental history lies the invented dialogue, based on what we do know and what we can surmise. We know that the dialogue took place, and we supply the words.

Although a skeptical questioner would ask the experimental historian, "How do you know? What is your evidence?" in fact the experimental historian is sometimes more critical and careful about evidence than a conventional historian. The conventional historian can write the story "from the note cards," and what we read is what the historian found. The experimental historian has to think a lot harder about every piece of surviving evidence, for all of it has to be used, not just repeated, to create the missing dialogue or scene.

Although they do not call themselves experimental historians, the authors of "microhistories" borrow certain experimental history techniques. As I wrote of Laurel Thatcher Ulrich's wonderful, prize-winning *A Midwife's Tale, The Life of Martha Ballard, Based on Her Diary, 1785–1812* (1991), in my *Sensory Worlds in Early America*, she

> transformed a slender and terse diary of midwife, mother, and businesswoman Martha Ballard of Hallowell, Maine, into a source that enables us to imagine the entire range of women's activities in early modern New England. We feel the cold of the winters' nights and the rough textures of homespun because Ulrich lived the story. She spent enough time on the upper Penobscot to enter Ballard's world. Ulrich's prose conveys her own intimate experience. She claims the diary speaks for itself—"One might wish for more detail, for more open expressions of opinion, fuller accounts of medical remedies or obstetrical complications, more candor in describing physicians or judges, and less circumspection in recording scandal, yet for all its reticence, Martha's diary is an unparalleled document in early American history. It is powerful in part because it is so difficult to use, so unyielding in its dailiness." In fact, it is with Ulrich's eyes, not Ballard's, that we see Northern New England at the end of the eighteenth century.

When artistry borrows from artifice, history can come alive.

On the other side of the nonfiction/fiction barrier, historical novels combine truth and lies to delight and amuse us with scenes that we could never have seen otherwise. The novelist depends upon the historian in these cases, pouring over historical accounts to describe accurately a place and time. The characters in the novel may be real historical personages or invented, or a combination of both, but what makes them come alive is the joint venture of novelist and historian. As Rhys Isaac wrote in his Pulitzer Prize–winning *Transformation of Virginia, 1740–1790* (1982): "The concepts—and the artistry—of all who have found ways to enter powerfully into alien worlds of experience, whether as novelists, dramatists, painters, literary critics, or social scientists, must be employed wherever they promise to be serviceable in the quest . . . to reconstruct something of the participants' worlds as they experienced them."

Borrowing historical insight from the novel is a two-way street. When he was testifying in his defense against a charge of copyright violation, historical novelist Dan Brown explained how he and his wife, Blythe, had used one history book:

> An important book for this early research [for Brown's *The Da Vinci Code*] was *The Hiram Key* by Christopher Knight and Robert Lomas. This book examines the role of the Masons and the Knights Templar in excavating and then hiding a cache of early Christian writings. It also mentions the family of Jesus (siblings as opposed to children), the origins of Christianity, the Gnostic Gospels, and Rosslyn Chapel, in Edinburgh. Looking back at my copy of *The Hiram Key*, I can see that either Blythe or myself has underlined passages that speculate as to the nature of what the Templars found and the subsequent impact on Christianity. We also underlined sections that deal with Constantine and the importance of Sol Invictus in determining modern Christian dates and practices.

Lest the reader think that the novel is itself a history, E. L. Doctorow, author of the best-selling historical novel *Ragtime* and others, replied that the reader who wanted historical truth should not believe every word in a novel. If art that fools the eye with false perspective and drama that recreates reality on a stage have value, and surely they do, the impact of art and drama come from trickery akin to fabrication.

Historical memoirs often perform the same magic act, crossing back and forth between fact and fiction. Had best-selling author James Frey admitted his work was more fiction than fact, he would have escaped the opprobrium heaped on him. In 2003 he published his memoir *A Million Little Pieces*. The book sold millions of copies, its tale of drug addiction and violent abuse followed by a courageous rehabilitation touching readers all over the country. His supposedly true story of suffering and redemption so moved the television celebrity Oprah Winfrey that she made his book a selection of her book club.

In 2005, the investigative Web site thesmokinggun.com discovered that Frey had fabricated significant portions of the memoir. For example, therapists at the rehab center he visited protested that his account of his stay included many falsehoods. In a story that is supposed to be true (as true as the memoir writer can recall), Frey had exaggerated, invented, and misrepresented events. He was never as bad a dude as he had portrayed himself in the book or on *Oprah*.

When first questioned about his memoir, he and his publisher insisted that everything in it was true and that he "stood by the essential truth of my book." After an embarrassing tongue-lashing by Winfrey on her television show, he admitted that he had fabricated much of the story, and in a note added to later printings he explained, "I wanted the stories in the book to ebb and flow, to have dramatic arcs, to have the tension that all great stories require," so "I altered events all the way through the book." A work of fiction inspired by events in his life became a memoir, and the rest was publishing history. But for us is the lesson a different one? Artful artifice had won readers' hearts and ennobled their lives.

Frey was not the first author to intentionally lie in a memoir and find that lying got a message across to readers that might not otherwise have been received. Reflect on Alex Haley's blockbuster best-seller, *Roots* (1976), supposedly based on a decade of research in America and Africa and Haley's own family's memories. This memoir's revelations about slavery and racism stirred the nation's conscience. Haley won the National Book Award and a Pulitzer Prize. The television miniseries based on the book won multiple awards and showed Americans in terms they could grasp the enormity of slavery's shamefulness. In fact, the central portion of the book, including the African materials, was almost entirely lifted from another author's work, and the rest of *Roots* was fiction. The background that Haley gave to interviewers was a lie, but from the book and the television version of the story millions of Americans learned about the horrors of slavery in a way they had not grasped before Haley's trickery.

Then there was Rigoberta Menchú, winner of the Nobel Peace Prize in 1992 for her attempts to protect her Indian brothers and sisters during the civil wars in Guatemala. She had documented her own family's earlier sufferings at the hands of racist government forces in her memoir *I, Rigoberta Menchú* (1983), a book that brought her and her people's plight to the attention of the reading world. In the book she asserted that she had grown up in a poor Indian peasant household, had never gone to school, and had been oppressed by rapacious landlords and that one brother and her father had been tortured, and both ultimately killed, by the ruling clique. She had watched as another brother died of malnutrition.

Then anthropologist David Stoll, working in the region of Guatemala that Menchú called home, found that key facts in her memoir were false. Her father was not the victim of landlords but was involved in a dispute with in-laws; she went to two prestigious boarding schools; and her brothers were not dead at all. Even her account of her early days as a labor organizer cannot be true, for she was in school at the time. The embroidery and outright fabrication brought her fame but, perhaps more important, turned attention to the plight of the real victims in a way that a straightforward account might not.

The genre of the faked memoir has a long history, throughout which the fabrication has enlightened and delighted readers. Long ago, the memoir was assumed to be a kind of fiction, a first-person novel. Famous twentieth-century authors like Lillian Hellman, Mary McCarthy, and Ernest Hemingway wrote memoirs in which critics found intentional factual errors. The misstatements work as literature, as fiction, however. What else would the reader expect from such literary giants?

Biographer Nancy Milford concluded, "In the end, maybe a memoir is no more about redemption than it is about the tricks of memory, the self-deceptions of age and the urgency a writer feels to say: This is the way I need to remember, this is how I wish I'd behaved, this is my false memoir as best I can write it." So true, wrote editor and memoir author Marie Arana of her own *American Chica*: "If there is such a thing as truth, I played with it. These were no calculated lies, but I shaped truth (as I understood it) to my own ends, used it for my own devices. I moved from the brain cells that remember to the cells that allow us to dream."

We are expected to know an artistic fiction when we see or hear it, and we do not expect to see it in a history book. The publisher classifies works as fiction or nonfiction, and there is where we find it on Barnes and Noble's shelves (though Barnes and Noble bookstores left Frey on the nonfiction bestseller shelf). We enter the playhouse or the movie theater accepting the fact that we will see fiction. Even when the play or the movie "is based on a true story," we know there will be invented dialogue and scenes. Indeed, when all is said and done, the fictional additions and alterations work when and precisely because they closely parallel the logic of truth, retaining logical form even when they are entirely false.

Our imagination, whether in the artist's eye or the author's pen, dances back and forth across the indefinite boundary between truth and lie. Could it be that reality itself crosses over this boundary in both directions all the time? To claim otherwise is to deny us the power to envision what we cannot prove and dream what we have not seen—and that is what makes history possible. The artistic lie is one retort to the impossibility of history.

Words That Lie

Another kind of falsification that the writing of history seems to attract is the **semantic error**. A semantic error does not just reflect ambiguity in the language; it arises from the fact that one of two or more meanings must be wrong. By indulging in the ambiguity we accept the fact that the statement or a part of the statement will not be true. Such tricks to the ear, like the optical illusion, make history fun to read.

Semantic error goes back to ancient myth and epic poetry. Ulysses in the Homeric epic was a trickster. He thought up the Trojan Horse—a deadly gift to the Trojans that depended upon their faith (and their gullibility) to destroy them. Foraging on an island on the way home from the war, he and a party of his men were captured by a one-eyed giant cannibal, a cyclops named Polyphemus. To save his men Ulysses told a clever lie—he gave his name as "Noman" and then put out the giant's eye. When the wounded giant summoned his tribe, they asked who or what had done him harm. He replied, "O friends, I die, and Noman gives the blow." They answered, "If no man hurts thee, it is the stroke of Jove, and thou must bear it." Ulysses was able to lead his men to their ships and the safety of the sea.

Ulysses' life-saving wordplay is an example of a pun. When we hear a pun, we are expected to groan. Polyphemus did. Everything from Japanese haiku poetry to Shakespeare to Ogden Nash is full of puns. A good pun poses a logical puzzle one part of which is untrue, because the two (or more) meanings of the pun deliberately create logical ambiguity. UCLA law professor Eugene Volokh has carried on a campaign, unsuccessfully, against puns in the titles of scholarly articles. With all due respect to his crusade, some of these are, frankly, hilarious. Out of respect to Professor Volokh and to protect the identity of the authors of the articles, I will forgo a list.

Puns can be the focus of logical puzzles. "When is a door not a door? When it's ajar." These semantic lies sometimes take the form of a phrase rather than a single word. It is the phrase that poses the ambiguity. "What animal can jump higher than a house?" The answer is that just about any animal can jump higher than a house because houses cannot jump.

In a "spoonerism" the first letters of two words in a common phrase are reversed, creating an entirely new meaning. The Reverend William Archibald Spooner was dean of New College, Oxford, and when not engaged in handling discipline at the college became famous for his slips of the tongue—so famous that he gave his name to them. You may never have uttered "a half-wormed fish" meaning to say "a half-formed wish," but then you probably had no desire to become famous for something like that either.

Then there are "malapropisms." Mrs. Malaprop, a comical character in Richard Sheridan's eighteenth-century English comedy *The Rivals,* innocently used the wrong word to describe people and things. (Actually, the name of the character was itself a kind of pun, based on the French *mal à propos,* meaning "inappropriate.") The words she chose, however, were hilariously and mischievously different from the ones she should have used. Her daughter, for example, was "as headstrong as an allegory on the banks of the Nile." She meant, one supposes, a reptile, not a popular type of medieval drama. You should beware of anyone trying to sell you furniture of "naughty pine."

In the oxymoron, from the Greek for "sharp-dull", a word or phrase contradicts itself. Most of the time, this example of wordplay arrives as a modifier and its noun. Shakespeare's *Romeo and Juliet* may hold the record for the most oxymorons in a single line of dialogue (or at least he's the consensus favorite): "O anything of nothing first create! / O heavy lightness, serious vanity! / Misshapen chaos of well-seeming forms! / Feather of lead, bright smoke, cold fire, sick health!" Shakespeare was also a master of puns, and in the example above he was well aware of what he was doing. Some oxymorons occur in common usage, rather like the way that arsenic, cyanide, or anthrax occur in nature. Among these are "top floor," a "small crowd," "fast food," and "tough love." Other, intentional oxymorons may be satirical commentary, like "business ethics." One may say that a familiar term or official title is an oxymoron to achieve this effect, as in "The 'Central Intelligence Agency' is an oxymoron."

What does this all have to do with lying in history? Most historians are also teachers of history. In the classroom, all history relies upon a lie. Words we say in a lecture (even with PowerPoint) and words on the page, even with pop-ups and overlays, and words on the screen, even with moving pictures, are two-dimensional representations of a world of four dimensions. We map reality onto flat surfaces. How can we make that flat depiction of a four-dimensional reality come alive? We use humor, twisting tales of history to twist the tails of our students. As our office doors reveal, we are not particularly adept at comedy, but small doses of puns and other wordplay help the more serious medicine of history go down.

James Axtell, a superb historical scholar and a much-admired history teacher at the College of William and Mary, put it this way: "Teachers of history have not only professionally challenging and socially important jobs, but immensely pleasurable ones as well. I want to emphasize not the pleasures that all teachers, whatever their subject, enjoy from time to time, but those particular to teachers of history." Axtell has a trick up his sleeve to involve the students in this enterprise: "As for my pedagogical and literary style, it's as mixed and complicated from day to day as anyone's, depending on the task to be done. But it tends toward—because I derive the most pleasure from—irony, wit, humor, and devil's advocacy. My goal as a teacher is to make myself *dis*pensable."

Richard Armour's two remarkable collections of historical nonsense sparked my interest in American history more than all the words of my teachers and all the books my teachers assigned in high school. *It All Started with Columbus* (1953) was wacky, irreverent, and curiously learned. Armour knew his history but refused to take it seriously. "The whites feared the redskins and considered them the forest's prime evil." John Smith was saved when the "fiery young daughter" of chief Powhatan "stepped in. We are not told what she stepped in." The Pilgrims "declined" to obey the kings of England and would have continued to decline if they had not left England. "The first four men ashore became our fourfathers."

Armour's purpose was not solely to entertain. He slipped messages into the mangled tales. "The first winter was cold, which was a distinct surprise to the Pilgrims. Indeed, they might not have survived but for the corn that was given them by friendly Indians. By a curious quirk of history, it has since become illegal for white men to give Indians either corn or rye." Not by accident, Armour wrote in the heyday of the McCarthy period, when any criticism of American history or values might lead to blacklisting or worse. Humor helped sugarcoat the social commentary.

Of course, sometimes our methods of using humor in the classroom come back to haunt us as students add their own inadvertent wittiness to our attempts at drollery. In the 1930s, Alexander Abingdon collected and published three volumes of history students' boners, among which are delightful unintentional puns, spoonerisms, oxymorons, and malapropisms. One student made the striking assertion that India had three major religions, "Buddhism, Brahminism, and idle worship." Another student, after a too-brief immersion in American Indian life, reported that "Indian squabs carry porpoises on their backs." More recent examination takers are still prone to take Mrs. Malaprop's advice to heart. Socrates, one student wrote, died of "wedlock" instead of the poison hemlock, perhaps a reference to his acerbic relations with Xantippe, his wife. Sir Francis Drake "circumcised" the globe, a painful and difficult alternative to his genuine feat of circumnavigating the globe. The U.S. Constitution was devised to secure "domestic hostility" instead of "domestic tranquility."

My own students give nothing away to their predecessors when it comes to the perfectly executed unintended pun. On a recent examination, one student insisted that a sure sign of a suspect's satanic powers at the Salem witchcraft trials was "being able to speak with tongues." A classmate's essay reported that Anne Hutchinson, the colonial Massachusetts religious dissenter, was guilty of "hearsay." Apparently telling tales was a more serious offense than heresy. Hutchinson, a third student believed, was a genuine "profit"—a slip of the pen that the famous German sociologist Max Weber (who thought that Puritanism spurred capitalism) would have appreciated. Historians are not above such punning, as shown by John Frederick Martin's *Profits in the Wilderness: Entrepreneurship and the Founding of New England Towns in the Seventeenth Century* (1991). To be fair to the author, I must say that the book is much better than its title.

The small still voice that is the scientific method planted in our brains whispers, "Wait, wait, this is not history. History cannot lie." But history is not just science, as the distinguished intellectual historian H. Stuart Hughes wrote in 1975: "The study of history offers living proof of the complementary nature of art and science." In fact, history is the only academic endeavor in which art and science are so inextricably intertwined. Hughes again: "The half-scientific half-artistic nature of their pursuits figures as a source of puzzlement and of difficulty in explaining to their colleagues in other fields" what historians really do. The historian cannot have science without art or art without science.

The artistic leap that allows us to see behind the cracked facade of what survives to what must have been there long ago, the imaginative fabrication that reenacts what is lost, the mesmerizer's trick of raising the dead that reaches out to students and draws them into our conspiracy to defeat the impossibility of history, those near-lies are an essential part of our teaching and study of history. They enable us to visualize what the far side of the bridge to the past might be. The other lies, the invented facts, the self-serving and the maliciously false arguments, should have no place in scholarship, though if one looks one can find them all too often.

6

The Politics of History
and History in Politics

[In] the fallacy of the political man [we] mistake people for
political animals who are moved mainly by a desire for power.
It reduces the complex psychic condition of men merely to their
political roles and shrinks all the components of the social
calculus to a simple equation of power, ambition, and interest.

—David Hackett Fischer (1970)

Fischer's warning about reducing the motives of political figures to a single cause is certainly worth our attention, but it runs in the
face of the origins of our profession. On the wall of the very first room
used to teach history to graduate students in America, at the Johns Hopkins University, hung a banner. It read, "History is past politics, and politics is present history."

Johns Hopkins University's newly appointed graduate history instruc-
tor Herbert Baxter Adams had borrowed the quotation from English historian E. A. Freeman because it captured Adams's, and his generation's,
notion of the purpose of history in the classroom. They had all witnessed
the horrors of the American Civil War. Surely the politicians of the 1850s
had forgotten vital lessons from the past? The history Ph.D.s who came
out of Adams's seminar and went into college teaching would pass on the
correct lessons of history to their students, the future leaders of the nation. It was that simple.

And that important. In 1886, George Bancroft, for nearly a half-century
the most popular and respected of all American historians, told the AHA,
"The object of our pursuit is one of the grandest that solicit the attention
of man. The movement of states over the scene of ever-succeeding action

is like the march of so many armies with their various civilizations for their banners: they themselves have faded away; their career, their enduring contributions to the sum of human knowledge, their men of transcendent genius, such as are vouchsafed to the race at great intervals of centuries, all come within the range of our pursuits." Great men, great deeds, great ideas, bound together in the rise and fall of states, were the proper subject of history.

The rise of the new profession of historian was a glittering prospect, and it drew to the graduate programs at Hopkins and elsewhere some of the brightest young minds in the country. But even as enrollments at the graduate schools grew, some students were finding the identification of history and politics too confining. By the beginning of the new century, with the first graduates establishing themselves in their own teaching positions, the call for economic history, social history, and cultural history was loud enough to concern the founders of the profession.

George Burton Adams, president of the AHA, was worried. In 1908 he told its members, "After three-quarters of a century of practically undisputed possession of our great field of study, during which the achievements of the political historian have won the admiration and applause of the world, our right to the field is now called in question, our methods, our results and our ideals are assailed, and we are being thrown upon the defensive at many points." Who were the barbarians at the gates? Hordes of political scientists, economists, geographers, sociologists, and psychologists, bringing with them heretical theories, an inclination for speculation, and the energy of youth. What should be done to repel this invasion? Well, perhaps "every attempt to unite the old and the new, to find a common standing-ground for all workers at what are really common tasks, ought to secure the hearty support of all historians. The men who try this from our side will be found however in most cases, I believe, to be the younger men."

Some of Herbert Baxter Adams's students became converts to the "new history." One, Frederick Jackson Turner, became president of the AHA in 1910 and told its members, "The transformations through which the United States is passing in our own day are so profound, so far-reaching, that it is hardly an exaggeration to say that we are witnessing the birth of a new nation in America. The revolution in the social and economic structure of this country during the past two decades is comparable to what occurred when independence was declared and the Constitution was formed, or to the changes wrought by the era which began half a century

ago, the era of Civil War and Reconstruction." The key forces and the crucial results were not political at all but social and economic. As Harry
Elmer Barnes triumphantly wrote in his *The New History and the Social
Sciences* (1922), "The very fact that the adherents of the older conventional
history feel compelled to cease scoffing at the contributions of the more
advanced and modernized historians . . . is most significant."

History was no longer simply past politics—but historians' politics, that
was another matter entirely. As the controversy over the old and the new
history at the turn of the century indicated, the politics of doing history
was inseparable from historians writing about politics. Worse, our work
could be deployed by politicians eager to have the authority of history at
their beck and call.

The Politics of Historians

As in any gathering of people, the discipline of history developed a politics of its own, riven with personal rivalries, ideological controversies, and
horror stories of vile book reviews, combative graduate school seminars,
and other atrocities. Some of these involved genuine disagreement about
the direction of the profession and the content of our histories. As I re-
counted in *Past Imperfect*, in the 1960s that politics became open warfare. A younger generation of historians came out of the graduate schools
fueled by a passion for equal rights for minorities and women and demanded that the academy open itself to reform. They called for and themselves created new histories, inclusive, diverse, and self-critical. As Warren Susman, one of these "new historians," wrote in 1964, "History is often
used as the basis for a political philosophy that while explaining the past
offers also a way to change the future. History thus operates ideologically.
But by the very nature of its enterprise and the kind of society that calls it
into existence, historical interpretation cannot be effectively monopolized
for long by any special class or group."

As the America of the 1960s was profoundly different from the America of all previous eras, so its history writing would reflect the new open-
ness and cultural diversity of the society and culture. Becker's "everyman"
was now truly a historian. The new history would also feature a quar-
relsomeness, suspicion of pandering to the public's desire for heroes and
heroism, and demand for methodological sophistication that set its members against one another and the movement against more traditional historians and schools of history.

Entrenched in history departments and the editorial boards of the major journals, the more conservative members of the profession were not amused by their juniors' antics. One of these mandarins, Johns Hopkins's David Donald, judged that the radical history was "not of sufficient consequence to merit extended consideration in the pages of our major professional journal." Still, he was tolerant in the way that a parent is tolerant of a wayward child: "Here, then, are the voices of the New Left—mostly neither new nor left. . . . The historical profession has already paid these writers more attention than they deserve." Thus "Let them . . . end their plaintive laments that the 'power structure' of the historical profession ignores them."

The struggle within the profession for control of its agenda continues. With the graying wayward children of the New Left now firmly in control of the editorial boards and the program committees of the major professional associations, conservative political and military historians claimed that "politically correct" social and cultural historians were taking over the professional organizations, with the result that national conference programs had an unfair slant. Some historians, like Marc Trachtenberg, accused the AHA itself of becoming "politicized." Eugene Genovese, a leading leftist historian who had moved far to the right, agreed. The AHA was "specialized, careerist, bureaucratized, and politically conformist." The demand for more studies on race, class, and gender to the exclusion of other fields to him "uncomfortably resembles the McCarthyism of the 1950s. It is being imposed by presiding cliques that have made ideological conformity the primary criterion for holding office."

Plainly, historians were crossing the line into politics with a capital P. There was plenty of precedent. The nineteenth-century European historians, men like Jules Michelet in France, Leopold von Ranke in Prussia, and George Babington Macaulay in England, were all apologists for the rise of the nation-state, not surprisingly their own. Respectively, they argued that history led directly to the glories of France (and the French Revolution), Prussia (and the Teutonic peoples), and England (especially the parliamentary system of government). In *The New History* Barnes lumped these and other giants of our discipline into a "political and nationalistic school of history." The categorization was accurate, given that von Ranke was appointed royal historiographer of Prussia in 1841 and Macaulay was a member of Parliament. Early twentieth-century historians were more professional but just as wedded to nationalism. Marc Bloch, for example, in the words of his biographer Carole Fink, believed that "history was a political subject."

In the United States, the most authoritative and popular historian of the nineteenth century, George Bancroft, was not only a celebrant of the rise of the United States but a Democratic politician, holding a number of political appointments. His twentieth-century successor as America's foremost historian (if three Pulitzer Prizes and two National Book Awards are any measure of greatness), Arthur Meier Schlesinger Jr., chronicled the presidencies of Andrew Jackson, Franklin Delano Roosevelt, and John F. Kennedy and served in Kennedy's administration. Schlesinger knew everyone who mattered and seemed to be in the right place at the right time to see politics in the making. For example, Truman, leaving the White House, was "very cheerful, scrubbed, and natty." Schlesinger always felt affection for the peppery warrior. Running for the presidency, John F. Kennedy was "impersonal in his remarks, quite prepared to see the views of interests of others." Schlesinger came to admire the man and regret the "mean spirited and bitter attacks" that biographers would make on JFK.

For Schlesinger, the politics of history and the historian's politics were inseparable. In *The Vital Center*, Schlesinger lamented that "western man in the middle of the twentieth century is tense, uncertain, adrift. We look upon our epoch as a time of troubles, an age of anxiety. The grounds of our civilization, of our certitude, are breaking up under our feet, and familiar ideas and institutions vanish as we reach for them, like shadows in the falling dusk." It was the historian's duty as a citizen to save the country from itself. "Our own objective is clear. We must defend and strengthen free society," a political act with a capital P as much as the more humble offering of opinions in another book. "It has become the duty of free society to answer these questions. . . . The rise of the social-welfare state is an expression of that sense of duty."

That state, and the commitment to its politics (in 1949), included "the expansion of the powers of government." It followed to Schlesinger that Roosevelt and Harry Truman were better models for America than conservative Republican critics of the New Deal. As for those critics of his views, Schlesinger wrote in 1996, "Being a historian has almost become a dangerous occupation. The public seems to have few inhibitions about passing judgment on the inner business of the historical community."

In the past few decades, other controversies have swirled around historians' roles in public events. On the occasion of the four-hundredth anniversary of the arrival of Columbus's little fleet in American waters; when the Smithsonian Museum of Air and Space proposed to open an exhibit on the *Enola Gay* and the end of World War II in the Pacific;

about the participation of historians in the debate over the impeachment of President Bill Clinton, critics howled in protest. The *Wall Street Journal* editorialized that "academics" were "unable to view American history as anything other than a woeful catalog of crimes and aggressions against the helpless peoples of the earth," and the *Washington Post* warned that something must be done to counter "the carping of elitists [historians] dedicated to tearing down national morale."

When Politicians Use History

If the historians have sometimes lost their objectivity (or simply rejected the notion of objectivity) in their quarrels with one another, politicians who use history have an even less enviable record. Alan Spitzer tells the story of one notorious blooper. In 1985, at the invitation of German Chancellor Helmut Kohl, U.S. President Ronald Reagan announced that he would visit Germany. The occasion was the Victory in Europe Day's fortieth anniversary, a sober time recalling the death of millions of men in arms, the end of Hitler's "Thousand Year Reich," and the murder of countless innocent civilians in German death camps.

But Reagan was in a forgiving—and forgetting—mood. On the list of places he planned to visit he included, at Kohl's suggestion, the military cemetery at Bitburg, resting place to, among other men, SS storm troopers. He did not elect to visit another of Kohl's suggested sites, the concentration camp at Dachau. When a storm of protest from all over the political spectrum in the states greeted the announced itinerary, Reagan turned to history to explain his choices. Because "the German people have very few alive that remember even the war, and certainly none of them who were adults and participating in any way, and they do, they have a feeling, a guilt feeling that's been imposed upon them," it was unnecessary to impose more of that guilt.

Reagan's history was curiously selective. People his age had fought in the war. Perhaps they had also participated in the "final solution" of the "Jewish problem." In any case, Reagan continued, the German people were victims too, persuaded to engage in "the awful evil started by one man." All the men in uniform were heroes who had sacrificed their lives to defend their beliefs. It was now time for reconciliation and, apparently, forgetting.

Reagan's history was inaccurate. Parts of it were fable, parts fabrication, parts gross oversimplification. Perhaps, as later critics hinted, Reagan was poorly informed. Or he was insensitive. But a simpler explanation is that Reagan wanted a strong West Germany as our ally in Europe, a bulwark against the Soviets. This was the same offer that conspirators against Hitler in 1944 were making secretly to the Allies. It was the basis for U.S. policy toward the rebuilding of West Germany after the war. Seen in the context of the military and diplomatic history of the Cold War, Reagan's history of the war was intended as a sop to conservative German opinion. It was an abuse of fact and interpretation, but it was not atypical. Bitburg was a highly visible case of a very old American phenomenon—the intentional misconstruction of historical meanings to gain political ends.

American political history, recent and distant, is replete with the mischievous use of history by one party or another for partisan ends. When the first national parties—Alexander Hamilton's Federalists and James Madison's Republicans—did battle in the 1790s, both men turned to recent history to spin their party's message. For in the political ideology that the revolutionaries inherited from England, standing political parties were at best self-interested cliques and at worst conspiratorial cabals. How to get around this obstacle? The very names that Hamilton and Madison adopted for their followings employed history. The Federalists, supposedly, were the true friends of the Constitution, because the federalists were the proratification party in 1787 and 1788. Anyone who opposed them (like Madison) must be enemies of the Constitution. It did not matter that Hamilton's views so upset the delegates to the constitutional convention in 1787 that he went home after expressing them or that Madison's views would become the core of the new document. The Republicans claimed to be the only real inheritors of the American Revolution. Their opponents thus had to be covert monarchists. It did not matter that all of the Federalists, even Hamilton, believed in the republican system of government and that many, like Hamilton, had risked their lives in the Revolutionary War.

When South Carolina "fire-eaters" led the state into secession after the election of Lincoln, in November 1860, they relentlessly charged him with a long career of race mixing. The message resonated throughout the Deep South and helped the secessionists in their drive to create a Confederate nation. Lincoln's Republican Party had its own message, an antipathy to slavery's expansion rooted in a history of slavery's evils that gained every northern electoral vote for Lincoln. Both sides deployed bits and pieces of history—quotations of speeches taken out of context, for example—to give political arguments the authority of historical truth. With both sides following the logic of their own message, compromise was impossible. Too late, Lincoln tried to apply the brakes, later ruing that "all dreaded it, all sought to avert it," but "the war came." It was a capsule political history that denied, in effect, the mistakes of an entire generation of politicians.

Perhaps one should not lament the misuse of history at the hands of the politicians. Politics is the act of gaining and exercising power, in which the old adage that "power corrupts" proves itself true over and over again. As Laurence Sterne tells readers in *Tristram Shandy*: "As the bilious and more saturnine passions, by creating disorders in the blood and humours, have as bad an influence, I see, upon the body politick as body natural—and as nothing but a habit of virtue can fully govern those passions, and subject them to reason," a large dose of history would seem the correct remedy for the corruptions of power. But the briefest survey of how politicians use history warns that a practical philosophy of history— our goal in this book—must define practicality in a different fashion than the politicians and their speechwriters.

Lessons in Logic Chopping

Recent history shows that politicians and political flacks have become masters of mischief with historical snippets. A bit of historical anecdote, a topically useful generalization, and a quotation or two out of context grace the politicians' rhetoric. They select that bit of evidence or story that will best chop up an opponent's argument and make him or her look a fool. If historical **logic chopping** is not going away, can a working philosophy of history offer countermeasures? If we can find some way to curb this urge to misuse history, we can make another important contribution to our philosophy of history.

The sad fact is that one does not have to look hard to find the same examples of political logic chopping that misuses history. Consider the **false question** and its twin, the **ad hominem**, as well as their traveling companion, the **straw man**. In the political version of the false question, one simply raises a question about one's opponent, preferably smearing him in a way that he cannot ever clean off. A little history makes the innuendo stick. "Did my opponent consort with the enemy? We'll just have to see." Not having made a declarative statement, but phrasing the insulting and often ludicrous smear as a question, the chopper is free from any taint of slander. After all, it was a question, and we (the listeners) are free to form our own opinion.

After Aaron Burr killed the Federalist Party leader Alexander Hamilton in a duel, the Federalists launched a campaign of vilification against Burr. The party's pet newspaper, the *Gazette of the United States,* followed Burr's travels in the West with one false question after another. "How long will it be before we shall hear of Colonel Burr being at the head of a revolutionary party on the Western Waters? . . . How soon will the forts and magazines and all the military posts at New Orleans and on the Mississippi be in the hands of Colonel Burr's revolutionary party?" Note how the initial speculation had become fact in the final speculation of the editorial. The newspaper's speculations fueled rumor, gossip, and then accusation that Burr plotted to sever the western states from the original thirteen. Indicted and tried in federal court for treason, Burr was acquitted, but he would never again hold public office. The false question had done its job.

The false question combines the loaded-question formula with an ad hominem attack. The ad hominem (literally "against the man") ignores the truth or falsity of your opponent's case and goes right after him: "Who are you to say that? You have no business coming here and making that argument." Such attacks may directly assault the qualifications of the speaker ("Of course we expect him to defend that position because he's a . . .") or be irrelevant to the question at hand ("Do you know that he's a . . . ?"). The effectiveness of the ad hominem derives from its demolition of one's opponent's credibility. When South Carolina Senator John C. Calhoun wanted to prevent the reading of antislavery petitions in Congress, in 1836, he told his colleagues, "We, the representatives of twelve of these sovereign States against whom this deadly war is waged, are expected to sit here in silence, hearing ourselves and our constituents day after day denounced. . . . As widely as this incendiary spirit has spread, it has not yet infected this body, or the great mass of the intelligent and business portion of the North; but unless it be speedily stopped, it will spread and work upwards till it brings the two great sections of the Union into deadly conflict." So, no need to read or consider the abolitionists' case.

A particularly nasty version of the false question relies upon a silly error in a long statement to dismiss, without disproof, the rest of the statement. I call it the "little mistake" version of the false question, and it goes like this: "How can we believe the rest of what you say when you misspelled Al Qaeda in the first paragraph?" This is a false question because it does not deal with the rest of the statement, much less offer evidence or argument to disprove the statement. The more outraged or dismissive the logic chopper is about the small error, the easier it is for him to ignore the rest of the message.

A media pundit found that author Gail Sheehy had on one occasion gotten President Bill Clinton's age wrong (by a year) in a biography of Hillary Clinton *(Hillary's Choice)*. The critic huffed that the error put the rest of the book's thoughts out of court, for if the author got this wrong, what else did she get wrong? If former Bush security advisor Richard Clarke got the reason for one terrorist's capture wrong, did it undermine the credibility of his book *Against All Enemies*? Yes, according to one critic. Demolition by false question, based on a little mistake in the author's own historical account.

To be candid, I have been a victim of the little-mistake version of the false question. In a review of a book I wrote on the 1741 slave uprising in New York City, the reviewer noted a numerical error in the number of slaves I claimed lived and worked in the city. If I had gotten this wrong, how could anyone trust the rest of the book? In fact, the reviewer had a more serious quarrel with my interpretation. He thought that slavery had its origins in racism. I thought and still think that it had its origins in the need for cheap and ready labor. To undermine my argument without engaging it directly, he fixed on the little mistake.

A cunning logic chopper can employ a straw man to abuse historical examples. A straw man is a scarecrow, fierce looking from a distance (at least to crows) but up close just old clothes stuffed with straw—no menace at all. The logic chopper willing to work a bit can build a straw man out of a variety of historical bits and pieces. Then the politician takes on the straw man instead of going after the arguments his opponent has actually made. The straw man never puts up a fight because he cannot. He is made of straw.

In the debates between Illinois Democratic Senator Stephen Douglas and Republican challenger Abraham Lincoln during 1858, both politicians stuffed and then beat straw men. Douglas, no mean debater, flailed away at Lincoln's supposed abolitionist leanings, knocking the straw out. As Douglas regaled his audience at the first round of the debate, on August 21, 1858:

In 1854, Mr. Abraham Lincoln and Mr. [Illinois Senator Lyman] Trumbull entered into an arrangement, one with the other, and each with his respective friends, to dissolve the old Whig party on the one hand, and to dissolve the old Democratic party on the other, and to connect the members of both into an Abolition party under the name and disguise of a Republican party. . . . Lincoln was to bring into the Abolition camp the old line Whigs, and transfer them over to [Joshua] Giddings, [Salmon P.] Chase, Fred[erick] Douglass, and Parson Lovejoy [all abolitionists], who were ready to receive them and christen them in their new faith.

When the first straw man, a supposedly abolitionist Republican Party dominated by a crew of "Black Republicans" (in fact, it was a free-soil party with abolitionists in it) was scattered to the wind, Douglas joyfully beat the stuffing out of another straw man, Lincoln's alleged belief in the equality of whites and blacks. "I do not question Mr. Lincoln's conscientious belief that the negro was made his equal, and hence is his brother [laughter], but for my own part, I do not regard the negro as my equal, and positively deny that he is my brother or any kin to me whatever." This was an effective debate tactic, as journalists on the scene recorded, but it was neither historically correct nor fair to Lincoln's views. Lincoln thought that all men were entitled to the fruits of their labor, but he did not believe in the equality of the races.

Lincoln in turn claimed that Douglas wanted to expand slavery into the North. Douglas had written the Kansas Nebraska Act, with its provision for the people of a territory to decide whether it should become a free or slave state. Lincoln focused on the text of the bill: It said, "It being the true intent and meaning of this bill not to legislate slavery into any Territory or State." Lincoln continued: "I have always been puzzled to know what business the word 'State' had in that connection. Judge Douglas knows. He put it there. He knows what he put it there for. We outsiders cannot say what he put it there for. The law they were passing was not about States, and was not making provisions for States. What was it placed there for?"

The straw man, here a single word, was now erected, and Lincoln struck it a mighty blow. "After seeing the Dred Scott decision, which holds that the people cannot exclude slavery from a Territory, if another Dred Scott decision shall come, holding that they cannot exclude it from a State, we shall discover that when the word was originally put there, it was in view of something which was to come in due time, we shall see that it was the other half of something." That something was nothing less than slavery imposed on the northern free states. "I ask the attention of the people here assembled and elsewhere, to the course that Judge Douglas is pursuing every day as bearing upon this question of making slavery national. Not going back to the records, but taking the speeches he makes, the speeches he made yesterday and day before, and makes constantly all over the country—I ask your attention to them." Douglas had no such intent, in part because he needed northern free-state Democratic Party votes if he wanted to fulfill his dream of becoming president, but Lincoln's straw man was already demolished.

Modern political leaders give nothing away to the two Illinois giants when it comes to beating on a straw man. President George W. Bush won many rounds against them. In one 2004 campaign speech, President Bush warned, "It may seem generous and open-minded to say that everybody, on every moral issue, is equally right, but that attitude can also be an excuse for sidestepping life's most important questions." Moral relativism was his straw man. In his 2006 State of the Union address, the president warned against a return to isolationism, arguing that "retreating within our borders" would leave "an assaulted world to fend for itself." Who was the isolationist for whom these lessons were meant? Mr. Straw Man.

Historical examples abound in another of the politicians' rhetorical techniques—**special pleading.** It suggests that certain cases or people should be excepted from general rules or even from the law. Special pleading may be "situational"—that is, claims for it may depend upon the time and place. This version of the **double standard** often occurs in politics. After the "Blackhawk Down" fiasco in Mogadishu, in 1993, Defense Secretary Les Aspin was forced to resign. The American forces in Somalia had not been given the right motorized weapons to do their job safely. When Secretary of Defense Donald Rumsfeld was asked about repeated instances of poorly armored vehicles leaving American forces defenseless against roadside bombs during the Iraq War ten years later, he testily replied, "You have to fight a war with the army you have, not the one you wish you had." He did not suffer any reprimand for his special pleading for serious problems with American military ordnance.

A little history helped Rumsfeld make his point. His defense of his and the administration's planning for the war was that he and his colleagues knew all about the pitfalls of a long war. According to one *Washington Post* reporter, he explained that "he did not dash heedless and underprepared into Iraq. Rumsfeld foresaw the things that could go wrong—and not just foresaw them, but wrote them up." The document was still classified, but it would prove—history would prove—that Rumsfeld was not a special pleader. Indeed, as the Rumsfeld-scripted official account explained, "It might help if Americans and their leaders were to show less arrogance and more understanding of themselves and their place in history. Perhaps more than any other people, Americans display a consistent amnesia concerning their own past, as well as the history of those around them."

Finally, one can slide down the **slippery slope** with a straw man clutched in one hand. A little history, polished the right way, helps. Take the following argument, implicit in a recent decision of the U.S. Supreme Court. The Court uses history all the time. The justices examine **precedents**, earlier decisions of the Court on past cases similar to the one they must decide at the moment. They also survey the events leading up to the case, in effect the case's own little history. If the case in front of them raises constitutional questions, they ask an additional set of historical questions: What did the framers of the Constitution and its amendments mean to say when they wrote those words? What did the words mean to people who lived then? Have those meanings changed over time?

What if, as may well occur, the High Court accepts the right-to-life position and decides that from conception the fetus is a person under the law? This means that the person in the womb has all the rights, privileges, and immunities of any citizen from conception. (It is not clear how this would fit with current citizenship law, for we become citizens when we are born here, not conceived here.) Now the pregnant woman is no longer just a prospective mother but the safekeeper of a human being already alive. We require that parents of living children provide those children with food, shelter, and some parental affection. Can we require this of the pregnant woman? If caffeine and cigarette smoking and alcohol use (as has been proven) harm fetuses, can we legally bar pregnant women from using these? Can we also require that they regularly visit the doctor to have checkups, stay in good health, and eat and exercise properly? Can we restrain their movements, even hospitalizing or jailing them if they resist these impositions on their personal freedoms? How much supervision might the state have to impose in order to protect the unborn child from its prospective mother? All this we might do following the slippery slope logic that pregnant women are not just individuals who might or might not bear a child but containers for living beings.

In *Carhart v. Gonzales* (2007), Justice Ruth Bader Ginsburg dissented from the majority opinion finding that the federal "partial birth abortion" ban was constitutional. She wrote "Today's decision is alarming. It refuses to take [earlier decisions on abortion rights] seriously. It tolerates, indeed applauds, federal intervention to ban nationwide a procedure found necessary and proper in certain cases by the American College of Obstetricians and Gynecologists. It blurs the line, firmly drawn in [prior cases], between pre-viability and post-viability abortions. And, for the first time since [*Roe v. Wade* was decided], the Court blesses a prohibition with no exception safeguarding a woman's health." Justice Ginsburg no doubt knew that a court in South Carolina had already followed this logic, each step linked to the previous step down the slope.

Such slippery slopes have two forms. Both require historical arguments. One is causal. A, if permitted, will lead to B, then B to C, and so on, and finally to X, an undesired result. This will happen more or less unstoppably. Thus we must not have A. If, for example, we let schools teach birth control to prevent teenage pregnancy, students will become familiar with sex, and then they will begin to experiment, there will be mistakes in birth control, and then we will have lots more teenage sex. So no sex education. Here the mistake lies in the assumption of the causal relation—a mistake all too common in historical scholarship.

The second kind of slippery slope is narrative—a progression from A to B through a series of very small steps. If God finds decent men in Sodom, argues Abraham, he should not destroy it entirely. The slope consists of how many men are enough. One thousand, one hundred, ten? The difference between the numbers is not really defined, nor is the logical connection between the final number and the sparing of Sodom. The number simply slides down the slope by itself (no cause needed).

Politicians often hurl arguments over the edge of this slippery slope. In 1956, southern politicians united in opposition to the desegregation decision *Brown v. Board of Education* (1954). They signed and published in the *Congressional Record* a "manifesto" one of whose central claims was a slippery slope greased with history. First, "We regard the decisions of the Supreme Court in the school cases as a clear abuse of judicial power. It climaxes a trend in the Federal Judiciary undertaking to legislate, in derogation of the authority of Congress, and to encroach upon the reserved rights of the States and the people." Actually, the Court's exercise of a kind of substantive due process (applying the Fourteenth Amendment to scrutinize the constitutionality of state regulations and **statutes**) went back to *Lochner v. New York* (1905), a decision knocking down state health, labor, and welfare regulations over fifty years before *Brown*. Among those regulations upheld at the time of *Lochner* were southern states' Jim Crow laws.

In the "Manifesto," education history also slid down the slope. "Without regard to the consent of the governed, outside mediators are threatening immediate and revolutionary changes in our public schools systems. If done, this is certain to destroy the system of public education in some of the States." That system of segregated education featured one dime spent for black schools for every dollar spent for white schools. What next? Would the Courts overturn southern state laws against intermarriage? (The High Court did in *Loving v. Virginia* in 1967.) And where would this lead? The Jackson, Mississippi, *Daily News* ominously warned after *Brown* was announced that "human blood may stain Southern soil in many places because of this decision. . . . White and negro children in the same schools will lead to miscegenation . . . and mongrelization of the human race."

Missing Words for All Occasions

If logic chopping is too tiring, there are other ways to use historical snippets. The slyest is **quoting out of context**. Quoting out of context can be very effective. Historians in training learn in their first graduate seminars that to understand the meaning of any document, one must take into account who wrote it, when, in what circumstances, and so on. In particular, one should not quote a piece of the document that contradicts its larger purpose or meaning.

Anyone whose words are published can expect to be quoted out of context. This often happens to historians' words when we are quoted by journalists. Some of that is inevitable. The telephone call from the reporter may go on for an hour, but only two lines of our conversation appear in print. Even our own publications and talks may be snipped into pieces and reassembled wrongly if the surrounding words pointed in a different direction.

In the course of hours of hearings on the impeachment of President Bill Clinton, a House of Representatives subcommittee listened to testimony of dozens of leading scholars and had before it hundreds of pages of these experts' research and opinion. Predictably, the witnesses took sides on whether Clinton's actions constituted impeachable offenses, but the journalists covering the hearings seized upon a single comment by Princeton historian Sean Wilentz and by quoting it out of context gave it an importance it did not have at the time. Replying in a testy tone of voice to a hostile congressman, Wilentz said that history would "hunt down and condemn" those in the House who voted for the impeachment for merely partisan reasons. Journalists feasted on Wilentz's unplanned comment, rendering it as a direct challenge to Republican members of the House instead of linking it to his larger point, that other hasty and partisan impeachments had not worn well over time.

Leaving out the context of a quotation can also alter what appear to be historical facts. For example, during the 2004 presidential campaign, Republican media handlers prepared an advertisement that used an editorial from "Kerry's hometown paper." The quotation from the paper was accurate, but the ad left out the fact that the paper, the *Boston Herald*, had endorsed Bush for the presidency in 2000 and did not much care for Kerry's position on the matter mentioned in the editorial. Political candidates' selective clipping and reprinting of snippets from friendly newspapers' editorials, in the process recasting an editorial opinion as if it were a fact, is another form of quoting out of context. The reader is not told that the newspaper words are part of an editorial (as opposed to news reporting or an investigative finding).

Changing the words in a quotation or making up a quotation and wrongly attributing it are forms of lying and belong in that category rather than quoting out of context, though both morally bankrupt acts are common on political blog sites. Leaving out words or taking words out of context can do as much damage to the truth as lying about who said what. Democratic politician Howard Dean is not always careful what he says, but critics made his comments even more censurable by taking them out of context. At the end of 2005, he told an interviewer, "The idea that we're going to win this war is an idea that unfortunately is just plain wrong." Republicans were outraged that the chairman of the Democratic National Party seemed to be giving comfort to our enemies, and Democrats thought that Dean was making them look unpatriotic. In fact, the comments were historical, part of his comparison of the Iraq War with the Vietnam War, a war that even the most patriotic observer (except for General Westmoreland) would concede we did not win.

Citing a past politician's words as support for a current policy is accurate only if the two contexts are the same. At a West Point commencement address on May 27, 2006, President George Bush, drawing a parallel between the contemporary threat of terrorism and the threat of communism in the late 1940s, compared himself to President Harry Truman by implication ("Fortunately we had a president named Harry Truman") and then made analogies between Truman's policy of supporting anticommunist governments in Europe and Asia and his own policies of invading Iraq and Afghanistan. When one reads the entire speech introducing the

"Truman Doctrine" at a joint session of Congress, on March 14, 1947, the importance of its context becomes clear:

> The gravity of the situation which confronts the world today necessitates my appearance before a joint session of the Congress. The foreign policy and the national security of this country are involved. One aspect of the present situation, which I wish to present to you at this time for your consideration and decision, concerns Greece and Turkey. The United States has received from the Greek Government an urgent appeal for financial and economic assistance. Preliminary reports from the American Economic Mission now in Greece and reports from the American Ambassador in Greece corroborate the statement of the Greek Government that assistance is imperative if Greece is to survive as a free nation.

Truman was asking for "foreign aid," the beginning of our policy of economic and technical assistance to help countries help themselves. "Greece is today without funds to finance the importation of those goods which are essential to bare subsistence. Under these circumstances the people of Greece cannot make progress in solving their problems of reconstruction. Greece is in desperate need of financial and economic assistance to enable it to resume purchases of food, clothing, fuel, and seeds. These are indispensable for the subsistence of its people and are obtainable only from abroad. Greece must have help to import the goods necessary to restore internal order and security, so essential for economic and political recovery." To be sure, there was a reference to "terror" in Truman's remarks, a reference necessary to instill the urgency of the events in the minds of members of Congress used to, and tired out from, the urgencies of World War II. "The very existence of the Greek state is today threatened by the terrorist activities of several thousand armed men, led by Communists, who defy the government's authority at a number of points, particularly along the northern boundaries."

Aid, assistance, support, but not an invasion of a foreign country was the core of the Truman Doctrine. Compare this to what President Bush told the cadets at West Point as he cited Truman and history in defense of the Iraq War effort: "You worked hard in the classroom and on the playing field to prepare for the rigors of combat. . . . The field of battle is where your degree and commission will take you. . . . The reality of war has surrounded you since your first moments at this Academy. More than 50 of your fellow cadets here at West Point have already seen combat in Afghanistan and Iraq." A military solution to the problem of national security, carried out on "the field of battle," was quite different from Truman's proposal. Through the process of leaving out context, Bush had materially altered Truman's doctrine from an alternative to war to, in Bush's words, "this new war."

Catchphrases use coded references to history to stand in for a more detailed recitation of events. They ignore context altogether. For example, the phrase *cut and run* applied to opponents of the Iraq War calls up the criticism of our departure from Vietnam. Such loaded historical words fill political oratory. On an early 2006 episode of the popular comedic current events program *The Daily Show*, host Jon Stewart pointed out the number of times that President George W. Bush used the term *victory* in a speech on the Iraq war. The U.S. occupation in Iraq was not going well, and the presidential advisory team had decided, after a series of polls, that Americans would support our continued involvement in Iraq if the president used the word *victory*, calling up images of World War II, instead of other key words like *democracy, peace,* and *freedom,* which had been staples of his speeches.

Ignoring context can easily lead to **Johnny one-note** or relentless **one-sidedness**. There are many examples of this same sort of one-sidedness, motivated by the desire to make a case for that side, in the history of politics. The abolitionist politicians before the Civil War were masters of this technique. In 1858, New York abolitionist and Republican senator William Henry Seward told a Rochester, New York, audience: "Either the cotton and rice fields of South Carolina and the sugar plantations of Louisiana will ultimately be tilled by free labor, and Charleston and New Orleans become marts of legitimate merchandise alone, or else the rye-fields and wheat-fields of Massachusetts and New York must again be surrendered by their farmers to slave culture and to the production of slaves, and Boston and New York become once more markets for trade in the bodies and souls of men." Strong language, untrue of New York and Boston (major ports of entry and exit for runaway slaves), and relentless in its condemnation of the South. Most cotton farm families in the South worked alone or with hired help (they could not afford slaves), just as most New England farm families depended on children and hired help in planting and harvesting seasons.

A form of one-sidedness is the **argument from consequences**. Politicians are like the rest of us: they not only look forward to good results but tend to argue from that expectation. History can be pillaged for unidimensional "lessons" that are actually arguments from consequences. Saying that we should accept the truth of a particular position because (if true) it would lead to a desirable end is no proof that the premise itself is true or that the desired end would occur. "We must be bringing democracy and peace to the Middle East. If we weren't, then the billions of dollars and the thousands of lives lost in the Iraq war would have been wasted." That is the semantic fallacy of arguing from consequences. The rejection of a premise just because its conclusion would be undesirable is similarly short-sighted. For example, "I don't believe in global warming. If it were true, our coastlines, our fuel supplies, and even our weather would be catastrophically affected. So there must be some other explanation for changes in climate and ocean temperature."

The most ludicrous (on purpose, to be sure) example of this type of reasoning from a negative consequence appears in the Marx Brothers' one political satire, *Duck Soup*. Rufus T. Firefly (Groucho) is the president of tiny Freedonia, menaced by its neighbor Sylvania. A diplomatic meeting between the two nations ends in failure before it even starts when Firefly, reasoning from negative anticipated consequences—"What if I extend the hand of friendship" to the president of Sylvania and he rejects it?—becomes so worked up at this prospect that he slaps Sylvania's president when he enters. A short and hilarious war follows. Real wars, brought on by such unthinking mixtures of logic and illogic, are rarely so bloodless.

Before one regards the argument from consequences as an example of that form of lunacy unique to the Marx Brothers, return to the 1836 speech that Calhoun made in the Senate against the abolitionist petitions. "However sound the great body of the non-slaveholding States are at present, in the course of a few years they will be succeeded by those who will have been taught to hate the people and institutions of nearly one-half of this Union, with a hatred more deadly than one hostile nation ever entertained towards another. It is easy to see the end. By the necessary course of events, if left to themselves, we must become, finally, two people." And so the petitions must not be read.

Thinking about consequences is not always reproachable. U.S. Supreme Court Justice Stephen Breyer's *Active Liberty* argues that judges should weigh the likely consequences of leaving a law in place or striking it down. What would happen, he muses, if rulings of the Court on which generations of Americans have relied were suddenly to be reversed? What would be the real-world consequences if the Court reached unpopular or difficult-to-enforce decisions? He is not the first justice to worry about this. Justice Felix Frankfurter taught that the Court has only a small store of political capital and must invest it wisely. That is why he, among others, feared that a sweeping decree in *Brown v. Board of Education* (1954) wiping out all state-sponsored segregation in public schools would be a mistake. He saw consequences that ranged from civil disobedience to outright violence in the Deep South. In his opinion on the abortion rights case *Casey v. Planned Parenthood* (1992), Justice David Souter wrote that one reason not to overturn *Roe v. Wade* was that so many women had come to rely on it as they planned their reproductive lives. Are all of these examples of the fallacy of argument from consequences? The answer is no. In no case do the justices argue that the premise is right because its consequences are desirable. Instead, they argue that the premise—the law or opinion—is desirable because its continued effect is desirable. In other words, they are connecting the foreseeable to the present, a perfectly logical thing to do.

In an editorial for the *New York Times* on July 18, 2007, Maureen Dowd expressed her frustration with politicians' use of history. Her target was President George W. Bush:

> The president mentioned in his speech Tuesday that he was reading history, and he has been summoning historians and theologians to the White House for discussions on the fate of Iraq and the nature of good and evil. W. thinks history will be his alibi. When presidents have screwed up and want to console themselves, they think history will give them a second chance. It's the historical equivalent of a presidential pardon. But there are other things—morality, strategy and security—that are more pressing than history. History is just the fanciest way possible of wanting to deny or distract attention from what's happening now.

Dowd's journalistic instinct to privilege the present over the past misled her. *Morality, strategy,* and *security* are empty words without an understanding of the past. Still, the litany of misshapen history in politicians' hands is an ominous warning of what politics can do to historical argument. It is also a salutary reminder as well that all argument has some politics to it, and a philosophy of history for our times insists that we be aware of our political biases. Those biases can easily—too easily—creep into our exchanges with other historians. Knowing how argument is misused in political history (including yesterday's news) helps us to see our own political stances. And make no mistake, even the isolated scholar in the Minotaur's cave of an archive has political views. Such views will—must—find their way into scholarship. Even the insistence that he or she is apolitical is suspect. Choice of topics, reading and selection of evidence, arrangement of argument, all of these derive from a point of view.

Our politics will lead us to disagree. As Haskell and Levinson wrote in their final reply to Alice Kessler-Harris:

> The principal justification for the existence of scholarly communities lies in their capacity to generate critical exchanges that are more intense than those that occur spontaneously in society at large, where the avoidance of disputes over fundamentals is often highly valued. But that is not to say, when it comes to criticism, that anything goes or that the cry "foul" should never deter us. Criticizing the logic and evidence of a dissenter's position furthers the debate and is entirely in keeping with scholarly traditions; trying in effect to silence (or to drown out) the dissenter is another thing altogether, and one deeply inimical to the principle of academic freedom.

Whether we regard historical scholarship and teaching as a "bully pulpit" for us to preach our views or cross our arms over our chests and put a finger to our lips to prevent our views from coming to light, a philosophy of history in today's contentious times demands respect for one another's views, if not consensus on political issues. Seeing the ease with which political commitment can slide into illogical argument, we should be wary of letting our own political commitments cause us to alter our findings, to remain silent when we should speak, or to condemn others for speaking their own mind.

Such political accusations among historians are not only unbecoming but unscholarly. Historians should share a canon of political good conduct. As the *Statement on Standards* of the AHA reminds all of us:

> Historians strive constantly to improve our collective understanding of the past through a complex process of critical dialogue—with each other, with the wider public, and with the historical record—in which we explore former lives and worlds in search of answers to the most compelling questions of our own time and place.
>
> Historians cannot successfully do this work without mutual trust and respect. By practicing their craft with integrity, historians acquire a reputation for trustworthiness that is arguably their single most precious

professional asset. The trust and respect both of one's peers and of the public at large are among the greatest and most hard-won achievements that any historian can attain. It is foolish indeed to put them at risk.

Although historians disagree with each other about many things, they do know what they trust and respect in each other's work. All historians believe in honoring the integrity of the historical record. They do not fabricate evidence. Forgery and fraud violate the most basic foundations on which historians construct their interpretations of the past. An undetected counterfeit undermines not just the historical arguments of the forger, but all subsequent scholarship that relies on the forger's work. Those who invent, alter, remove, or destroy evidence make it difficult for any serious historian ever wholly to trust their work again.

The internal politics of history undermine the entire project of constructing a philosophy of history for our time, but the working trust that is the watchword of the *Statement on Standards* suggests that the political may not be the last word. Whatever politics individual historians have, a decent respect for our common endeavor mandates that we give the other side the time and space to make its best case. Then, and only then, building a bridge to the past becomes a common endeavor.

7

Historians in the Marketplace

The best response is the number of people who buy it [*Undaunted Courage*] and the royalty checks that come in. The next best response is the people who write and say, "I read your book and I took the family out on the trail." That means a lot.

—Stephen Ambrose (2002)

Stephen Ambrose was one of America's most beloved and best-read historians. He knew that history is big business in America and that historians and their work are commodities in the marketplace. Most teachers of history depend upon their salaries to pay the bills, but best-selling works of history routinely sell in six figures and may bring as much as one-million-dollar advances on royalties to popular authors like Ambrose. According to Robert Townsend and the AHA's journal *Perspectives*, in 2003, 10,439 new history books hit the market. In 2004, 9,662 more new titles arrived. The number of books had grown 50 percent since 1993, the first year in which totals of history books were compiled. In 2004, there were 181,199 books published in all fields. By my count, that makes history books about 5.5 percent of all books published each year.

There are nearly ten thousand members of the Organization of American Historians and half again more members of the AHA, but professionally trained historians are not the sole proprietors of history. Over one hundred thousand men and women teach history in the public and private secondary schools. As Harvard's Laurel Thatcher Ulrich told an interviewer not long ago, "We need to have a little a bit of humility to recognize people can do what they want to with the past. Historians do not own history."

History is popular entertainment. The History Channels, the history theme parks and restorations, museums, and living museums on historical sites bring in billions of dollars and millions of visitors each year. As the *Newsweek* issue of April 30, 2007, on the four hundredth anniversary of the Jamestown settlement proclaimed, near the pit where archeologists were digging up the shards of pots, "You'll see a historic American community coming back to life." For the American who loves reading history or visiting historical sites and parks, history is not impossible at all.

The recognition of the fact that history and historians are market commodities raises practical questions for our philosophy of history—questions that traditional philosophies of history ignored. What are our professional and ethical obligations as purveyors of goods in the market?

The legal standard for sellers is laid out in the Uniform Commercial Code (UCC) that the American Law Institute and the National Conference of Commissioners on Uniform State Laws prepared in the 1940s and has been adopted, at least in part, by all but one state. The gist of the UCC is that we should honestly label and sell fairly our product. There is "an obligation of good faith" (UCC sec. 1-304). The consumer has a right to know exactly what he or she is buying. In short, our students and readers have to be able to trust us and our work.

But a more recent form of analysis of commercial dealings based on "law and economics" theory tells us that we may weigh risk versus gain in deciding how to package ourselves and our product. We are told to weigh the risk of discovery of misconduct and its associated loss of reputation and future prospects against the gain that any particular choice of conduct might bring. In other words, we need to calculate the likelihood that a shortcut or a fabrication or some other generally disapproved conduct would be discovered. Is that risk worth taking for the rewards that the misconduct might bring? If we are willing to pay the price of discovery, then the gains from the misconduct are worth the risk entailed.

In terms more familiar to historians, should we adopt some version of Herbert Spencer's "first principle" of happiness and freedom? As Spencer wrote in *Social Statics; or, The Conditions Essential to Human Happiness Specified* (1851), the "first principle" of human happiness is that every man should be free to do what he will, save to infringe the freedom of another man. And "if every man has freedom to do all that he wills, provided he infringes not the equal freedom of any other man, it is manifest that he has a claim to his life: for without it he can do nothing that he has willed; and to his personal liberty: for the withdrawal of it partially, if not wholly, restrains him from the fulfilment of his will." Should we adopt a "survival of the fittest" attitude toward competition with other historians for jobs, publication contracts, and the other rewards that the market can offer?

Risky Business

Recent events offer some anecdotal answers to these questions of market conduct. There is a huge market for history textbooks for grades K–12. Texas alone spends over four million dollars a year on its history textbooks. California spends more. Historians and their publishers who succeed in writing textbooks for that market can reap significant financial rewards. Writing for that market means catering to the desires of state school boards in states like Texas and local school boards elsewhere. That, in turn, means shaping the text to omit certain episodes and avoid certain terms that will offend the potential adopters of the text and enhancing or emphasizing other episodes that will gain the adopters' approval.

In 2001, conservatives, according to the *U.S. News and World Report,* were aghast when Texas adopted statewide a high school text that lauded the courage of an African American sailor at Pearl Harbor but did not mention the heroism of Ethan Allen. (It may be that Seaman Dorie Miller, played in the movie *Pearl Harbor* by Cuba Gooding Jr., was a less controversial figure than Ethan Allen. Miller died later in the war when his ship was torpedoed. Allen spent part of his war in prison and offered his services to both sides at one time or another.) But Texas was not done. As Alexander Stille reported in "Textbook Publishers Learn: Avoid Messing with Texas," a piece for the June 29, 2002, *New York Times:*

> *Out of Many,* the work of four respected historians, is one of the biggest sellers among American history college textbooks in the United States, but it is not likely to be available to Texas high school students taking advanced placement history. Conservative groups in Texas objected to two paragraphs in the nearly 1,000-page text that explained that prostitution was rampant in cattle towns during the late 19th century, before the West was fully settled. "It makes it sound that every woman west of the Mississippi was a prostitute," said Grace Shore, the Republican chairwoman of the Texas State Board of Education. "The book says that there were 50,000 prostitutes west of the Mississippi. I doubt it, but even if there were, is that something that should be emphasized? Is that an important historical fact?"

Should the authors of a textbook up for adoption in a huge market agree to make the changes that the state board of education wants? They said no. They gave up the lucrative option of conforming to their customers' preferences. They did not opt out of the market, but they elected not to participate in this transaction. "The publisher, Pearson Prentice Hall, has quietly withdrawn the book from consideration by the board. Wendy Spiegel, a vice president for communications at the company, said it had another textbook that better fit the state's curriculum. . . . Peggy Venable, director of the Texas chapter, said executives at Pearson Prentice Hall withdrew *Out of Many*, because they 'wisely didn't want to jeopardize their larger sales in the state by having that book as its poster child.'" One notes that the publisher's conduct more closely fit the Spencerian model than the historian-authors' conduct.

Should historians seeking to market a general program of historical studies for grades K–12 conform their views to political currents? In the 1980s, a series of factual (multiple-choice) tests on American history given high school students revealed that they were woefully ignorant of the most basic information about our past. That proved to educator Diane Ravitch and others that the schools needed more extensive history offerings. The University of California at Los Angeles won the grant from the National Endowment for the Humanities, with chairman Lynne Cheney making the choice, and set about assembling experts to write standards. The chair of the National History Center, Gary Nash, had a good deal of experience and a strong track record in writing history textbooks for high school. His approach included many of the ordinary people—immigrants, ethnic minorities, women, laborers—that older textbooks had omitted. While a basic facts approach might have remedied the low test scores of the students, Nash wanted an end to the "false dichotomy between facts and conceptual analysis." Democratic ideas were both real and visionary. History was not just narrative but "interpretation of narrative," "depth," and "contingency and complexity." A simplistic notion of "progress" was a "trap that many survey history textbooks still lay for students," as was the older focus on "winners." A program of "active learning and critical inquiry" using primary sources would enable students to "write and speak their own minds" instead of passively absorbing what teachers or textbooks said.

Cheney had other ideas. Years later, she judged that the National Standards Nash had published "reflected the gloomy, politically driven revisionism" that had become "all too familiar on college campuses." In addition, the heroes were all gone, replaced by minor figures. Enduring values were gone too; only oppression remained. On October 20, 1994, her op-ed piece entitled "The End of History" graced the back pages of the *Wall Street Journal*. In it, she ridiculed the standards for elevating the National

Organization of Women, the Sierra Club, and Harriet Tubman in importance above the Constitution, the U.S. Congress, and U. S. Grant (though in fact these were subjects of students' essays from the "Examples of Student Achievement," not the standards themselves). The result, she judged, was a "grim and gloomy" account of America that could give comfort only to the "politically correct."

Nash refused to cater to the politicians. As a mass-market project, the National History Standards were a disaster and even after extensive revision are not widely used. At Department of Education "Teaching American History" seminars for middle and high school teachers of history, I discovered that the teachers had never heard of, much less seen, the Standards. Nash had not withdrawn himself from the market, but he refused to let one vocal segment of the marketplace dictate what he and his coworkers would write.

But the lure of the marketplace can lead historians astray. Consider the following hypothetical. You are a popular historian. Your previous books have sold well. You can command a hefty "advance" payment against the anticipated royalties of your next book from a trade (commercial) publisher. These advances are paid in installments, but in recent law cases the courts have ruled that you can keep the portion of the advance already paid you if you have made a good-faith effort to produce the book. Now you have choices to make—market choices.

To whom do you (or your agent) offer the book? Top-level university (academic) presses have trade capacity and will work to get your book into bookstores as well as sell it to scholars and put it in classrooms, but rarely do their books hit the best-seller lists. You decide to go with a trade publisher. There's another advantage to this choice. Trade publishers make the decision to put you in print "in house." In other words, the editors read the work and make the decision to publish themselves. Academic presses send your manuscript out to two or three readers for assessments. Even if these are favorable, the manuscript will require some revisions. Then your manuscript has to meet the approval of the academic press's board of editors, a distinguished group of humanists and scientists who probably know little about your topic. A trade house can get your manuscript into the bookstores in four to six months. Academic presses average a little over a year from accepted manuscript through copyediting and page proofs to finished book.

What topic should you select for your trade press book? The most popular topics—biography, military history, Civil War, and World War II era—beckon, for they will always have a market, but you know that you have very little new to say about them. Should you spend years searching for new documents and giving progress reports at conferences (where others may hear what you have found and "scoop" you)? Or will you spend the bulk of your time collecting and pouring over what your predecessors have written, copying down on note cards quotations from primary sources in their pages, along with some of the best passages that they wrote?

You decide to do a biography of Abraham Lincoln or a book on the D-Day invasion. You know that as soon as you finish this book you can sign a contract for another book. In fact, your income is dependent more on the advances than on royalties, because even modest advances (say mid-five figures) will probably exceed the 10 or 15 percent of the net sales that you would get from royalties over the lifetime of the book. That is another reason to choose the trade publisher, as a matter of fact. Most academic histories do not sell enough copies (the average is around 1,200) for anyone—university press publisher or professor-author—to get rich on them.

Most academic press histories, to judge from the acknowledgments and other anecdotal evidence, took nearly a decade to research and write. You do not have this luxury. You need to move along fairly quickly. Those other books, with their juicy quotations from the documents or interviews and their fine prose summaries, are starting to look more inviting, and your borrowings from them begin to pile up on your desk. Relying on what you have read in the other books' pages is becoming more appealing every day.

As a contribution to scholarship, your book should say something, in fact lots of things, that are new or should uncover evidence that your predecessors did not see or use. But all the market choices that have brought you to this point in your work—the choice of topic and publisher, the size of the advance—press you to take the shortcut. Should you? On April 5, 2002, Coleman Warner of the New Orleans *Times-Picayune* interviewed David Rosenthal, Simon and Schuster's publisher, about his author Stephen Ambrose. Rosenthal told Warner that "popular and academic history are different animals, that an Ambrose book gets less of a prepublication combing for factual accuracy than would an obscure thesis submitted to a history journal. 'We take it on faith that an author is accurate,' Rosenthal said. 'Our purpose here is not to create an academically vetted book. It is to create a book which is readable, accurate, sensible and compares favorably to the genre.'"

Stephen Ambrose was a superb storyteller who catered to the general audience even though he had been a professor of history at the University of New Orleans. His output was prodigious. With help from his family he was turning out a book every two years. His topics were presidential biography, adventure, and war. When in 2002 he was accused of **plagiarism**—copying portions of his books from other authors without fully or fairly labeling the degree of borrowing—his editor at Simon and Schuster, Alice Mayhew, told him, he said, to keep on writing. Rosenthal agreed. "At Simon and Schuster, the plagiarism issue seems to be having no effect on sales of Ambrose's works," Rosenthal said. "We cannot wait for his next book." All of them had the same commercial stake in his continued productivity. They had made a market choice that his questionable techniques would not particularly reduce his sales. They were right about the sales, as his critics were right that he was a veteran serial plagiarist, but was their calculation one that our philosophy of history should applaud?

Believe it or not, even in this day of stern admonitions against plagiarists, it is possible to compose a defense of borrowing without attribution. The parts of that defense are almost as old as printed books. When an unnamed "gentleman" suggested that James Kirkpatrick had cribbed language, form, and theme for his book-length poem *Sea-Piece* (1750) from classical texts, he bristled: "Here it seems difficult for a Mind, imbued with the least Generosity, not to express a just Contempt for the invidious Pains" of those who "by an Imputation of Plagiarism" denounce as a "crime" what has been "very customary in the scribbling world." In fact, "a frequent similarity would be the more inevitable, where both, happening to employ themselves on the same historical subject, had equally determined to preserve the received Circumstances and Connections of it." In short, everyone did it, and even if copying was not "customary," similarities of phrasing and similar uses of the same primary sources were inevitable.

Lest one of the those uncharitable readers whom Kirkpatrick decried reply, "Well, that was then, but not now," consider the following two much more recent cases. Biographer and history professor Stephen Oates tells the first story. It "began in 1990–1991, when a literary critic, a professor of classics, an associate professor of criminology, and two historians publicly charged that I had plagiarized in writing *With Malice toward None*, my life of Lincoln. They cited as evidence similarities of phrases and short bits of factual matter between my account of Lincoln's early years and that in Benjamin Thomas's 1952 biography *[Abraham Lincoln, A Biography]*."

The charge soon became public knowledge, and Oates waged a vigorous defense against the charge. His colleagues in Civil War and Lincoln studies obtained letters defending him, based largely on the letter writers' assessment of Oates's professional and personal character. He contested the investigation of the matter conducted by the AHA's Professional Division (he was not a member of the AHA and so refused to participate in the inquiry there) and in the press. Ten years later he was still advancing the argument that "in fact, there are no guidelines for what is sufficient acknowledgment of sources in popular biographies and histories. Thousands of such works including a great many on Lincoln have been published with no footnotes and no bibliographies at all." Thomas had written five books on Lincoln and had provided only minimal references. Oates had merely used the same primary sources as Thomas and so, inevitably, had fashioned similar depictions.

Michael Burlingame, one of Oates's accusers, replied in a series of paired quotations from Oates and Thomas. A sampler:

> Stephen B. Oates: "tugging on their slender sweeps to avoid snags and sandbars . . ."
>
> Benjamin P. Thomas: "giving an occasional tug on the slender sweeps to avoid the snags and sandbars . . ."
>
> Stephen B. Oates: "Tad . . . ate all the strawberries intended for a state dinner. The steward raged at the boy and pulled his hair . . ."
>
> Benjamin P. Thomas: "Tad ate all the strawberries intended for a state dinner; the steward raged and tore his hair . . ."
>
> Stephen B. Oates: "the McCormick reaper episode had been one of the most crushing experiences of his life . . ."
>
> Benjamin P. Thomas: "he remembered his snub at Cincinnati in the McCormick reaper case as one of the most crushing experiences of his life . . ."

Whatever the reader decides about these and the other close paraphrases in the two works, the point for our purposes is that Oates and his publisher, Harper and Row, then a major New York City trade house, knew that the Lincoln project was a winner. Oates, then only in midcareer, was proving a commercially successful biographer. He had already written a biography of John Brown, two books on the Texas frontier, and, two years before *With Malice toward None,* a biography of the slave rebel Nat Turner. Oates took but two years to spin out the Lincoln book, 492 pages long. There followed, in fairly short order (within ten years), a short book on the Civil War, a 560-page biography of Martin Luther King (1982), another book on Lincoln, a 434-page revised biography of John Brown, and an edited book on how to do biography. Biographers typically spend decades on books as long as Oates's on Brown, Lincoln, and King. By contrast, Oates's productivity matched Ambrose's. Surely author and publisher might be excused for asking: Why spend an extra year or two or three finding ways to say something in different words when Thomas had said it so well?

In the last essay of the collection he edited, *Biography as High Adventure,* Oates wrote, "For me, biography has not only been high literary and historical adventure, but deep personal experience as well. I have lived through four human lives besides my own, something that has enriched me beyond measure as a writer and a man." Perhaps Oates's choice of verb—*enriched*—was unfortunate in the light of the later accusations, for while there was no particular scholarly need for another biography of Lincoln, there are other ways that highly successful commercial biographies enrich their authors.

A second case: consider what Judge Richard Posner has to say about plagiarism, bearing in mind that the judge is one of the avatars of law and economics theory, in which the ethical value of any conduct is weighed by the impact it has on the marketplace. "The idea that copying another person's ideas or expression (the form of words in which the idea is encapsulated), without the person's authorization and without explicit acknowledgment of the copying, is reprehensible is, in general, clearly false." Why? Because "this is a general characteristic of government documents, CEOs' speeches, and books by celebrities." Judge Posner might have added university presidents, men of the cloth, and others in high places. For example, he went on, then-Senator John F. Kennedy's Pulitzer Prize–winning *Profiles in Courage* was a "managed book." "Many judicial opinions are of this character. It seems likely that many multivolume treatises by (that is, nominally by) law professors are 'managed books' in which most of the actual writing is done by student research assistants . . . though I am guessing; I have no actual evidence." (Posner was being charitable—there is evidence that some of these books are indeed collaborative efforts in which nominal authors merely acknowledge the written contributions of their research assistants.)

For Posner, plagiarism "is a label attached to instances of unauthorized copying of which the society, or some influential group within it, disapproves." If fraud or copyright infringement or some other form of loss of property rights is involved, then the plagiarism is indeed censurable, and if the student or author gains from the fraud, then it is an offense. "A professional historian who 'authored' a managed book without disclosure of the fact would be committing a fraud because his fellow historians would think he'd written it himself." Misrepresentation of a product is the sin, not misconduct in the writing.

Plagiarism of Ambrose's sort may not be palatable to even the most cynical defenders of Spencerian behavior, or law and economics theory for that matter, but another kind of market-based shortcut is rarely condemned, even by the most scrupulous of historians. In the acknowledgments to her Pulitzer Prize–winning book on Franklin and Eleanor Roosevelt in the World War II era, *No Ordinary Time,* Doris Kearns Goodwin revealed, "This book would not have been possible without the research help of Linda Vandergrift. . . . Her diligence in digging through the archives, her love of detail, and her passion accompanied me every step along the way." The two women reassembled for Goodwin's *Team of Rivals: The Political Genius of Abraham Lincoln* (2005). Once more Goodwin admitted: "I owe an immense debt once again to my great friend and indefatigable assistant Linda Vandergrift." In the acknowlgments for her best-selling *Founding Mothers: The Women Who Raised Our Nation* (New York: Morrow, 2004), Cokie Roberts reported, "I couldn't do it without the help of my old friend Ann Charnley." Charnley did the research, aided by Roberts's niece Abigail, and the footnotes were supplied by Annie Whitworth.

One usually thinks of historical work as the research and writing of history. If time is of the essence and the market beckons, it makes sense to assemble a team of researchers, fact checkers, and other aides. The author then becomes something of a compiler, putting together the pieces that others have found into a pleasing pattern. Should this kind of collaborative labor be addressed in a philosophy of history? One very useful answer comes from the market itself, or rather from an academic tool often used to make market decisions.

Let the Buyer Beware?

One might reply to the danger that faces a buyer of our history in the marketplace: *Caveat emptor* (Let the buyer beware). Is there not within a more sophisticated, modern set of ideas about market decision making some other basis for controlling historians' behavior? I suggest that **game**

theory, and in particular the variant known as the **prisoner's dilemma**, provides one plausible resolution to academic dilemmas otherwise resolved in unethical fashion.

The term prisoner's dilemma was coined by Albert Tucker, a mathematician at Princeton University, to help explain game theory to his students. Before World War II, a number of brilliant mathematicians, in particular Johann Von Neumann (one of the giants of early computer programming) figured out that decision making could be reduced to a kind of mathematical game. After the war, with the world teetering on the abyss of global nuclear war, the need to find minimum-risk strategies in the Cold War between the Western powers and the Communist bloc led some mathematicians to turn to game theory. At "think tanks" like the U.S. government–funded RAND Corporation in California (short for "Research ANd Development"), mathematicians sought reliable predictive models to take the guesswork out of the behavior of nations. Game theory convinced American policy planners that a first strike against an enemy would lead to retaliation.

At RAND, in 1949, Merrill Flood and Melvin Dresher thought up the prisoner's dilemma and applied it to a wide range of military, economic, and political situations to weigh risks and opportunities for world peace and economic progress. The people at RAND, by 1949 a private nonprofit outfit, spread word of their achievements. Tucker learned of the puzzle, his name for it caught on, and it in turn popularized game theory. John F. Nash, one of Tucker's students at Princeton, would carry the theory to new heights of sophistication in his 1950 dissertation and win the Nobel Prize in economics in 1994. His story is told in the book and the movie *A Beautiful Mind*.

In a noncooperating game, various players make decisions to maximize their own gains. Are there mutually beneficial, rational outcomes to such games, or are their outcomes inherently and irretrievably unpredictable? Nash found that there was a rational outcome to every such game, in what later game theorists termed the Nash equilibrium. Such an equilibrium is not a thing but a set of predictions about how the players will make their decisions. Nash proposed that if all the players had the same information available to them—the same "playbook," as it were—and all were rational, then the game could come to a point where no player could further extend his or her gains against what the other players had gained. There are a lot of assumptions here, and in the half-century after Nash proposed his theory many modifications and variants of it have appeared.

But the basics are clear and applicable to historians. Imagine, for example, that you are revising the chapters of a book on the philosophy of history for our times. As you revise each chapter, all the others look shabby by comparison. So you revise another chapter. All the other chapters (including the one you just finished) look poor by comparison. When revising a chapter, any chapter, no longer improves it relative to the other chapters—in game theory lingo, when revising no longer extends any chapter's advantage over the other chapters—you have reached a Nash equilibrium. Nash's thesis is that such an equilibrium can be reached in every rationally played game—or, for our example, every process of revision of a book's chapters. It does not tell the game players when the equilibrium will exist, any more than it tells an author when to stop tweaking the text and submit the manuscript to a publisher, but it does reassure us that there will be a time to put the manuscript into a padded mailer and send it off.

Implicit in Nash's formulation was a moral and psychological dimension to decision making. Players must be consistent in their views of their own aims and their views of other players' aims throughout the game. This requires a degree of self-awareness and a shared culture among the players. Historians have these qualities. As individuals we are aware of our aims and work to obtain those aims rationally. We share a common culture of honesty and integrity embodied in the AHA's *Statement on Standards*. But historians' conduct in the market is not always entirely rational. Not everyone shares all the same values. Not everyone has all the same information. Not every decision is made rationally. The hand skips, the mind wobbles, and rationality trembles. One can model the likelihood of this kind of deviation from Nash equilibrium by applying the prisoner's dilemma to historians' choices in the marketplace.

We confront one form or another of the prisoner's dilemma every day. The best-known version is the one on the police procedural television show, in fact the one that Tucker used to introduce the game to his students. The police have arrested and brought to the station house two or more suspects for the same offense. They put each in a separate interrogation room and tell each one, "Here is a onetime offer. The first of you to take it will get a guaranteed reduced sentence. You have to agree to testify against the other prisoner. If they take it first, you will do a long stretch in the penitentiary." If neither talks, the police will not be able to convict anyone of anything. But each suspect cannot know what the other will do. If one suspect stays silent while another agrees to the deal, he is the big loser. Cooperation with the police seems to offer the best outcome, called the dominant choice, and seems to be the rational one. But the best outcome for both suspects is to say nothing, or deny everything. Then both walk out of the station. The trick is that the rational decision for one player is the irrational one for both.

Now you may think to yourself, What's wrong with choosing the option that is best for me? One of the sayings attributed to the Talmudic sage Rabbi Hillel is that "if I am not for myself, then who should be for me?" For example, if I am not confident enough of my work to submit it for publication and the possibility of criticism or even rejection, then who should stand up for my abilities as a scholar? We should not forget the second half of the saying, however: "If I am just for myself, then what kind of person am I?"

How many times every day have we fumed at the person who makes the selfish choice in the everyday version of the prisoner's dilemma? The person who insists on making the left turn at the light, sticks out in traffic, and creates gridlock; the person who holds up the entire line at the checkout counter trying to empty his pocket of pennies; and the person who takes all the chicken tikka at the Indian buffet instead of a portion, leaving everyone else in the restaurant to wait for another tray to arrive from the kitchen are all examples of me-first thinking that, if it becomes a rule, would create true social gridlock.

History is replete with examples of individual selfishness endangering entire communities. When English traders introduced southeastern Indians to European trade goods in exchange for deerskins, the natives were eager customers. Although their traditional customs entailed hunting the deer as a group and then sharing the bounty of the hunt with everyone, the chance to obtain trade goods caused individuals to hunt for themselves. The result was the overhunting of the deer and the neglect of communal responsibilities. Indians starved as animal populations were reduced to critically low levels. The decision to promote one's own interest endangered the survival of the village.

When the game is played not by individual players but by whole peoples or nations, it gets a lot more complicated, much like actual historical events. Still, the best common outcome (the **greatest good for the greatest number**) may not correspond to what seems the rational choice of one people or nation. For example, if two nations have a choice of peace or war with one another, peace is the best outcome for both, but if one goes to war upon the other, it may obtain desired territory and resources not available through peaceful relations. Thus the rational decision looks like going to war. But if both nations reason this way and go to war against one another, neither has an advantage over the other, and the outcome is the ruin of both. Thus the result of what appears to be a rational decision for one is actually the irrational decision for both.

For all its abstractness and potential complexity, the prisoner's dilemma is not just an abstract formulation or a game. It is history in game form. In terms of individual nations' aims versus the global good, the prisoner's dilemma is repeated in every imperial venture, every decision to exploit the natural resources of underdeveloped nations, every deployment of a technological advance. When corporate and political leaders put short-term preferences and economic interests (for example, jobs in polluting industries) ahead of long-term interests (for example, in environmental survival), they are playing the prisoner's dilemma.

Historians' Gamesmanship

Historians face their own version of these dilemmas. Are they to copy from another's unpublished work or seminar paper or public lecture and beat the other author into print? Repeat old stories without adding anything new just to publish? Share their research findings? Work toward a better history in common ventures, or go it alone? The urge to scoop one's colleagues is promoted by the system of publication and tenure that rewards individual effort, but concealing findings from others working in the same field, sometimes for years, while the historian gets the book ready, sets back the common endeavor.

Hiring in history departments is extremely competitive. For an entry-level tenure track position in twentieth-century American history my department received over two hundred applications. Of these, nearly fifty applicants had, on paper, experience, publications, and quality education equal to or better than that I had when I was hired thirty years ago. We can give an interview to only a dozen of these wonderfully well-qualified people, bring only three or four to campus, and hire but one.

What if one of the applicants decides to cheat? If everyone who applies is strictly honest in his or her application, then no one has an unfair advantage. But if someone lies about educational achievements or publications, then he or she may gain an advantage over all other candidates. Against this course of action one must lay the risk that a lie will be discovered, but the potential gain may outweigh the risk in the applicant's mind. If all the applicants lie, then no one has an advantage. What should the applicant do?

The Nash equilibrium suggests an answer. Where would all the players find equilibrium, where no player could gain an advantage anymore against the others if one cheated? If one cheats, then others must cheat if they are to gain against those still playing by the rules. There is no equilibrium as everyone starts and keeps on cheating. Is this a desirable outcome for any one of the cheaters? No. They have not gained anything from their cheating, except an increased risk of exposure. If, however, everyone plays by the rules, no one gains anything further against the other players. Thus cheating is not a rational act for anyone.

Information about the rules, as required in Nash's formulation, is open to all the players. Everyone who interviews for a job, and everyone who recruits for a job, has the same playbook. The AHA's *Statement on Standards* says that "historians are obligated to present their credentials accurately and honestly in all contexts. They should take care not to misrepresent their qualifications in resumes, applications, or the public record. They should apply the same rigor and integrity in describing their own accomplishments as their profession applies to the historical record itself." In short, professional ethics require that applicants be truthful, and lying undermines the entire foundation of academic hiring.

What happens when departments search for a position—for example, in twentieth-century U.S. history—but have an agenda that they do not reveal in the advertisement? For example, they may wish to increase their minority presence or the number of women in the department. Such information may be available to some candidates but not to others, or it may be inferred from the nature of the job description but not spelled out. According to the *Statement on Standards,* "Employment decisions always involve judgments. But, except in those cases in which federal law allows a specific preference, institutions should base hiring decisions as well as all decisions relating to reappointment, promotion, tenure, apprenticeship, graduate student assistantships, awards, and fellowships solely on professional qualifications without regard to sex, race, color, national origin, sexual orientation, religion, political affiliation, veteran status, age, certain physical handicaps, or marital status."

Does game theory help explain how the department should act in this case? The rational decision in the short term, much like taking the deal the police offered or going to war, would be to cull the applicant pool, reducing it to just those individuals who fit the hidden description. But thinking in terms of the Nash equilibrium, what if every search proceeded in this way—for example, discriminating against women because the department did not want any more women, or not considering individuals because of their religious affiliation (or requiring all applicants to subscribe to a creedal test before allowing their candidacies to go forward)? What would the result of such decisions be? The result would be that hiring was based no longer on merit but on the perceived fit of individuals in a department for entirely or largely nonprofessional reasons. Individual departments would decline in status as they refilled their ranks with only certain kinds of racial or religious groups. The status of the profession would decline as well, as individuals of merit considering a career in history realized that their job prospects depended not on merit but on personal characteristics. Something of this sort has, in fact, happened in the historical profession. That is why hiring is not now in a Nash equilibrium.

Consider now the game from the perspective of the potential hiree. He or she is valued by more than one department. When history departments compete for an individual who has "outside offers," the individual can maximize his or her gain by playing the two (or more) departments against one another. The individual tells the department that has made the offer that he or she wants very much to come, then tells the current employer that he or she very much wants to stay. The applicant has maximized his or her value by "bidding up" the stakes. Historians successful at this game will tell disgruntled colleagues that they have to "go on the market" to gain similar advantages in pay and teaching load.

What happens if everyone adopts this decision? Everyone in the department becomes a marketable (or unmarketable) commodity. Does this lead to equilibrium, with everyone reaching the stage where no further decision will bring a reward? No. Instead, it leads everyone to repeat the process of seeking outside offers every year, the very opposite of equilibrium because now the end of the game, the Nash equilibrium, is not obtainable. Instead, there will be endless rounds of seeking outside offers.

By rewarding such conduct, in effect measuring individual merit by how attractive the individual is to other departments, the home department and the departments attempting to lure the candidate also find themselves in a state of disequilibrium. They cannot predict who will stay and who will depart, and they face the problem of keeping faculty from leaving—or recruiting new faculty—every year.

Can the Nash equilibrium help us with the problem of cheating in publication? Yes. For example, I recognize that there is a market for another biography of U. S. Grant, but there is little new to say. I find an old biography, whose author has passed away, and liberally borrow from it for my own book. Borrowing cuts the time my project takes to complete. My book is a commercial success. I have won at the prisoner's dilemma. The cheater has gained an advantage in the marketplace, but if that decision is rational then all others in the same situation, rationally, should cut and paste books together from other books. Setting aside the copyright violation question, the result is not the Nash equilibrium but an ever-escalating process of unoriginal works masquerading as new. The reading public may be satisfied, but it too is being cheated. Buyers are paying for new books that are in fact retreads. And there is no stopping the fraud.

These simple applications of game theory to historians' conduct in the market suggest a series of important additions to our philosophy of history. If and only if historians recognize that we are in but not of the market, that we should not mimic or encourage the worst features of the nineteenth-century notion of free markets, we can protect ourselves and our work against irrational decisions. True, some of these collective behavioral choices go against our ingrained habits. Some merely require that we recognize our mutual dependency.

Take the question of collaboration among historians. As I have mentioned, for the most part, historians are solitary laborers. They work alone, write alone, and alone submit their final product for judgment. Yet at that point they become part of a vast collaborative or collective process. They read portions of their work as papers at conferences, and fellow panelists or "commentators" provide constructive (or on occasion not-so-constructive) responses. When the historian submits an article to a learned journal, the editor sends it out to expert readers for their advice. Should it be published? How can it be improved? The leading journals routinely ask five or six outside readers to vet a submission. The historian who sends a manuscript to an academic publisher can expect at least two and sometimes more outside readers to advise the press, and the author, of the manuscript's value.

Throughout this entire process, the helpers—outside readers, referees, and even colleagues who set aside their own work to help with ours—are not immediately rewarded. Refereeing article submissions for a journal, for example, is uncompensated. It takes time and effort away from one's own work. But we do it in the expectation that when we submit, someone else will take time from his or her work to read and comment on ours. This collaborative, collegial effort is not simply the exchange or barter of services. Historians who do not write and submit articles to journals nevertheless make themselves available as referees of submissions. Historians who are not planning to submit a book manuscript in the near future will still set aside their research and make time to help a publisher and an author improve the author's work.

In such collaborative efforts, the whole is greater than the sum of its parts, a goal of game theory as well. A philosophy of history for our time would make space for this kind of work and credit sharing, not moving history away from its traditional reliance on the solitary scholar in the archive so much as acknowledging that even the solitary scholar depends upon many other scholars, editors, and publishers to bring any piece of work to completion.

Similarly, game theory reminds us that treating potential hires on their merits, rather than on preconceived notions of compatibility or quotas for various groups, makes the playing field fair for everyone. Affirmative action hiring may still be necessary because a department has a long history of discrimination against certain groups that needs to be remedied, because students would benefit from a diversity of teaching styles and research interests that a particular department lacks, or because a government agency has mandated certain kinds of hiring. Otherwise, hidden agendas, secret handshakes, and special interests simply prevent the realization of the Nash equilibrium—there will always be a way for an individual to better his or her own situation relative to others'.

Finally, game theory reveals that the immediate gains of cheating in all forms are soon offset by the loss to the individual and to the reputation of all historians. No one will quite forget that Stephen Ambrose plagiarized, and a decent man and fine historian will always bear its stigma. If we cheat, everyone in the end loses because no one will trust what historians say. We lose our authority as a discipline along with our respectability as individuals. Cheating, the prisoner's dilemma tells us, will always bring a bad outcome. A bridge to the past built upon such unsound foundations cannot last.

8

Uncertainties

> There are no longer any certainties either in life or in thought. Everywhere confusion. Everywhere questions. Where are we? Where did we come from? Where do we go from here? What is it all about?
>
> —Carl Becker (1926)

Becker wrote these words in a letter to the editor of the Cornell University student newspaper when students complained of a lack of certainties in their coursework. Adrift in the moral permissiveness of the "lost generation" of the 1920s, students looked to history and found only relativism like Becker's. He was sympathetic but replied that history provided them, and him, no comfort.

Historians today once again face a crisis of uncertainty. As I wrote in *Past Imperfect*, the 1980s had begun with one of the giants of our profession, Bernard Bailyn, at the helm of the AHA, calling for a "retelling of stories," a reunification of all the many highly technical findings of the younger generation of new historians. He was confident that this synthesis could be attained, and he devoted his address at the annual convention to a brief summary of the many highly specialized fields that needed to be incorporated into the story.

The 1990s ended with Joyce Appleby's very different presidential address to the association: "Today, we confront a challenge. . . . The static in our conversation with the public comes not from an inappropriately positivistic view of history but from its very opposite—confusion about the nature of historical knowledge and the amount of credibility it deserves. Such confusion can well incite indifference, even antagonism."

So it had. In the face of a storm of criticism of academic history and historians, Appleby desperately wanted the public to understand how historians had, in the years since 1980, changed the very foundation of how historical knowledge was acquired. "You can't learn what history has to impart if you start with a false idea of what history is and how historians—amateurs and professionals alike—acquire knowledge about the past. Even worse, without this understanding, you become susceptible to rumors of cultural warfare and academic conspiracies. Doubts about the validity of historical knowledge having been registered, they must be addressed."

Her appeal to a common "historical method," suspiciously close to the "scientific method" of the late nineteenth century, did not persuade anyone that we could dodge the uncertainty problem's two prongs. The first concerns our use of words. Do the words historians use to describe the past actually correspond to things? Can we trust our language to reflect reality when our reality is no longer "there"?

The second problem is, if anything, even more vexing. Even if we can be reasonably comfortable with the words we use, are there any patterns in the past that we can discover? Without such larger, organizing structures, we could not cross the bridge to the past because the other side would be entirely without order or sense to us. Surely all the "revisions" of history by each generation of scholars are proof that historical scholarship is never final. But one could ask whether there is finality out there, somewhere. If we could be reassured on that score, then perhaps we could say that historical knowledge may not be certain but that it approaches certainty the way that the integration of the points on a curve approaches the precise calculation of the curve itself.

Naive Realism?

Historians cannot do without words. We title arbitrary spans of time like centuries and decades with particular names—the American century, the Reagan decade—and give names to periods, eras, and ages. We raise scattered events to the level of movements and collate collections of individuals into parties, sects, and communities. With a flourish of our pens we can turn a civil war into a revolution and a mob into a gathering of demonstrators. With such confident gestures, we assume that our words are things and that things are adequately captured in words.

Perhaps naively, most historians assume that words and things are inextricably tied together and that our words thus correspond in some way to reality. In the theory of "naive realism" one would say that what we see, hear, and otherwise sense is "out there" just as we perceive it. Historians should be wary of such one-to-one mapping of word to sense data to thing because we know that words are cultural artifacts and that individuals from different cultures may not describe the very same thing in the very same way.

An example from my book *Sensory Worlds in Early America* (2003) will illustrate my point. The Micmac of Nova Scotia passed down a legend of how they met French mariner Jacques Cartier's little fleet off the coast in 1534. (Of course the dates and the identity of the newcomers were not part of the Indian story.) One morning, the Micmac people gathered on the bank and saw a peculiar little island, with trees on it, float close to the shore and then stop. In the trees were bears. But when the Micmacs ran to the edge of the water with their bows and arrows to shoot the bears, they magically turned into men and climbed into a strange-looking canoe to row to shore. Only when the French took a number of the Indians aboard the ship did they realize that it was manmade.

The French recorded that encounter as well, and what they saw was quite different from what the Micmac saw, just as their culture was different from the Micmac's. The French assumed that the "two fleets of savage canoes" that approached them on July 6, 1534, had a warlike purpose. In Cartier's words, though the natives

> all came after our longboat, dancing and showing many signs of joy, and of their desire to be friends . . . we did not care to trust to their signs and waved to them to go back . . . and seeing that no matter how much we signed to them, they would not go back, we shot off over their heads two small cannon. On this they began to return towards [the shore], after which they began to come on as before. And when they had come alongside our longboat, we shot off two fire-lances which scattered among them and frightened them so much that they began to paddle off in very great haste.

The Micmac hunters and the French explorers reacted to what they saw, and later recalled it, in entirely different ways precisely because their prior experiences and technologies were so different.

History teaches us that seeing is culture bound: we see what we are taught to see, not what is "out there" for all to see in the same way. Great thinkers have pondered a parallel question throughout Western history. Is what any of us, then or now, sense real, or is it the shadowy reflection of an ideal thing that we can never see? Idealists like the Anglo-Irish eighteenth-century philosopher and Anglican cleric George Berkeley thought words reflected the ideas in our heads. There were no abstract ideas outside our minds. As he wrote in his *Treatise Concerning the Principles of Human Knowledge* (1734):

> It is indeed an Opinion strangely prevailing amongst Men, that Houses, Mountains, Rivers, and in a word all sensible Objects have an Existence Natural or Real, distinct from their being perceived by the Understanding. But with how great an Assurance and Acquiescence soever this Principle may be entertained in the World; yet whoever shall find in his Heart to call it in Question, may, if I mistake not, perceive it to involve a manifest Contradiction. For what are the aforementioned Objects but the things we perceive by Sense, and what do we perceive besides our own Ideas or Sensations; and is it not plainly repugnant that any one of these or any Combination of them should exist unperceived?

Words were not things, for different peoples had different words for the same thing. "It is evident to anyone who takes a Survey of the Objects of Humane Knowledge, that they are either Ideas actually imprinted on the Senses, or else such as are perceived by attending to the Passions and Operations of the Mind, or lastly Ideas formed by help of Memory and Imagination, either compounding, dividing, or barely representing those originally perceived in the aforesaid ways. . . . So long as I confine my Thoughts to my own Ideas divested of Words, I do not see how I can easily be mistaken." We could never prove that there was a world out there, independent of our thoughts (except that God would not fool us, and that was good enough for Berkeley). "To me, I say, it is evident that the Being of a Spirit infinitely Wise, Good, and Powerful is abundantly sufficient to explain all the Appearances of Nature."

If what we see and hear at this moment is not what is "out there" but exists only in our minds, what then is history? Without a "now" that we share, how can there be a shared "then"? For the historian wants us to believe that we share a world with one another, and his or her account of that world, if not certainly true, at least might be true. There could be no gradual building of historical knowledge because such a structure would exist, if it could exist, only in the individual mind, and everyone's idea of it would be particular to that individual. As Berkeley wrote, "Whenever I attempt to frame a simple Idea of Time, abstracted from the succession of Ideas in my Mind, which flows uniformly, and is participated by all

Beings, I am lost and entangled in inextricable Difficulties. I have no Notion of it at all."

Berkeley's view of ideas and time has become something of a curiosity, but in the years after World War II, when so many of the traditional assumptions about rationality in Western philosophy were in shambles, a new school of skeptical thinkers (sometimes termed **deconstructionists**) rejected the notion of a truth outside language. Often reviled, more often misunderstood as gamesmen or debunkers merely, without a positive program, in fact they were deep thinkers many of whom had seen too much history. For history then was memory of the unthinkable horror of the Holocaust. They were suspicious of the claims of nations and parties that reality was simple, that it could be strictly categorized, and that everyone fit in one box or another defined by the state.

For Jacques Derrida, time was "conceived in terms of the present, and can mean nothing else." Meanings in texts could travel through time, from text to text, but text was all there was. History was indeterminate, time collapsed, as writer of text and reader of text became one. There was no fixed meaning to historical terms, at least meaning fixed in a context outside the language. If this seems enigmatic, Derrida would have been the first to concede, as he did in his last years, that he was forever "questioning myself [about] unanswerable questions." As Richard J. Evans has posed in his *In Defense of History* (1999), the ultimate resting place of such theories was that "authors can no longer be regarded as having control over the meaning of what they write. . . . In history, meaning cannot be found in the past; it is merely put there, each time differently, and with equal validity, by different historians." Let the reader beware, or let the reader delight—for the text belonged to the reader. In the end, we were left with a less optimistic and self-assured version of Bishop Berkeley's idealistic skepticism, in which there was no benign deity to assure us that our readings of our own consciousness were right.

There was (as one might suspect after reading chapter 6) a political side to this, for most deconstructionists were highly suspicious of government. The power of the state expressed in its archives, or its armies, extended to the power to fabricate history. Derrida, for example, grew to manhood in Algeria during the Second World War, persecuted for being a Jew, and was educated in a France still reeling from the consequences of collaboration and occupation. In short, one might, with something less than charity, hint that the deconstructionist perception of the use and misuse of language was the result not of the inherent qualities of language but of the terrible experiences of war, occupation, and national dishonor. As David Roberts has concluded about the deconstruction movement in its dying days, "Critics grew more aggressive, portraying deconstruction as discredited, its earlier vogue as an embarrassment, to be explained in terms of the idiosyncrasies of French intellectual life and American literature departments."

Supplying this context for the "willful extravagance" of the deconstructionists' ideas does not rob the critique of its power. But deconstruction of a historical past may open the door to entirely partisan (and not coincidentally, self-serving) claims about the past. If, as John Tosh warns, "the aspiration to recreate the past [in scholarly accounts] is an illusion," then who is to say that any particular narrative or assessment is any worse, or better, than its rivals? "Wuz you dere, Charlie?" is the battle cry of both skeptics and true believers. The skeptic dismisses all history as "bunk," while the true believer knows what really happened despite all scholarship to the contrary.

Category Mistakes and False Concreteness

Can our philosophy of history save itself from such a fundamental challenge to all historical knowing? Enter Gilbert Ryle, a noted Oxford philosopher, and the author in 1949 of a remarkable book entitled *The Concept of Mind*. In it he introduced what he called the **category mistake** with a story. He showed a visitor Oxford, pointing out the students, the colleges, the library, and all other things real. The visitor then asked him, in genuine bewilderment, where the "university" was. Ryle explained that this was a category mistake, an assumption that the university had to be something other than the sum of its constituent parts.

It was the same mistake we make when we say that the "mind" is different from the all the conscious functions of the brain. We have put a "ghost" into the machine. Take, for example, one of the lodestars of Western historians, the idea of progress. If progress was a steady (or even an unsteady) rise in the standard of living, the material and technological mastery of nature, and creature comforts, then it could be weighed against the spread of horrific warfare and its modern weapons. The historian could compile evidence for either side. If progress was a concept, however, a ghost in the machine, in which unseen history marched toward better days, then no evidence would suffice to prove or deny it. Progress in the mind of the historian would be meaningless.

This category mistake might apply to much of what historians have written about great movements in the past. For example, to call the growing industrial infrastructure of nineteenth-century England an "industrial revolution" may be adding one word too many to what we can enumerate. We can show our reader the factories, the workers, and the capital investment, and we can even point to the changing mentality of all concerned, but where was the revolution? Change in technology can be demonstrated, but at what point does the change become so profound that it amounts to a revolution? We get away with such general terms because we all use them and accord one another the professional courtesy of these coinages. I fear that if we performed strict tests of the category mistake on our synthetic works of history we would find many ghosts in our machinery.

A second challenge to casual historical categorization is the **fallacy of false concreteness**. It antedated Ryle's. The English mathematician Alfred North Whitehead named it at the beginning of the twentieth century. Simply put, saying something exists so does not make it so. This should be a troubling insight for historians, for much of the time we have no surviving proof of motive, causation, and other vital parts of our accounts. Naming does not create episodes, events, or shared consciousness. By calling the 1880s the Gilded Age or the 1980s the "me-first generation" we show our own views, we judge, but we cannot create a thing by naming it. Mark Twain was perhaps justly infuriated by the gaudy display of the new rich, surrounded by abject poverty, in the cities of the 1880s. The critics of the yuppies may have found in their coinage a similar moral comfort. But the words are not things.

For the historian, false concreteness is a minefield we navigate every day. Long ago, marvels that we scoff at today were taken not only as real but as direct revelations of the purpose of a higher power. The medieval historian wrote of angels and miracles and the divine power behind them. Medieval scholars authored tracts to explain why the marvelous had to be real. While the secularism of the vast majority of modern scholars is a kind of armor against these very old examples of wonder, we have replaced them with our own. We mistake the political entity of the state for a cultural wonder we call the nation. We mistake the working government for a concrete polity. We write of the history of freedom, the history of private property, the history of rights as though these were things in themselves, when in fact they are our mental constructs.

A more sophisticated attack on category mistakes and false concreteness belongs a group of European philosophers called the **logical positivists**.

These men were concerned with what science could verify in our language. If something could not be verified, then naming it was just making a noise. In this class they put everything in metaphysics and religion that could not be tested in the real world. Did history belong there too?

In his classic work *Language, Truth, and Logic* (1946), English philosopher Alfred Jules Ayer explained what the logical positivists required. A rational belief was defined "as one which is arrived at by the methods which are now considered reliable." There was no absolute standard for rationality or reliability, but "we trust the methods of science because they have been successful in practice." Reliability then became the "degree of confidence" one might have in any proposition about the real world, and this confidence derived from "observation." But how could this be applied to historical events, which could not be directly observed?

Ayer had a ready answer: "Propositions referring to the past have the same hypothetical character as those which refer to the present." To be precise, "our knowledge of the past" had the same "hypothetical character" as our knowledge of the present, to be gained "pragmatically." Just as every proposition about the present was a hypothesis that might be disproved, so there was no past "objectively there." History was nothing more or less than a set of propositions subject to proof by means similar to scientific proof.

But how could one prove by a **verification test** what one could not subject to any verification tests? If every statement about the past was a proposition, and the confidence one had in any proposition was dependent upon success in practice, and success in practice was measured by observation, historical statements could not be verified at all. Ayer had left historical knowledge in a perfect circle, a train on tracks going around and around, never stopping at a station of fact or truth. Only his reference to **pragmatism** hinted at a way to get off this train to nowhere.

A Pragmatic History

The beginning of an answer to these challenges to historians' words came from an unexpected quarter. Although America is not known for its academic philosophers, in a development parallel to that of European positivism, indeed anticipating it somewhat, late nineteenth-century American philosopher Charles Sanders Peirce took a hard look at our own "truths." His philosophy he called "pragmatism," and it is especially suspicious of the loose use of empty words.

In a 1905 essay entitled "What Pragmatism Is," Peirce offered readers his valedictory version of the pragmatic way of knowing: "The theory that a conception, that is, the rational purport of a word or other expression, lies exclusively in its conceivable bearing upon the conduct of life. . . . If one can define accurately all the conceivable experimental phenomena which the affirmation or denial of a concept could imply, one will have therein a complete definition of the concept, and there is absolutely nothing more in it."

That definition, so succinct and final in itself, poses a twofold problem for the historian. If, as Peirce's friend and fellow pragmatist William James told an audience at Boston's Lowell Institution, in 1907, reality is not a given but "is still in the making, and awaits part of its complexion from the future," how is history possible? The past is changing even as the historian attempts to penetrate its secrets. The historian cannot define experimental conditions for testing any particular account of that past, for not only are its fullness and original context largely lost, but what does remain is constantly changing. All we have are irreproducible fragments constantly in flux.

Worse, the historical student of three-dimensional people and things is largely dependent on two-dimensional documents. On these one finds, not people and things, but words that are, well, just words. The American historian's dilemma is even more excruciating, for our most treasured words, like *democracy, equality,* and *rights,* seem to have no concrete reality at all. While the emanations of these words do have real-world impact, the concepts themselves cannot be subject to pragmatic experiments. They cannot be verified. Should they be thrown out with the bathwater of mysticism and the occult?

One of the foremost of the later pragmatists, Columbia University philosopher John Dewey, tackled this dilemma. He believed deeply in democracy and equality—but how could these foundational values be defended by a pragmatist? The answer for him lay in the way that these values should be taught. In 1916, Dewey's *Democracy and Education* proposed that

> a society which not only changes but which has the ideal of such change as will improve it, will have different standards and methods of education from one which aims simply at the perpetuation of its own customs. To make the general ideas set forth applicable to our own educational practice, it is, therefore, necessary to come to closer quarters with the nature

of present social life. . . . We cannot set up, out of our heads, something we regard as an ideal society. We must base our conception upon societies which actually exist, in order to have any assurance that our ideal is a practicable one. But, as we have just seen, the ideal cannot simply repeat the traits which are actually found. The problem is to extract the desirable traits of forms of community life which actually exist, and employ them to criticize undesirable features and suggest improvement.

In short, the answer was an inquiry of an entirely different kind, into the values themselves.

What did this mean for the possibility of historical certainty? Dewey wrote that "all history is necessarily written from the standpoint of the present." It is not hard to see the basis for that generalization—any historian writing about the past is at the time of his or her writing in the present. For Dewey, that meant that the present was always (forgive the pun) present in our histories. "Present-mindedness," writing about the past with the problems and values of the present in our heads, is one of the fallacies that David Hackett Fischer condemns. To answer that we do not live in the past, that the evidence we use exists in the present and that our actions (remember that pragmatism assigned meaning to verifiable things) are in the present, does not convince critics of presentism. We can, of course, simply abjure presentism, banish it loudly to the last circle of scholarly hell, but that does not mean it goes where we send it. For if Dewey is right, no amount of denial by the historian of present-mindedness suffices. We are stuck. Our selection of material, our emphases, our use of words, our point of view, all of these arise out of our present state of mind.

How does such a presentism enable a philosophy of history for our time? At stake in such an inquiry is much that we value in our history and our laws. There might be no philosophical proof that "all men are created equal, and endowed by their creator with certain inalienable rights." Moreover, our history reveals the contradictions and uncertainties in such pronouncements. The man who wrote those ringing opening words of the Declaration of Independence owned slaves and did not free the vast majority of them. By contrast, groups of slaves in New England took those words and repeated them in petitions for freedom, and against their own economic interest New England slaveowners agreed that slavery could not be sustained in a revolutionary republic.

American pragmatism fits a philosophy of history for our time not because we can follow Peirce's rules, or because we buy into all of Dewey's presentism, but because pragmatism allows us to explore how our founding ideals work in practice. Thus, for historical pragmatism, equality is not some distant goal but a verifiable fact. When groups are denied equal status in the law, in the public arena, even in radio and television access, remedies in the real world, through the courts and the legislatures, provide it. Freedom is visible every day, or if not, we demand to know why. Our laws permit us not only to speak out but to be (relatively) safe from government oppression. When overzealous political agencies step over that line, a step toward tyranny, we have the means to protest. Liberty, the pursuit of individual goals of happiness and economic opportunity, can also be pragmatically measured and tested in the real world. If those goals are not always attainable, at least they are visible. With some exceptions, our system of rule, our freedoms, and our rights do not exhibit false concreteness and category mistakes.

All of this should reassure historians looking for a working philosophy of history today. We need to be confident that we are not playing a shell game with words, thinking words instead of things. Pragmatism reminds us that our terms must be grounded in real experience, must correspond to a world we all share. History that is so in love with its own jargon, so bent upon being abstruse, that ordinary readers cannot follow it is a structure of category mistakes and false concreteness. Academic history too often falls into this error, with professors writing for a handful of other professors. Our philosophy of history demands transparency, a respect for the educated lay reader. And when we achieve this literary clarity, we also take one more step away from impossibility and one step closer to that other side—the past. For a history that speaks to the millions is a history of those millions. Such historians can cross the bridge into this past far more comfortably than historians wedded to arcane theories and obscure terminology.

But what if chaos rules on the far shore?

Proving Uncertainty

Imagine a great archeologist whose legendary exploits took him all over the world in search of storied treasures. On one of these expeditions he sought a box that had in it the secret of all knowledge. He found the box and opened it. Inside was a single piece of yellowed papyrus with the words: "The box is empty." Slamming down his fedora, the adventurous scientist looked all around to see if someone had beaten him to the box's contents. No one was there. The paper was the secret itself. If it was true, and the box was empty, then there was no paper. He had spent too many years in the field and was imagining the end of his quest. But there it was. If it was false, and there was something in the box, then it was the paper, and it said that the box was empty. Our frustrated hero sold the box at the local native market and set off in search of a rumored wooden ark of mysterious power.

Let's add a layer of complexity to the mysterious box's contents. It is called the "Greek paradox" because the ancient Greeks sneered that their Cretan commercial rivals were "always liars," the source for which information was a certain Cretan! The piece of paper inside the box says, "This statement is false." Now the writing is referring not to the box but to itself. If what it tells us is true, then the statement is false. If it the statement is false, then the opposite must be so—the statement is true. According to Aristotle the statement cannot be both false and true, so which is it? The answer is that you cannot decide from the statement itself whether it is true or false.

For logicians this puzzle opened the way to explore the limits of deduction. Think of the statement on the paper as a mathematical system (that is, a type of mathematics like geometry, algebra, calculus, or the like) filled with smaller statements. We'd like to know whether those statements can be proved true or false simply by referring them to one another—in other words, by staying within the system itself. That is the nature of proof by deduction, and it is the question that the Viennese mathematician Kurt Gödel attacked in the 1920s.

Gödel was something of a puzzle himself, plagued by mysterious nervous breakdowns and given to oracular pronouncements that even his equals could not fully comprehend. He was born and educated in early twentieth-century Vienna. A math prodigy, he became a professor shortly after earning the equivalent of his doctorate, in 1933. He proved that in all really big mathematical systems based on **axioms** some propositions cannot be proved or disproved within the axioms of the system. (Geometry and calculus were not big enough to be affected—their internal logic is airtight.) This conclusion, called **Gödel's paradox**, knocked over hundreds of years of attempts to prove that there were ways of putting all of mathematics into perfect logical systems. He had proved, with unassailable logic, that the logic of mathematics was incomplete.

The proof made Gödel famous but not happy. His unsettled state of mind was not relieved when the Nazis arrived in Austria. They kept mistaking him for a Jew (he wasn't) and harassing him, so he came to the United States and found a home at the Institute for Advanced Study in Princeton, New Jersey. There, according to Rebecca Goldstein's *Incompleteness: The Proof and Paradox of Kurt Gödel*, he baffled just about everyone who had the temerity to ask him about his work, an effect that, naturally, added to his aura. The fact that no one understood his answers gave them a kind of authority beyond their own incompleteness. Despite more breakdowns, he continued to produce superb mathematics until his death in 1971. Long after his death people who had met him were still telling anecdotes about him. His work still stands, his "incompleteness" proof a model of the power of reason in a twentieth-century world of war and persecution that had, by just about every other standard, gone mad.

If the most elegant of our intellectual achievements—mathematics— was incomplete and indeterminate, what could we say about the messy real world we inhabit? Return for a moment to the Greek paradox, the piece of paper with the statement that it was false, and apply it to law and politics. How often do we hear a media pundit tell us that the media cannot be trusted to tell the truth? In a more serious vein: We live in a tolerant society, but one that has boundaries. Can we tolerate those who deny the very fundamentals of our tolerance? When neo-Nazis demanded the right to hold a rally in the largely Jewish Chicago suburb of Skokie, the American Civil Liberties Union defended that right and the courts upheld it, even though, had Nazis come to power, they surely would have denied to their opponents the rights of free speech and assembly, starting with the lawyers of the ACLU. During the McCarthy era, many liberal intellectuals were faced with a similar dilemma. The Stalinist Soviet Union punished dissenters with internal exile, jail, and death. Should advocates of Soviet life be permitted to teach in the United States?

The dilemma reappears in the indeterminacy of the very idea of free speech. Could a society committed to free speech allow speech that might, if unchecked, lead to the downfall of that society? Conservative pundit and author David Horowitz does not see any puzzle here and advertises his attack on opponents of the Iraq War, *Unholy Alliance,* by inverting the paradox: "Not all dissent is equal, and Americans whose actions are calculated to give aid and comfort to the butchers who murdered 3,000 innocent people on September 11, 2001 are not patriotic at all. . . . They are, in fact, quite the opposite"—an example of all-or-nothing fallacious thinking and guilt by association, but surely a paradox that cannot be ignored.

Chaos

What Gödel's paradox was for mathematics, the second law of thermodynamics, better known as **entropy,** and **chaos theory,** are to natural phenomena. Entropy is a theory, not a fact, but a well-established theory from its first exploration in the nineteenth century. According to the man who introduced the idea, German physicist Rudolf Clausius, entropy is energy not available for use. Although complex in its mathematical formulation, entropy can be compared to our common experience that there is never enough time in the day to do all the things we had planned. Hard as we try to get everything done, efficient as we try to be, a certain portion of our efforts is always wasted.

Such energy loss, according to some scientists, is a proof of the disorderliness of the universe. Hence a logically determined law proves that logical laws are ephemera. As energy is dissipated, more and more variations on every structure and form appear. For example, heat ice and it changes to water. By heating the solid you are expending energy. The molecules in water are the same as those in ice, but in liquids molecules can be arrayed in many more ways than in a solid like ice. The heat energy is spent creating disorder. This disorder increases over time. The universe has been around for quite a while, and thus entropy has been at work all that time, making a hash of atomic and subatomic arrays and causing us to lose one of every pair of socks we own. Some physicists have predicted that the end of time will come when entropy has finished its labors and there is no more energy left, or when we finally give up looking for our lost haberdashery.

Geneticist Richard Dawkins poses the same proof of a disorderly universe at a lower level of generality. "In a universe of electrons and selfish genes, blind physical forces and genetic replication, some people are going to get hurt, other people are going to get lucky, and you won't find any rhyme or reason in it, nor any justice. The universe that we observe has precisely the properties we should expect if there is, at bottom, no design, no purpose, no evil, no good, nothing but pitiless indifference."

Chaos theory suggests the indeterminacy of even simply plotted actual events like the weather. In fact, chaos theory began with the age-old problem of how to predict the weather. It turned out that if very small variations occurred in the initial conditions in any developing weather system, the outcome could vary tremendously. This was an "intuitive" result: in other words, pretty much common sense if you paid any attention to weather predictions on the television or radio. The prediction or forecast was right some of the time, but the longer the span of time between the prediction and the event, the greater the likelihood of a mistake. The theory was popularized as the "butterfly effect": the wind created by the flapping of a butterfly's wings in Brazil might, through a complex series of events, end up causing a tornado in Texas. The movie *The Butterfly Effect* dramatized this phenomenon—you simply could not predict how events developed when the smallest alteration at the start of the sequence had such impact on the end result.

A mathematician named Benoit Mandelbrot pushed the theory a little further. He was interested in fluctuations in commodities' prices, and he argued that no matter how closely the data were studied, little variations in it were always missed. The same was true for any attempt to plot the exact shape of a coastline. No matter how precise the plotting, small variations in the actual coastline were missed. An infinite series of closer and closer plots got closer and closer to the reality, but the infinite series of adjustments (being infinite) had no end. Absolute precision escaped us in the real world, just as absolute completeness could not be had in the largest closed systems of mathematics. Logic did not lead to a confirmation of rationality but proved irrationality.

The story of chaos theory had one more unexpected plot twist. The indeterminacy the theory proposed was itself rule bound: that is, there were rules for indeterminacy. Although this seems self-contradictory, it is not. Instead, it is a characteristic of all of the great logical puzzles. They may not seem to have satisfactory answers at first, but tackling them forces us to engage in deep reasoning.

Chaos theory bred **fractal theory** or "self-similarity." These forbidding names describe something quite simple. Big things are composed of smaller versions of themselves. Look at the branches of a tree. Then look at the veins of a leaf from the tree. They are similar. Examine the bronchial tubes in our lungs. Then use a microscope to look at the blood vessels that supply the bronchial tubes. They reproduce the form of the bronchial tubes. Even more startling, the ratio of the little versions to the larger objects in some cases is exactly 4 2/3 to 1. Every time you look at a smaller part of the whole, the ratio reappears. This is not true for all objects, but it is true enough to give a name to those that exhibit this remarkable quality—Mandelbrot sets.

Fractal theory itself is quite precise, even modest in its claims, but one can go a little beyond it to suggest powerful connections between miniature worlds and galaxies. For example, in the nineteenth century some scientists believed that "ontogeny," the development of the embryo in the womb, recapitulated "phylogeny," the evolution of adult ancestral forms. In other words, each individual goes through the same developmental stages as the human race itself. We know more about embryos now and no longer regard the ontogeny/phylogeny comparison as biologically sound, but as a metaphor it still tells us that each infant carries within itself the evolutionary achievement of the entire species.

History's Uncertainties

At the turn of the twentieth century American philosopher Georges Santayana opened his five-volume work *The Life of Reason* (1906) with "In which of its adventures would the human race, reviewing its whole experience, acknowledge a progress and a gain? To answer these questions, as they may be answered speculatively and provisionally by an individual, is the purpose of the following work." For him, human reason was both a process of individual thought and a reflection of the progress of the Western mind. Tutored by Gilbert Ryle and Alfred North Whitehead, we might be suspicious of such general terms as *reason* and *mind,* but no one can deny the attractiveness of Santayana's analogy between each individual's quest for meaning and the larger history of Western philosophy. As Santayana himself said, "A philosopher could hardly have a higher ambition than to make himself a mouth-piece for the memory and judgment of his race."

Fractals, embryonic development, and even Gödel's proof all supply a pattern or design. That is exactly what the historian does—supply a pattern or design. The contents are not entirely fixed, for within the design the precise elements may not be easily identified. The pattern, the design, originates not in nature itself but in the interaction of the real world and the historian's mind. Thinking it so does not make it so, but thinking about patterns and designs allows a kind of order within uncertainty. Perhaps our desire to predict weather, fluctuations in key market indicators, and other natural phenomena does not prove that there are immutable natural laws governing such events, any more than medieval philosophers' search for God proved that God existed, but as Gödel himself wrote, near the end of his life, "Reason itself does not err." The error for a philosophy of history for our times would be to doubt that historians can bring a kind of order to the past world.

So our philosophy of history must content itself with a measure of uncertainty. Patterns are acceptable but not completeness, or any philosophy that insists on every event and movement fitting neatly into a predesigned niche. Confident that our words do reflect a reality and re-assured that we can find patterns in the past, we are almost done with our bridge-building effort.

9

Historians Confront
the Problem of Evil

Our moral . . . opinions . . . [arc] inconsistent with a serious and
disciplined empirical inquiry into what actually happened. [They]
would make it into a handmaid of moral philosophy.
                                        —David Hackett Fischer (1970)

Historians know all about evil. Our subject is a primer of it.
The evil that individuals, groups, and nations do to one another, and to
themselves, the casual evil of neglect, the fierce evil of discrimination, the
almost incomprehensible evil of genocide are the stuff of history. Fischer
warned that writing our moral views into our history impermissibly confused present with past. But for many historians evil events demand moral
judgment. Such events pose a variant of the old **problem of evil**. If all
causes are God's will, if his providence directs the course of events, then
how could a good God who is all-powerful let evil happen to innocents?

Setting aside for a moment the arguments for and against providential
history, immoral evil choices are the historical acts of real people in real
time. Whatever the historian's own religious beliefs, evil is not just a problem for the religiously observant historian. It must be addressed in any
modern philosophy of history, for too much is at stake today in the way
history is used to make and defend far-reaching policies for any of us to
ignore the problem of evil.

See No Evil?

We often choose sides when we write history, looking for our friends in
the past. We cast our narrative in lights and shadows, revealing our moral

sensibility as we denounce evil. History becomes our podium to praise the worthy and consign the unworthy to their place in the circles of hell. To George Fisher, president of the AHA in 1898, it hardly needed repeating that "it is one office of the historian to weigh in the scales of justice the merits of historic persons. It belongs to him to gauge the qualities of the men and women who act their parts on the public stage." John Emrich Lord Acton, Regius Professor of Modern History at Cambridge, in 1895 exhorted his students "never to debase the moral currency or lower the standard of rectitude, but to try others by the final maxim that governs your own lives, and to suffer no man and no cause to escape the undying penalty which history has the power to inflict on wrong." In short, the historian was to be the judge of past morality. Neither Fisher nor Acton believed that moral principles varied with time and place. Instead, the highest good was the protection of human life and the promotion of human happiness, a value system (they believed) that transcended historical particulars.

Fisher's and Acton's views are alive and well. In the wake of the Vietnam War, historians returned to the theme of moral judgment in history. Gordon Wright's 1975 AHA presidential address was frank about the issue. "The idea of consciously reintroducing the moral dimension into history runs counter to the basic training of most historians, and probably to their professional instinct as well. Each of us has some strong views on the general subject of morality; each of us knows the dangers involved in making moral judgments in our work, or even suggesting a need for them." But the times were wrong for such timidity. "Neither our audience nor the condition of the world in which we live any longer allows us the luxury of escape into a Proustian cork-lined ivory tower free of dust, microbes, and values. . . . No doubt those of us who profess contemporary history have found the dilemma sharpest; whoever must deal with the more brutal aspects of the Hitler or Stalin era, or with the devastating mass impact of mechanized total war, finds it hard to restrain some expression of that righteous indignation."

One cannot predict where this historical indignation will go, however, or who will feel it. As Wright conceded, his liberality might make moral judgments harder to pronounce, but "Our conservative colleagues—at least those who are self-consciously conservative—have had it easier; a good many of them have always been quite openly committed to a system of absolute values, religiously or ethically based, by which the events of the past can be confidently judged without the least embarrassment." In a June 1, 2002, commencement address at West Point, President George W. Bush returned to historical examples to explain how moral judgment belonged in any recounting of the past:

> Some worry that it is somehow undiplomatic or impolite to speak the language of right and wrong. I disagree. Different circumstances require different methods, but not different moralities. Moral truth is the same in every culture, in every time, and in every place. . . . There can be no neutrality between justice and cruelty, between the innocent and the guilty. We are in a conflict between good and evil, and America will call evil by its name. By confronting evil and lawless regimes, we do not create a problem, we reveal a problem. And we will lead the world in opposing it.

One might object that the story of historical writing reveals a movement away from such moralistic thinking into the realm of the dispassionate and scientific study of the past. Marc Bloch, who knew Acton's work, objected: "Now for a long time, the historian has passed for a sort of judge in Hades, charged with meting our praise or blame to dead heroes." While such an Olympian pose must satisfy "a deep rooted instinct . . . such labels become an embarrassment. Are we so sure of ourselves and of our age as to divide the company of our forefathers into the just and the damned? How absurd it is . . . elevating the entirely relative criteria of one individual, one party, or one generation to the absolute." But times and events change men's minds, and Bloch wrote on July 8, 1940, to his co-worker and fellow patriot Lucien Febvre, "It is useless to comment on the events. They surpass in horror and in humiliation all we could dream in our worst nightmares."

There are, to be sure, historians determined to see no evil, or at least, no evil that we see. As Bloch reflected, what may appear evil to us did not necessarily appear evil to our predecessors. In 1839, as European Americans swept west, Democratic Party spokesman John O'Sullivan assayed the doctrine of "Manifest Destiny." Manifest Destiny explained and defended the dispossession of the natives without mentioning them. The lesson was a moral one, and history was the primer:

> What friend of human liberty, civilization, and refinement, can cast his view over the past history of the monarchies and aristocracies of antiquity, and not deplore that they ever existed? . . . America is destined for better deeds. It is our unparalleled glory that we have no reminiscences

of battle fields, but in defense of humanity, of the oppressed of all nations, of the rights of conscience, the rights of personal enfranchisement. . . . We have had patriots to defend our homes, our liberties, but no aspirants to crowns or thrones; nor have the American people ever suffered themselves to be led on by wicked ambition to depopulate the land, to spread desolation far and wide, that a human being might be placed on a seat of supremacy.

O'Sullivan's history lesson tutored Americans in their future endeavors. "Yes, we are the nation of progress, of individual freedom, of universal enfranchisement. . . . We must onward to the fulfilment of our mission— to the entire development of the principle of our organization—freedom of conscience, freedom of person, freedom of trade and business pursuits, universality of freedom and equality." The policy that O'Sullivan and the Democratic Party espoused in particular was the annexation of the newly independent republic of Texas. Its former rulers, the Republic of Mexico, and its current occupants, the Native Americans, simply stood in the way of that mission and thus had no place in O'Sullivan's history lesson, much less was their dispossession an evil.

In the 1880s, with the replacement of the Indians by European farmers, ranchers, and miners all but complete, a young Theodore Roosevelt wrote in his *Winning of the West* that the "spread of the English-speaking peoples over the world's waste spaces [that is, the places where Indians, Asians, and Africans lived were wasted] had been not only the most striking feature in the world's history, but also the event of all others most far reaching in it effects and its importance. . . . Much yet remained to be done before the West would reach its natural limits and would fill from frontier to frontier with populous commonwealths of its own citizens." Indians could not be citizens, nor could they be part of commonwealths. It was inevitable, indeed good that the ruling race of northern Europeans would bring democracy, Protestantism, and free enterprise to the West. Hence there was no evil in the displacement of the primitives.

U. B. Phillips was in the early years of the twentieth century a leading historical authority on slavery. Though born and reared in Georgia, Phillips earned his Ph.D. at Columbia University in New York City and taught from 1902 to 1908 at the University of Wisconsin and then at Tulane University. His *American Negro Slavery* (1918) was widely respected by other historians when it appeared. In his pages, slaves constituted "a lowly caste" whose "natural amenability" had led to their enslavement.

The moderation and general fairness of their masters were requited by the slaves' loyalty and even affection for their owners. There were exceptions—revolts and crimes—but few of these resulted "directly from the pressure of slave circumstance." In general, slaves were happy darkies, well kept, safer in slavery in the southern states than in their native Africa—on "the master's premises, where the back yard with its crooning women and multi-colored children" displayed a delightful domestic scene, and the master himself was "paternalistically inclined" (how else could there have been so many "multi-colored children"?). Phillips's sources were those of the master class, criminal courts records, plantation diaries, and newspapers, but he was confident that slaves would have agreed that slavery represented a minor evil, if an evil at all.

While most historians of any quality will not dispute the horror of the "final solution" imposed on the Jews of Europe by Hitler and his subordinates, a hot debate rages over responsibility for this holocaust. Was Hitler simply a mad genius who imposed his malign will on a mesmerized German people (recall President Reagan's speech at Bitburg), or were the vast majority of them knowingly and willingly complicit? Anti-Semitism was certainly a prominent theme in German culture before Hitler's rise to power and contributed to his success. But did racialist views lead Germans to genocidal acts? Can an entire nation be condemned for the actions of individuals in it?

Certainly for those who supported the Nazi "purification" of Europe in the years before World War II, including a number of racial historians, the annihilation of the Jews was not only a good but part of the greater plan of European history. For example, Adolf Bartels, a literary historian and professor of history, argued that the Jewish influence in literature and art debased the pure Aryan and must be eradicated. For him, there was no evil like the Jewish presence in the midst of the ruling race.

Such relativism on the problem of evil can induce a form of historical amnesia, or worse, delusion. Holocaust deniers like Britain's David Irving, a historian, removed the evil of the Holocaust from the world's history with a few strokes of the pen, or tried to, and when historians like Emory University's Deborah Lipstadt challenged him in her *Denying the Holocaust: The Growing Assault on Truth and Memory* (1994), he sued for defamation in England. Irving had written, according to Lipstadt, that "'Jews are not victims but victimizers' and that 'they 'stole' billions in reparations, destroyed Germany's good name by spreading the 'myth' of the Holocaust, and won international sympathy because of what they claimed had been done to them." This was standard fare for the troop of Holocaust deniers. Lipstadt regarded Irving and his many books as dangerous, for he seemed, at least to some of his readers, to be a legitimate historian. He certainly offered documentary materials and primary sources to back up his claims. When closely examined, however, they turned out to be bogus.

Irving's suit against Lipstadt, whose book was published in England by Penguin (giving English courts jurisdiction) came to trial in January 2000. After over a year of preparation and trial, Lipstadt, almost bankrupted by the trial and emotionally exhausted, won a great victory. A parade of leading twentieth-century European historians demolished Irving's use of evidence, establishing that what he wrote was not history and hence that Lipstadt was not libeling him by calling him an apologist for Hitler. Justice Charles Gray issued a strongly worded decision. Irving was and had been for thirty years "an active Holocaust denier, anti-Semitic, and racist, and associated with right-wing extremists who promoted neo Nazism." Irving had "persistently and deliberately manipulated historical evidence" to portray Hitler and his movement in a favorable light and to deny the horrors of the concentration camps.

What Lipstadt had said of Irving was true, a defense to Irving's suit for libel. In Britain, the burden of proving the truth of a publication falls on the author. There is no requirement of reckless indifference to the truth and no exception for public figures, as there is in the United States. But in Britain, again unlike the United States, the loser, in this case Irving, must pay the legal fees of the winner. Irving appealed, unsuccessfully, and faced over 1.5 million pounds in legal fees.

Lipstadt herself was elated, exhausted, and vindicated, but her victory was more than hers. Irving started it—bringing a suit that denied both the immorality of history and the amorality of some historians. Why he lied about the Holocaust, and why he brought the suit, are stuff for psychohistorians. Lipstadt's motivation also lay beyond mere defense of her writing. It lay in the defense of the moral power of history. As she wrote about the aftermath of the trial, "For a long time after the court battle was over, I felt pain when I thought of the many people who had watched Irving ravage their memories. . . . I felt not just pain, but also a certain sense of privilege. I was reminded of the fact that Jewish tradition highly values acts of loving-kindness. . . . Taking care of the dead is called *hesed shel emet* [mercy and truth], the most genuine act of loving-kindness." It is an act that everyone performs when they remember parents, children, loved ones, teachers, and leaders' lives. Lipstadt had performed that *mitzvah* (blessing) for the victims and the survivors of the Holocaust.

But no courtroom victory in a single case can change the perceived benefits to some of seeing no evil. Recent Japanese history textbooks have all but erased mention of Japanese mistreatment of prisoners of war, the use of local women in occupied countries as prostitutes for Japanese troops, and the pillage of civilian centers like Nanjing. The Japanese experimentation with germ and chemical warfare during the war has likewise vanished from the Society for History Textbook Reform's model edition. One of the major themes of the new Japanese history is to blame the Chinese for the Japanese invasion of China. No apology is necessary for those against whom no evil was committed. Proving that turnabout is neither fair play nor good history, new Chinese history textbooks have erased the horrors of the Cultural Revolution, along with all but one brief mention of Mao Zedong's name, in the effort to polish Communist China's international reputation. His name, along with the Communist Revolution, the wars of imperial conquest, and other jarring events before 1979, has been banished, replaced with glowing tributes to globalism and international trade.

Another dodgy version of seeing no evil is finding silver linings. The carnage of the Crusades opened up trade in the Mediterranean, bringing on a rise of standards of living, the introduction of modern ideas of commerce, and the sharing of scientific and mathematical knowledge among Christians and Muslims. The horrors of the plague were followed by a period of growth and relative prosperity. The decimation of Native American peoples by Europeans (and European pathogens) enabled Western civilization to blossom in the New World. Recasting events in this way, jiggling time frames, ignoring immediate human costs, and evading "what might have been" make it easier to swallow the bitter pill of our inhumanity to one another.

Tackling Evil

The historical thinker who professes a religious faith or believes in some form of divine spark in our species finds the problem of evil particularly vexing. Throughout history religious thinkers have combined history and theology to wrestle with the problem. The Judeo-Christian tradition is a historical one as well as a theological one, in which a linear history runs from creation to a final judgment day. Within this historical account Jews and Christians, among others, do not believe that evil is natural and un-avoidable because the gods or natural powers are morally neutral. Jews and Christians believe that God is the source of all moral law, God is om-nipotent (all powerful), God loves us and created us in his image, and thus God must have simultaneously forbidden the doing of evil and had the power to banish all evil. That is the logical contradiction that makes the problem of evil a prime subject for Western religious history.

A dwindling number of genuinely devout historians have to wrestle with the traditional formulation of the problem: If God created the world, he must have created evil. If he was and is omniscient (all-knowing), he must have known that evil things would happen, that we would do evil to one another, and even that the problem of evil would puzzle us. But if he loves us, and wants us to do good, why then is there so much evil in the world?

Theologians have used history to address this historical dilemma, and because theologians are real people, acting and thinking in historical time, their answers become part of the history of religion. In this sense, the problem of evil leaves historians in search of a philosophy of history chas-ing our own tails. For the intellectual history of devout attempts to answer the problem leads to faith in God's will, or providence, not to a resolu-tion in human terms: in short, a complete rejection of the logical puzzle and a reassertion of faith. God is all-powerful, all-knowing, and good. He knows what is going on, and one must trust in him. What appears to be evil may not be evil at all but in any case is all part of his plan. Evil may serve his purposes. If we choose evil we are violating God's desire, but he left us free to do so.

This argument especially appealed to St. Augustine, bishop of Hippo in the fifth century CE. Before his conversion to Christianity, he had dallied with many religious and philosophical systems, always looking for the so-lution to the problem of evil. An avid reader, he studied history for clues. His *City of God* (410) was as much about Rome as the heavenly city. "But the earthly city, which shall not be everlasting . . . has its good in this world, and rejoices in it with such joy as such things can afford. But as this is not a good which can discharge its devotees of all distresses, this city is often divided against itself by litigations, wars, quarrels, and such victories as are either life-destroying or short-lived." He found solace in Christianity in part because the combination of an all-powerful God and human free will made sense to him. Man is sinful, depraved, fallen be-cause of Adam's disobedience to God's instructions. Evidence from history proved that proposition. Goodness comes through God's love of his fallen children. Evil comes from men.

Augustine wrestled with the problem but did not pin it. Original sin provides no easy answer to the problem of evil. We may deserve anything and everything bad that happens to us. Still, if we are depraved at heart, saved from eternal damnation only by the grace of God and the intervention of Jesus, then there is something worth saving in us, and the problem of evil reappears. In any case, today, many liberal theologians and many religious groups have rejected the idea that we are inherently sinful.

In the Reformation, a historical episode that tried souls and bodies in the name of a true faith, Christians once again tackled the problem of evil. Calvinists, radical reformist Protestants who believed in predestination (the idea that God chose before the Creation who would be saved and who lost), found that the problem of evil was not a problem at all. Everything was God's will. The problem, however, then shifted from a soteriological one (am I saved?) to a psychological one—endless rounds of self-recrimination and uncertainty about whether this or that person was among the saved, what signs, what "assurance" one could trust, and when and how one could gain this seal of grace.

For example, when in the early 1630s a portion of the Boston congregation, led by its minister, John Cotton, and prominent members of the church like Massachusetts Bay governor Henry Vane and the Hutchinson family, rejected the idea that assurance could be safe without an experience of grace, they set the colony of Massachusetts Bay on fire. Other ministers insisted that preparation through study and action gave hints of God's will. The Boston "free grace" party replied that these lukewarm Christians might be living in a "covenant of works" too close to the Roman Catholic sacramental forms. A series of trials and expulsions ended with John Cotton pulling back from the extremity of his views, Vane returning to England, and the Hutchinsons heading for cooler climes.

The argument of predestination provides at least a partial answer to the puzzle of natural evils as well as moral ones—why the innocent child dies from a terrible disease and why thousands of good people may perish in an earthquake, flood, or volcanic eruption. According to the answer based on predestination, God has his reasons for allowing natural disasters. We simply cannot know his mind. Attempts to use Holy Scripture to speculate about this—for example, to show that this life is simply a preparation for the world to come (as in 2 Corinthians and Job)—may comfort the bereaved, but they do not resolve the problem.

But more and more religious history—the story of past generations' attempts to resolve the problem of evil—is written by scholars who are not especially religious. As Edward Whiting Fox in 1955 introduced E. Harris Harbison's essay on the Reformation for a new series on Western thought, "Harbison has at once described the crisis of faith and conscience which wracked western Europe at the beginning of our modern era and set it firmly in the context of the political and social struggle which constitutes the history of the sixteenth century . . . a test case of modern sociological history in its effort to demonstrate that ideals and guiding principles are not fully understandable apart from the men who held them nor the men wholly comprehensible as individuals divorced from the society in which they lived." Harbison himself gave a concrete example of this "modern sociological history" when he wrote, "One of the most difficult tasks of the historian is to discover how and why a complex set of ideas like those of Luther captures men's minds." Neither Fox nor Harbison considered—indeed, neither was particularly interested in—telling the Reformation story from the inside as either a victory of God's will or a defeat of revealed Christian truth. That would not have been historical scholarship.

Arnold Toynbee's magisterial *Study of History* offers some insight into the retreat of the historians from anything resembling a providential interpretation of evil. Speaking of intolerance and religious violence, he wrote: "This great blot upon our Western Civilization in the early modern age presents . . . an extraordinary contrast to the rapid yet sure-footed contemporary progress of the same society in other directions; and the fact that religious intolerance, in this time and place, was not merely an absolute evil in itself, but was also a glaring anachronism no doubt accounts in part for the unprecedented excesses to which it ran in the latest chapter of its history in the West." Toynbee had his own explanation for the problem of evil—organized religion itself was the source of moral evil. Gibbon had returned.

I teach the early history of English Puritanism and have some passing acquaintance with the literature in the field. I cannot think offhand of any of the fine volumes on Puritans in England or early America that adopts their own view of their mission. That mission was certainly historical; indeed, it defined Christian history. As Edward Johnson wrote in his contemporary *Wonder-Working Providence of Sions Saviour* (1654), "Christ Jesus intending to manifest his kingly office toward his churches more fully than ever yet the sons of men saw . . . begins with our English nation . . . and therefore in the year 1628 he stirs up his servants as the heralds of a king to make his proclamation for volunteers." The Puritan migration was a holy mission, commissioned by Jesus to save the faith. A half-century later, Cotton Mather introduced his *Magnalia Christi Americana, or, The Ecclesiastical History of New England* (1702): "I write of the wonders of the Christian religion, flying from the deprivations of Europe, to the American strand, and assisted by the Holy Author of that religion, I do, with all conscience of truth . . . report the wonderful displays of his infinite power, wisdom, goodness, and faithfulness, wherewith his divine providence hath irradiated an Indian wilderness."

Not one of the modern chroniclers of the remarkable Puritan religious experience, superb historians themselves, all deeply and sympathetically immersed in the Puritan literature, from Perry Miller in the first half of the twentieth century through Stephen Foster, David Hall, and Michael Winship at the end of the twentieth century and the beginning of the twenty-first, shared that millennial vision or that faith (and fear) in God's particular intention for the Puritans. Of all of these scholars, Winship takes the theological conversations of the Puritan ministers most seriously, indeed at their word, yet even (or especially) he has no truck with anything resembling a providential view of events or the problem of evil. Anne Hutchinson as much as accused her ministerial persecutors of being unregenerate men, and they in turn came to regard her as not only wrong in her theology but damned for her lies. Regarding this, Winship's conclusion floats above the invective, a distant perch not of angels on high but of a jury box of dispassionate, secular scholars: "[The controversy] was about interference with the revelation of greater depths to the Gospel and with a prophetess of God raised up for some great purpose, or it was about the harassment of brethren and sisters who were basically sound, if holding some absurd points. . . . It was about the need to oppose papist doctrine. . . . It was about ministers who kept Christians chained to the Law when they should have been experiencing Gospel liberty." Winship certainly does not share either side's view of the controversy or claim any insight of his own into God's purpose in visiting these trials on his Chosen People.

Even historians with deeply held religious convictions shy away from the providential view of historical evil. If they interlard their accounts with moral messages, these come from the mouths of their subjects, not from God. George Marsden, Pulitzer Prize–winning biographer of the great Puritan divine Jonathan Edwards, is far more sympathetic than Winship and most of the other students of Puritanism to the project of "Christian scholarship." As he has written in *The Outrageous Idea of Christian Scholarship* (1997):

> The heart of human sinfulness is in our achievements, in the illusion that we can be our own gods, a law unto ourselves, creating and controlling our own reality. Such perspectives ought to transform religiously-committed scholars into dissenters from many theories taken for granted in current academia; it should make them critical of viewpoints, especially strong in the arts and literature, that emphasize human freedom and creativity as the supreme values. Although of immense worth, these human gifts will reach their highest expressions when exercised within a sense of the limits of the individual in relationship to the community, the created order, and ultimately to God.

But when he came to sum his contribution to the vast literature on Edwards, Marsden conformed his words to the secular rather than the theological canon: "One of my hopes is that this book may help bridge the gap between the Edwards of the students of American culture and the Edwards of the theologians. . . . As a biographer attempting to understand Edwards first as an eighteenth-century figure, I have been working most directly as a cultural historian. Yet I have been doing this always with an eye on the theological question, taking his thought seriously as part of the larger Christian tradition." Yet this tradition of faith and obedience found itself only in the margins of his pages. "My belief is that one of the uses of being an historian, particularly if one is part of a community of faith, is to help persons of such communities better understand what they and their community might appropriate from the great mentors of the past. . . . Everything is, of course, time-bound." In short, pray as if everything depended on God; write history as if everything depended on human agency.

For Sydney Ahlstrom, the foremost historian of American religion in our time, hope was stronger than despair. Writing in the last days of America's wrenching entanglement in the Vietnam War, an era that caused many right-thinking people to question whether our history had gone wrong, Ahlstrom found in our religious history a sermon of hope. His final passages urged "the reader" adopt a "life style and moral stance" that recapitulated the best in the American religious tradition, for "the American people, in their moral and religious history, were drawing on the profounder elements of their traditions, finding new sources of strength and

confidence, and thus vindicating the idealism which has been so fundamental an element in the country's past." A study of the history of religion
was a good thing. It could elevate the spirit and tutor the moral sense.
But any legitimate history of American Christianity required "a constant
concern for men, movements, and ideas whose origins are very remote in
time and place." Even a religious history that praised faith had to be the
story of people and their ideas, not the story of God's providence.

Though they do not have available in their histories the theologians'
answer to the problem of evil, scholars like Marsden and Ahlstrom hint
that the study of history provides comfort. Historians face evil in its
plainest garb. But taking providence out of the story of our past reduces
evil to more recognizable dimensions. It is us. History, free of the brooding omnipresence of a superhuman evil, shows that evil is our own doing. History also demonstrates that we are capable of mastering our aggressive and hurtful urges. Standing naked like this, without the garments
of divine origin and the promise of heavenly afterlife, human history is
an even grander subject—and a more frightening one to many. A return
to the comfort of religion might reduce the shock of such realizations.
Some popular historians have assayed that course. They have found in the
founding fathers, in Lincoln and other national leaders, and in Civil War
and World War II soldiers a faith in a benevolent and caring God, which
then becomes proof that the problem of evil is only in our minds.

If providence can no longer be relied upon as the ultimate explanation of
evil, what takes its place? I propose that we accept with humble resigna-
tion the role that irony plays in history. In the penultimate scene of the
Monty Python movie *The Meaning of Life*, a dinner party is interrupted by
a surprise visitor, and an element of all our history becomes apparent.

> Grim Reaper: I am the Grim Reaper.
> Geoffrey: Who?
> Grim Reaper: The Grim Reaper.
> Geoffrey: Yes, I see.
> Grim Reaper: I am death . . .
> Angela: Who is it, darling?
> Geoffrey: It's a "Mr. Death" or something. He's come about the reaping? I
> don't think we need any at the moment.
> Angela: Hello. Well, don't leave him hanging around outside, darling. Ask
> him in . . .

Debbie: Well, isn't that extraordinary? We were just talking about death only
    five minutes ago . . .
Grim Reaper: Be quiet! . . . I have come for you.
Angela: You mean . . . to—
Grim Reaper: Take you away. That is my purpose. I am death.
Geoffrey: Well, that's cast rather a gloom over the evening, hasn't it?
. . . .
Geoffrey: Now, look here. You barge in here, quite uninvited, break glasses,
    and then announce, quite casually, that we're all dead. Well, I would re-
    mind you that you are a guest in this house, and—
Grim Reaper: Be quiet! . . .
Debbie: Can I ask you a question?
Grim Reaper: What?
Debbie: How can we all have died at the same time?
Grim Reaper: The salmon mousse.
Geoffrey: Darling, you didn't use canned salmon, did you?
Angela: I'm most dreadfully embarrassed.
Grim Reaper: Now the time has come. Follow. Follow me. . . .
Debbie: Hey, I didn't even eat the mousse.

As Debbie discovered, there is a chance element in all human events,
unpredictable, certainly amoral, which has nothing to do with the moral
merits or demerits of individuals or groups. She is in good company. Did
the Indians lose to the Europeans because the Europeans were God's chosen people and the Indians red devils? Hardly. The Indians lost because
the Europeans brought with them a dead man's chest full of pathogens—
measles, mumps, chicken pox, smallpox—to which the Indians had no
natural immunities. Europeans did—paid for by hundreds of generations
of living with and sleeping alongside the pigs, sheep, and other domesticated animals that sired these pathogens. Worse, when the Europeans arrived with their hogs, cattle, sheep, horses, rats, cockroaches, bacteria, and
viruses foreign to the New World, those species colonized the land faster
than the immigrants.

Did millions of Africans earn or merit the brutalities of chattel slavery in the Americas? Hardly. They were not particularly suited by nature
or nature's God to toil for others' gain. Instead, the lucrative Portuguese
and Spanish sugarcane plantations had an almost inexhaustible a need for
labor, and the existing African slave trade had the means to service that
need. No sugar, no African slaves in the New World. When historians

recognize that element of unpredictability, they are able to see how moral judgment becomes hindsight, and tragedy can lead to sermonizing.

The Grim Reaper takes them all, even Debbie, who did not eat the salmon mousse. The lesson is plain—not everything is going to be explained. It is in that gap between our partial knowledge, no matter how diligently we pursue our researches, and the vast detail of the historical past, the gap into which Debbie's death falls, that we find the problem of evil. If we knew more, perhaps we would understand why certain people and certain groups came to decide to do evil. Such knowledge would not cure the past harm and might not even palliate it, but it would explain. And that, for us, would be enough.

Such universal and detailed knowledge is beyond the historian's ken. It may be in God's mind, but it will never be in ours. We must content ourselves with the recognition that we have chosen a field of study that will sometimes make us almost unutterably sad and other times shaking with fury. The recognition of the irony of history will remind us of our own limitations and will make us humble. We will celebrate justice when we see it in our researches and welcome charitable acts when we can chronicle them.

Conclusion

A Bridge to the Past

The past is a foreign country . . . unvisitable and unconquerable. . . .
Historical experience is not the deluded and blithely arrogant
conviction that we have experienced the past as people in the past
experienced it. Rather, it is the experience of a rift, a break, between
what we are now and what others were then.

—Alan Megill (2007)

History is impossible. Nothing I have written or could write
will change that brute fact. We cannot go back in time. But doing history,
studying the past, is not impossible. If we complete the bridge from present to past, we must confront this final challenge that Megill poses. There
is a striking scene near the end of the movie *Indiana Jones and the Last
Crusade* in which Indiana Jones must cross a yawning chasm to reach
the cave that houses the Holy Grail. He must have faith in his quest, and
that faith requires he take a step into what appears to be empty space.
He does, and finds solid ground—a bridge to the other side. What we
need to complete our philosophy is a step of faith onto the bridge we have
constructed.

Where does such a faith arise? Surely after all we have said here, not in
the jargon of arcane academic methodologies. When Erasmus dedicated
his *In Praise of Folly* to his English host, Thomas More, both men knew
that the real purpose of the essay was to get its readers to think about the
folly that knowing philosophy or rhetoric could save a man when faith
could not. Erasmus: "All Christian religion seems to have a kind of alliance with folly and in no respect to have any accord with wisdom. Of
which if you expect proofs, consider first that boys, old men, women, and
fools are more delighted with religious and sacred things than others, and

to that purpose are ever next the altars; and this they do by mere impulse of nature. And in the next place, you see that those first founders of it were plain, simple persons and most bitter enemies of learning."

No historian will rest a working philosophy on pure faith alone, certainly not the faith of holy fools, but neither should that philosophy rest in the arrogance that history is akin to pure reason. In October 2006, a blue-ribbon committee of Harvard's undergraduate teachers called for a collegewide course requirement entitled "Reason and Faith." In December, they retreated. Their colleague, Steven Pinker, had put his finger on the sore spot in their proposal. "The juxtaposition of the two words makes it sound like 'faith' and 'reason' are parallel and equivalent ways of knowing, and we have to help students navigate between them. But universities are about reason, pure and simple. Faith—believing something without good reasons to do so—has no place in anything but a religious institution, and our society has no shortage of these."

A powerful indictment, if somewhat broad. For Harvard also leads its young charges into realms of the imagination where reason has little place. We believe a good many things "without good reasons to do so": to expect another to love us for a lifetime; to spend that lifetime writing poetry; to run into burning buildings to save perfect strangers; to believe that peace is possible. To argue that knowing is "about reason, pure and simple" is to forget that history is a little short of that "pure and simple" truth. As the distinguished physicist Lawrence M. Krauss reminds us, "There is undoubtedly a deep need within our psyches to believe in the existence of new realms where our hopes and dreams might be fulfilled, and our worst nightmares may lie buried." History is one of those realms, filled with human hopes and dreams, nightmares too.

Is our faith in the possibility of history merely a dream, then? Have we returned to Oscar Handlin's valley, surrounded by unreachable peaks? Stephen J. Gould was one of the most beloved and widely read biologists of the second half of the twentieth century. He offered us the concept of the evolution of species as a series of punctuated equilibria, sudden spurts in the development of genetic variation often taking place in nature's backwaters, as an alternative to Charles Darwin's idea of evolution as a long process featuring only the gradual appearance and success of new traits. Gould also believed that the most rigorous scientific defense of evolution did not rule out a faith that we could penetrate beyond scientific certainty to know more than met the eye. In making the case for revealed religion in "Nonoverlapping Magisteria," an essay in 1997 commenting on Pope

John Paul II's belief that Catholicism and evolution were not mutually exclusive, Gould wrote, "I have some scientific colleagues, including a few prominent enough to wield influence by their writings, who view this rapprochement of the separate magisteria with dismay."

If I were to make a similar argument for history's faith, I think I would find a similar upwelling of criticism. But consider that faith itself need not have a canonical object. We can have faith in our ability to know a world different from our own without bringing in an immanent deity. If organized religion is not a way to "know" anything about history, reason and its modern proxy "science" without basic humane values can just as easily lead to acts of unkindness and intolerance as unreasoning dogma can. Such values in the end analysis are based on little more than a faith in our common goodness, along with a faith in ourselves. Such faith can lead us to love, to aspire, and to sacrifice.

The structure of the bridge between the present and the past, including the segments of the span supplied by reasoned argument, near-fallacy, the use of hypotheticals and other loaded questions, literary artifice, a sense of political context, the willingness to cooperate, and a pragmatic acceptance of useful categories and configurations to accommodate uncertainty, is almost completed by the recognition that doing history presents us with the logical paradox of a yearning for certainties in an uncertain world. There is evil. There is good. And the outcome of the struggle between them—a struggle the historian can chronicle but cannot referee—is governed by chance and circumstance. The problem of evil is only the last of the results of this paradox. It is a paradox we can overcome with a due confidence in our own abilities and a recognition of our limitations. Then the bridge to the past, approached with reason, girded with literary skill, aware of the politics in its foundational piers, spanned with categories rooted in real life, suspended by moral awareness, is decked and paved with faith—faith that we can know enough; faith that what we know is enough; faith that the effort is worthwhile for us and for those who read us.

What is the philosophy of history for our time? It is that it is safe to go back into the archives, safe to return to the classroom and the lecture hall, safe to sit at the word processor or to lift the pen over the yellow pad, safe to go to the library and take out a history book or buy one on Amazon. com. It is safe to teach and write and read and listen to history. Something happened out there, long ago, and we have the ability, if we have the faith, to learn what that something is.

Deborah Gershenowitz, my editor and a student of history herself, asked early in the production of this work, "What is your personal philosophy of history?" A fair question, but one I found, even after all I had written, not so easy to answer. The words of the beautiful ballad "How to Handle a Woman" from *Camelot* came into my mind. The way to handle history is simply to love it. That is not hard. To paraphrase Henry David Thoreau, history is the stream we all go fishing in. We are the product of history and we make history. Though most of us occupy only a very small place in it, leaving behind us the scant documentary record of our aspirations and achievements (and our failures too), we are the stuff of history. It is that single, necessary fact that enables us to know about the past and demands that we seek out its truths.

If this little book provides some help in understanding this lesson, then it has done its job, and I mine, though in a famous commencement address delivered in 1837, "The American Scholar," Thoreau's patron and fellow Transcendentalist Ralph Waldo Emerson warned us against relying on authorities—particularly those who told us to read their books and all would be well! "The writer was a just and wise spirit: henceforward it is settled, the book is perfect; as love of the hero corrupts into worship of his statue. Instantly, the book becomes noxious: the guide is a tyrant." This book is only a starting point. The rest, reader, is up to you.

Glossary

A note to the reader: these are the bolded words and terms from the preceding pages. The definitions given below refer to the use of the words on those pages. Many of the words have other definitions, but these are omitted here.

AD HOMINEM: literally "against the man," a personal attack.

AFFIRMING THE CONSEQUENT, FALLACY OF: reasoning that the premise is correct because the conclusion is so.

ALL-OR-NOTHING (BLACK-AND-WHITE, EITHER-OR) FALLACY: an argument with no middle ground.

ANALOGY: a comparison that has the form "If A is like B, then A has a particular characteristic in B."

APPEAL TO AUTHORITY: let's settle this dispute by asking someone who knows.

ARGUMENT: in logic, a statement or series of statements purporting to be so. Not a yelling match.

ARGUMENT FROM AUTHORITY: it is true because an authority figure says so.

ARGUMENT FROM CONSEQUENCES: the premise is true because I want the consequence to prove true.

ATLANTIC CITY (GAMBLER'S HOPE) FALLACY: I've been losing, so the odds say I'll win on my next throw. I'll keep on betting.

AXIOM: a rule in a closed logical system: for example, in geometry, "The whole is greater than the part."

BEGGING THE QUESTION: assuming the truth of what you are supposed to be proving; circular reasoning.

BIG LIE: a boldface untruth, told with the intention of fooling lots of people.

CATEGORY MISTAKE: the error of assuming that the name of a collection of things is a thing itself.

CHAOS THEORY (BUTTERFLY EFFECT): the discovery that minute changes in initial conditions may lead similar events to result in widely different conclusions.

CIRCULAR REASONING: a statement chasing its own tail, proving its truth by reasserting its premise.

CLUSTERING ILLUSION: the fallacy of thinking that a cluster of events must be related to some other, nearby event.

CONCOMITANCE, FALLACY OF: mistaking proximity in time or place for cause.

CONTRAPOSITIVE: in formal logic, "If p then q, then if not q then not p."

CONVERSE: in formal logic, "If p then q, then if q then p."

DECONSTRUCTIONISTS: a group of literary critics and philosophers who ignore the context of texts in favor of the timelessness of texts.

DEDUCTION: in logic, reasoning from a definition or an infallible rule to a particular case.

DENYING THE ANTECEDENT, FALLACY OF: in logic, "If p then q, not p, therefore not q."

DOGMA, DOGMATISM: the claim that an authority is always right and must be accepted as such. It helps to be infallible on the subject.

DOUBLE STANDARD: do as I say, not as I do.

EMPIRICIST: someone who reasons from inference; the opposite of the metaphysician.

ENTROPY: the second of the three classical laws of thermodynamics. Energy in the universe is not conserved; instead, it is in a steady process of dissipation. In other words, don't waste your energy, you will not have it tomorrow.

EXPERIMENT: testing a hypothesis through the use of controls and repetition.

EVIL, PROBLEM OF: why, if God loves us and is good, is there evil; why do the innocents suffer?

FALLACY: a mistake in logic, word use, or reasoning.

FALSE CAUSE: mistaking motives or excuses for causes.

FALSE CONCRETENESS, FALLACY OF: wishing cannot make it so, and coining a term does not do it either.

FALSE IDENTIFICATION FALLACY: argument based on incorrect or misleading association of A and B.

FALSE QUESTION, FALLACY OF: a demeaning hypothetical in question form.

FORMAL LOGICAL FALLACY: a mistake in formal logic; a form of statement that violates the rules of propositional reasoning.

FORMAL (PROPOSITIONAL) LOGIC: a calculation of validity of statements based on a set of rules.

FRACTAL THEORY: the theory describing how certain physical structures in nature (fractals) repeat themselves in miniature.

GAME THEORY: a series of strategies for making decisions that accounts for other players' decisions as well.

GÖDEL'S PARADOX: there are some large axiomatic mathematical systems whose axioms' truth cannot be determined within the system itself; a theory of inherent indeterminacy.

GREATEST GOOD FOR THE GREATEST NUMBER: the mantra of John Stuart Mill's nineteenth-century philosophy of utilitarianism.

GUILT BY ASSOCIATION: the accusation that one's adversary is hanging out with the wrong crowd.

HASTY GENERALIZATION: a statement about an individual or a group based on insufficient information, often demonstrating stereotyping.

HINDSIGHT, FALLACY OF: explanations of events based on their outcome; Monday morning quarterbacking.

HYPOTHESIS: a proposition that can be proved true or false through empirical tests.

HYPOTHETICAL: known contrary-to-fact statement, often used as a teaching device. Not to be confused with *hypothesis*, which is a potentially true statement a researcher is testing.

IF-THEN ARGUMENT: if p then q.

INDUCTION: see *inference*.

INFERENCE: reaching a conclusion based on gathering of evidence, laboratory tests, or other empirical means.

INFORMAL LOGICAL FALLACY: a mistake in reasoning based on other than formal logical rules. See also *near-fallacy*.

INVERSE: in formal logic, "If not p then not q."

JOHNNY-ONE-NOTE (ONE-SIDEDNESS): relentless harping on one side of a complex issue; single-mindedness.

LAW OF CONTRADICTION: in Aristotelian logic, "A cannot be not A."

LAW OF THE EXCLUDED MIDDLE: in Aristotelian logic, "Either A or not A."

LAW OF IDENTITY: in Aristotelian logic, "A is A, and evermore shall be so."

LOADED QUESTION: the you-can't-win-however-you-answer-it question.

LOGIC: not easily defined. I'm tempted to say that we know it when we read or hear it, for its reasoned tone, its careful movement from premise to conclusion, and its concern for clear and convincing relationships between the parts of arguments.

LOGIC CHOPPING: using logical tricks to defeat an opponent.

LOGICAL POSITIVISTS: members of a school of twentieth-century philosophy using analysis of language to challenge metaphysics.

MAGIC: controlling nature through charms, spells, and other invisible means; a form of popular entertainment using hidden mechanisms and sleight of hand.

NEAR-FALLACY: an argument or method of argument that sails close to fallacy, and can easily be used to argue wrongly, but may also be correct.

NON SEQUITUR: asserting that A follows B when in fact B has no factual relationship to A.

OBJECTIVE (OBJECTIVITY): judgment based, in theory, upon deduction from commonly accepted principles; in law, the "rational man" standard. In history, the ideal of historical-mindedness, or seeing the world through our subject's eyes.

PARADOX: on its face, a puzzle or contradiction.

PHILOSOPHY OF HISTORY: a much-contested term, not to be confused with *historical method* (the rhetorical, research, or other devices used to compose history). A philosophy of history is an exploration of how we know about the past. The plural version of the term, *philosophies of history*, suggests the study of existing theories rather than the putting forward of one's own theory.

PLAGIARISM: the practice of claiming another's words as one's own creation or original expression.

POISONING THE WELL: insinuating, before the debate has begun, that an opposing argument or debater is unfit.

PRAGMATISM: an American philosophy asserting that meaning can be based only on empirical verification; sometimes confused with practical thinking.

PRECEDENT: that which has gone before; in our legal system, the rule or standard laid down in prior appellate court decisions that may be applied to subsequent cases.

PREDETERMINISM (DETERMINISM): the causal theory that everything that happens is covered by one or more general laws.

PREMISE: a statement of fact or opinion that may or may not be true.

PRESENTISM (PRESENT-MINDEDNESS), FALLACY OF: seeing the past in terms of present values or needs, overemphasizing in the past what survived to the present.

PRISONER'S DILEMMA: the popular name given to one of the varieties of game theory.

PROPOSITION: in formal logic, a statement.

QUOTING OUT OF CONTEXT: abstracting a portion of a text from the whole in such a way that the argument of the original text is misrepresented.

RATIONALITY: acting in reasonable fashion, conforming one's behavior and thinking to one's own or others' best interests.

RATIONALIZATION: in psychology, a defense mechanism to hide the actual basis for one's actions. Also, a form of lying.

REDUCTIONIST: employing the strategy of explanation that fits all cases into one category and provides for all events a single story line.

REGRESSION (STATISTICAL) FALLACY: assuming that any one case will resemble the majority of cases.

RELATIVIST: in historical scholarship, arguing that all historical studies' perspective and bias grows out of the time and place in which they were written; in ethics, arguing that moral judgments are also determined by time and place.

RHETORICAL QUESTION: a question to which one already knows the answer, or whose answer is obvious from the question.

RULE OF THUMB (REASONING BY DEFAULT): basing action or belief on a generalization or on prior experience.

SAMPLE: a single case of or a selection from a larger number of cases.

SAMPLING FALLACY: reaching a conclusion about an entire population of people or things based on an atypical portion of the whole.

SCIENTIFIC METHOD: what scientists are supposed to do to test their theories, using hypothesis and experiment. It now has a status rivaling religious dogma.

SELF-FULFILLING PROPHECY: after hearing the oracle speak, our actions make the prediction happen.

SEMANTIC ERROR: an error or ambiguity in usage of language—for example, a pun.

SKEPTICS' FALLACY: in logic, "If p is not true, then q cannot be true."

SLIPPERY SLOPE: an argument that moves to its conclusion through a series of linked hypotheticals.

SPECIAL PLEADING: arguing for exceptions to a general rule.

STATUTES: acts of legislative bodies, often misspelled as *statues* for some mysterious reason.

STEREOTYPING, STEREOTYPICAL THINKING: a demeaning and misleading hasty generalization about a group or its characteristics.

STRAW MAN: a fake position created for the sole purpose of its demolition.

SUBJECTIVE (SUBJECTIVITY): a rule of judgment based on individual preferences or values.

SWEEPING GENERALIZATION (DICTO SIMPLICITER): overgeneralization; reaching a general rule from too few cases.

SYLLOGISM: in formal logic, "If A is B and B is C, then A is C."

TRUTH: a fact or conclusion provable in the real world or asserted as a universal without proof.

UNREPRESENTATIVE SAMPLE: see *Sampling fallacy.*

VALID (VALIDITY): a logical relationship.

VERIFICATION TEST: the philosophical version of the infamous slogan, "If it doesn't fit, you must acquit." For a word to have meaning, its sense must be testable in the real world.

WHAT IF?: a question that poses a contrary-to-fact premise, allowing us to explore variations of explanations for what actually did happen.

ZEALOTS, ZEALOTRY: the extreme of dogma put into action. Never having to say you are sorry, cut and run, or admit error as you slay your enemy, or he slays you.

A Very Brief Bibliographical Essay

Even novelists are including bibliographies in their work these days, so while this book is meant for general readers and does not have those troublesome and odd-looking little numbers in the text or the crabbed and overstuffed pages of endnotes, a very brief bibliography is certainly in order. It is part tribute to the works that have inspired the essay above and part guide to the materials I have used. Some of the material comes from thirty-odd years of teaching notes, the time I have been in harness teaching history to college students. I have included passages from other books of mine, including *Past Imperfect: Facts, Fictions, and Fraud in American History* (New York: PublicAffairs, 2004), *Sensory Worlds in Early America* (Baltimore: Johns Hopkins University, 2003), and *Seven Fires: The Urban Infernos That Reshaped America* (New York: PublicAffairs, 2006). Other bits and pieces came from conversations with friends and colleagues.

I have given references in the text to sources quoted but have omitted page numbers when the text is available on the Web. The bibliography indicates the version or translation of the text I used. Readers of Erasmus's *In Praise of Folly* (Ann Arbor: University of Michigan Press, 1958), quotations on pp. 4 and 143, and Edward Hallett Carr's *What Is History?* (New York: Knopf, 1962) will see my debt to their erudition. When I went to graduate school, Carr was the standard short work on historical method. I found it fascinating and still do. Quotations from it come from pp. 33, 35, and 133. Jacques Barzun and Henry F. Graff's *The Modern Researcher* (New York: Harcourt Brace, 1957) was a little dry, but it has gone through multiple editions, so someone out there must be assigning it to classes. Like Barzun and Graff, most of the books students are assigned these days focus solely on methods—how to research a topic, how to prepare a paper, and the like. These come in little sealed packages, "shrink wrapped" with huge and expensive textbooks in history. I've even coauthored one myself, *Reading and Writing American History*, 3rd ed., 2 vols. (2003). A nice, earnest, but not entirely convincing attempt to go beyond deconstruction is Joyce Appleby, Lynn Hunt, and Margaret Jacob's *Telling the Truth about History* (New York: Norton, 1994). I have in the past asked my graduate students to read portions of Peter Novick's spicy yet morally profound *That Noble Dream: The "Objectivity Question" and the American Historical Profession* (New York: Cambridge University Press, 1988). The quotation came from p. 17.

Finally, those of us who remember Richard Armour's *It All Started with Columbus* and *It Would Have Startled Columbus* (New York: McGraw Hill, 1953) (quotations from pp. 6, 7, 8, and 9 of the former) and Dave Barry's *Dave Barry Slept Here: A Sort of History of the United States* (New York: Random House, 1989) will recognize the tone of respectful irreverence in the pages above.

Legal references are courtesy of Lexis.com, combined federal and state cases. The *New York Times* articles can be found online at www.nytimes. com. The AHA presidential addresses all are online at www.historians.org, the AHA Web site.

The chapter epigraphs come from Carl Becker, *Detachment and the Writing of History*, ed. Phil L. Snyder (Ithaca, NY: Cornell University Press, 1958), pp. 65, 44, and 157; David Hackett Fischer, *Historians' Fallacies: Toward a Logic of Historical Thought* (New York: Harper, 1970), pp. 200, 78 (and on Nevins, pp. 46–47); Allan Nevins, *The Gateway to History*, rev. ed. (New York: D. C. Heath, 1962), p. 238; Frederick Jackson Turner, *The Frontier in American History* (New York: Holt, 1935), p. 3; Bernard Bailyn, *the Intellectual Origins of the American Revolution* (Cambridge, MA: Harvard University Press, 1967), pp. 9, 20–21; Gertrude Himmelfarb, "Postmodernist History" [1994], reprinted in *Reconstructing History: The Emergence of a New Historical Society*, ed. Elizabeth Fox Genovese and Elisabeth Lasch Quinn (New York: Routledge, 1999), p. 80; Stephen Ambrose quoted in Susan Larson, "Undaunted Courage," New Orleans *Times-Picayune*, October 6, 2002, Living section, p. 1.

Wilhelm Dilthey, *Pattern and Meaning in History*, ed. H. P. Rickman and translated by B. G. Teubner (1911; repr., New York: Harper, 1962), p. 140, opens the preface, and rightly so, for Dilthey was one of the most profound premodern thinkers about historical method. I am grateful to Monty Python Ltd. for allowing their material to become public and fair use exception in our copyright laws for allowing me to quote snippets.

For Handlin's revealing personal reminiscence in the Introduction, see Oscar Handlin, *Truth in History* (Cambridge: Harvard University Press,

1979), pp. 38–39. Allan Megill's collection of earlier critical pieces, *Historical Knowledge, Historical Error: A Contemporary Guide to Practice* (Chicago: University of Chicago, 2007), quotations on pp. x, 13, and 213, came to hand as I was near the end of this essay, but I have read it with awe and some dread. I am not sure that I qualify as one of Megill's "true historians" (something like Molester Mole's secret list in Walt Kelly's *Pogo* strip, to be feared but not revealed), but I hope so. At any rate, I think I fit the description he gives of the "dinosaurs" who learned method before the "cultural turn" revealed that Foucault and his comrades were models to be copied. Hayden White, *The Content of the Form: Narrative Discourse and Historical Representation* (Baltimore: Johns Hopkins University Press, 1990), pp. 1, 49, buries its pessimism about knowing the past under layers of philosophical debris—hard going, but the message comes clear: history is just a form of rhetoric.

Daniel Little, "Philosophy of History," Stanford Encyclopedia of Philosophy, http://plato.stanford.edu/entries/history/, posted February 18, 2007, is the source of the introduction's quotation on the philosophy of history. Bury, Fustel de Coulanges, and von Ranke appeared in my dog-eared copy of Fritz Stern, ed., *The Varieties of History* (New York: Meridian, 1956), on pp. 208, 178, and 55. G. R. Elton, *The Practice of History* (New York: Crowell, 1967), tells us not to worry about historical truth. The quotations are from pp. 17 and 46.

Marc Bloch, *The Historian's Craft*, trans. Peter Putnam (New York: Vintage, 1953), pp. 22 and 47 and, on moral judgments (discussed in Chapter 9), 139 and 140, is a book of luminous wisdom and is still inspiring after all these years. Carole Fink's *Marc Bloch: A Life in History* (Cambridge: Cambridge University Press, 1989) is excellent and admiring. In Chapter 9, the quotation on Bloch's view of history as politics appears on p. 249, and Bloch's letter to Febvre on evil is reproduced in part on p. 205.

Jacques Barzun's lament in the Introduction appeared in *Clio and the Doctors: Psycho-History and Quanto-History* (Chicago: University of Chicago Press, 1974), p. 3. John Tosh's *The Pursuit of History*, rev. 3rd ed. (New York: Longman, 2002), finds the comparison between history and the sciences "perhaps somewhat contrived" (p. 178). Quite right. The philosopher Morris R. Cohen had the last word, though he published sixty years ago and is rarely read today. He concluded that history was simply a distinctive way of "organizing human knowledge." Cohen, *The Meaning of Human History* (LaSalle, IL: Open Court, 1947), p. 41.

Barbara J. Shapiro's *A Culture of Fact: England, 1550–1720* (Ithaca: Cornell University Press, 2003), mentioned in chapter 1, discusses the rise of the profession of history and its "facts" on pp. 34–62, with quotation on p. 34. George Creel recalls his motives in *World War, 1914–1918* (New York: Harper, 1920), p. 5.

Socrates extols reason in Plato, *The Republic,* trans. Benjamin Jowett (Oxford: Clarendon Press, 1888), p. 327. The standard scholarly edition of the three volumes of Aristotle's *Organon* is Harvard University Press's (1938–52). For Aquinas, see Anton Charles Pegis, ed., *Basic Writing of Saint Thomas Aquinas* (New York: Random House, 1945), p. 23. Thomas Paine's *Age of Reason* [1795] is in *The Complete Writings of Thomas Paine* (New York: Citadel, 1945); the quotation is from p. 596. *The Philosophical Writings of Descartes,* trans. Anthony Kenny (Cambridge: Cambridge University Press, 1991), vol. 1, p. 120, supplies Descartes's method, and p. 200 connects our powers of knowing to a good God. John Locke, in *Essay Concerning Human Understanding,* ed. Kenneth P. Winkler (Indianapolis: Hackett, 1995), p. 313, supplies another way of knowing.

Edward Gibbon's *Decline and Fall of the Roman Empire* (Whitefish, MT: Kessinger, 2004), vol. 3, p. 548, summarizes the case for religion as a (malevolent) cause. John Marshall, *The Life of George Washington* (Philadelphia: Crissy, 1836), vol. 1, p. 108, is the source of the quote from Washington. Peter Oliver, *Origin and Progress of the American Rebellion,* ed. Douglas Adair and John A. Schutz (1781; repr., Stanford University Press, 1961), 148–49, offers the loyalist counterargument. Hegel can be found in *Hegel's Science of Logic,* trans. A. V. Miller (London: Routledge, 2002), p. 82. Francis Fukuyama, *The End of History and the Last Man* (New York: Harper, 1992), p. 215, notes the contradiction in national history based on universal principles.

On atrocities (there were more than we once thought) in the English Civil Wars, see Barbara Donagan, "Atrocity, War Crimes and Treason in the English Civil War," *American Historical Review* 99 (October 1994): 1137–66. Thomas Hobbes reveals the secrets of *Leviathan, or, The Matter, Form, and Power of a Common-wealth Ecclesiastical and Civil* (London: Routledge, 1885), on p. 85. John Aubrey told the story about Hobbes. See *Brief Lives,* ed. Anthony Powell (New York: Scribners, 1949), p. 150.

Like Cohen, Karl Popper was not a historian, but *The Poverty of Historicism* (1957; repr., London: Routledge, 2002) is a classic statement of the humane limitations of historical inquiry. The quotations are from pp. 46 and 81. John Hobson, *Imperialism: A Study* (London: Nisbet, 1902), 241, explains why imperialism was a necessary good. I used Laurence Sterne, *The Life and Opinions of Tristram Shandy, Gentleman* (Ware: Wordsworth, 1996); quotations in Chapters 1 and 6 are on pp. 8 and 236 respectively.

The reference to "institutes" in Chapter 1 can be explored more fully in Robin Wilson, "New Centers Bring Tradition to a Study of U.S. History," *Chronicle of Higher Education,* March 16, 2007, p. A10. The quotation from Festinger appears in Leon Festinger, *A Theory of Cognitive Dissonance* (Evanston, IL: Row, Peterson, 1957), p. 18.

Most textbooks and treatises on formal logic are above my head. For the basics provided in Chapter 1, I have relied on Thomas Gilovich, *How We Know It Isn't So: The Fallibility of Reason in Everyday Life* (New York: Free Press, 1993); Robert Todd Carroll, *The Skeptic's Dictionary* (New York: Wiley, 2003); and Howard T. Kahane and Nancy Cavender, *Logic and Contemporary Rhetoric,* 10th ed. (Belmont, CA: Wadsworth, 2006).

I read Fischer's *Historians' Fallacies,* discussed in Chapter 2, when I was just starting my teaching career, and its lessons remain with me. Three years later, I came upon Ernest R. May's *"Lessons" of the Past: The Use and Misuse of History in American Foreign Policy* (New York: Oxford University Press, 1973), a reminder that readers of history can mistake its teachings.

Daniel Boorstin's *The Americans: The National Experience* (New York: Random House, 1965), pp. 55, 183, 191, makes hasty generalizations about slaves. David M. Kennedy's *Freedom from Fear* (New York: Oxford University Press, 1999), p. 380, makes a hasty generalization about FDR, but it is a reasonable one. Justice Hugo Black's words are repeated in Peter Irons, *Justice at War: The Story of the Japanese American Internment Cases* (Berkeley: University of California Press, 1983), p. 357.

Francis Parkman generalized about northeastern Indians partly on the basis of his experiences with the Plains Indians he met as a Harvard undergraduate years before he began writing his magisterial *France and England in America.* He was also, as a Boston Brahmin, a tried and true Anglophile. The quotation can be found in *Parkman,* a collection of portions of his books from the Library of America (New York: Library of America, 1983), p. 369. Henry Cabot Lodge published his speech, with its view of race, in *Speeches and Addresses of Henry Cabot Lodge, 1884–1909* (Boston: Houghton Mifflin, 1909), p. 262. David Landes's far more sophisticated stereotyping appears in his *The Wealth and Poverty of Nations: Why Some Are So Rich and Some So Poor* (New York: Norton, 1998), pp. 512–13.

The story of the National History Standards presented in Chapter 2 comes from my *Past Imperfect,* pp. 98–114, but students of this episode should consult Gary B. Nash, Charlotte Crabtree, and Ross E. Dunn, *History on Trial: Culture Wars and the Teaching of the Past* (New York: Vintage, 2000). Newt Gingrich speaks to us in "Why Pearl Harbor Is Still Relevant—Now More Than Ever," May 14, 2007, www.humanevents.com/article.php?id=20715.

On abortion proponents, I used David Garrow, *Liberty and Sexuality: The Right to Privacy and the Making of Roe v. Wade* (New York: Macmillan, 1994); James Risen and Judy L. Thomas, *Wrath of Angels: The American Abortion War* (New York: Basic Books, 1998); and my own *Roe v. Wade: The Abortion Rights Controversy in American History,* coauthored with N. E. H. Hull (Lawrence: University Press of Kansas, 2001).

The highly charged exchange about book reviews and reviewers mentioned in Chapter 2 comes from the "Communications" pages of the *American Historical Review* 105 (2000): 1871–72. The dueling professors X and Y are, respectively, Alan M. Dershowitz (www.alandershowitz.com) and Norman Finkelstein (www.normanfinkelstein.com). Though their Web sites are not recommended for the faint-hearted, the reader may search them, as I did, for the comments quoted above and many more like them. The tenure battle story appears in Jennifer Howard, "DePaul U. Turns Norman Finkelstein Down for Tenure," *Chronicle of Higher Education,* June 11, 2007, p. A5.

My source for Chapter 2's story behind the brief in *Webster* was a conversation with James C. Mohr, the lead author. For the Robert Caro quotations, see *The Power Broker: Robert Moses and the Fall of New York* (New York: Knopf, 1974), pp. 1161–62. Paul Johnson, *Modern Times: The World from the Twenties to the Eighties* (New York: Harper and Row, 1983), p. 659, describes war and economics; David Halberstam, *The Fifties* (New York: Fawcett, 1993), p. 144, is the source of the quotation on suburbia. Bernard Bailyn's call for the narrative synthesis came at the 1981 AHA meeting and was published as "The Challenge of Modern Historiography," *American Historical Review* 87 (1982): 1–24. The quotation is from p. 12.

In 1963, at the University of Rochester, Willson H. Coates told the students in his historical methods course about his rule of thumb. I was impressed then and remain so now. Coates was a historian's historian—kindly, precise, and above all wise. James McPherson, ed., *The Atlas of the Civil War* (Philadelphia: Running Press, 2005), p. 142, reports the figure of seven thousand. Gordon Rhea, *Cold Harbor: Grant and Lee, May 26–June 3, 1864* (Baton Rouge: Louisiana State University Press, 2002), p. 386, estimates three thousand casualties. For Westmoreland, see Patricia Sullivan, "General

Commanded Troops in Vietnam," *Washington Post,* July 19, 2005, p. A1. Renata Adler's *Reckless Disregard* (New York: Knopf, 1988) is a classic.

Paul Cameron is the subject (and author) in many blog sites. For the quotation in Chapter 2, see www.splcenter.org/intel/intelreport/article.jsp?aid=587. R. R. Palmer speaks of comparisons and changes in word usage in *The Age of Democratic Revolution: The Challenge* (Princeton: Princeton University Press, 1959). The quotations are from pp. 13 and 21.

The Gary Becker/Richard Posner blog, January 23, 2005, featured Judge Richard Posner's comments on profiling Hispanics. See www.becker-posner-blog.com/archives/2005/01/comment_on_prof.html.

For Chapter 3's quote on the blundering generation, see James G. Randall, "The Blundering Generation," *Mississippi Valley Historical Review* 27 (1940): 7, 8. Not by accident, the piece appeared as the United States teetered on the brink of entering World War II. Randall concluded that "in the present troubled age" policy makers ought to pay more attention to the horrible realities of war than its heroic romances (pp. 27–28). The presidential debate in which Michael Dukakis expressed his opposition to the death penalty can be found at www.debates.org/pages/trans88a.htm.

Malkin and Coulter quotes in Chapter 3 appear in Web sites plugging their books as well as Ann Coulter's *Slander: Liberal Lies about the American Right* (New York: Crown, 2002), p. 6, and Michelle Malkin at www.jewishworldreview.com/michelle/malkin100401.asp. Philip Roth bares his soul in *Operation Shylock: A Confession* (New York: Simon and Schuster, 1993). The quotation is from p. 397. David Horowitz quotations come from his Web site, frontpagemag.com. See David Horowitz on Marable at www.frontpagemag.com/Articles/Read.aspx?GUID'66E73ED7-4575-49E4-AE9B-17F7B5A57F51. The original blurb for the book by Horowitz on his frontpagemagazine.com has disappeared from the Web, confusing observers who are trying to figure out what the critics of the book are saying. The disappearance of the original blurb is also an object lesson in the dangers of using Web sites as sources!

Boethius consoles us in *The Consolation of Philosophy,* trans. Joel Relihan (Indianapolis: Hackett, 2000), pp. 7–8. *The Apologia and Other Works of Socrates* is the reprint of the superb Benjamin Jowett translation (repr., Whitefish, MT: Kessinger, 2004); the quotation is from p. 14.

Jefferson included Logan's oration in his *Notes on the State of Virginia,* ed. William Peden (1785; repr., Chapel Hill: University of North Carolina Press, 1955), p. 229. The reply to Governor John Henry of Maryland, dated December 31, 1797, appears as Appendix III in the J. W. Randolph edition

(Richmond, 1853), p. 243. Jefferson's concern for "past revolutionary history" was somewhat self-serving. After all, it was his life story. The quotation comes from a letter from Jefferson to Joel Barlow, April 16, 1811, reprinted in Albert E. Bergh and Andrew Lipscomb, eds., *The Writings of Thomas Jefferson* (Washington, DC: U.S. Government Printing Office, 1903), vol. 13, p. 44. For more on the framers' views of history, see my *Revolution and Regeneration: Life Cycle and the Historical Vision of the Generation of 1776* (Athens: University of Georgia Press, 1983).

Richard Dawkins shared his views on religion, in response to 9/11, in *A Devil's Chaplain* (New York: Houghton Mifflin, 2003), p. 157.

On population increases in early modern cities (discussed in Chapter 3), see Allan Sharlin, "Natural Decrease in Early Modern Cities: A Reconsideration," *Past and Present* 79 (1978): 127, 128. Robert Cowley, *What Ifs? of American History: Eminent Historians Imagine What Might Have Been* (New York: Putnam, 2003), p. xiii.

On "Murphy's Law," see Arthur Bloch, *Murphy's Law,* 26th ed. (New York: Penguin, 2003); on "the Peter Principle," see Laurence J. Peter and Raymond Hull, *The Peter Principle* (New York: Morrow, 1969); on "Parkinson's Law," see C. Northcote Parkinson, *Parkinson's Law* (Boston: Houghton, 1957)—all classics. On Cleo's snout, see Daniel Boorstin, *Cleopatra's Nose: Essays on the Unexpected in History* (New York: Random House, 1994), p. ix. Edward Ayer's *In the Presence of Mine Enemies: War in the Heart of America* (New York: Norton, 2003), p. 148, explores but one of the many ironies in the coming of the Civil War.

Chapter 4's discussion of the collapse of the Twin Towers draws on *The 9/11 Commission Report: Authorized Edition* (New York: Norton, 2004), p. 339. The paraphrase from my *Seven Fires: The Urban Infernos That Reshaped America* (New York: PublicAffairs, 2006), pp. 366–68, is still chilling reading to me. On Hume's idea of causation, see *Treatise of Human Understanding,* bk. 1, p. 171. Steven Pinker, *The Stuff of Thought: Language as a Window into Human Nature* (New York: Viking, 2007), pp. 189, 190, is the source of the quotations on time, cause, and space.

Karl Marx's *Poverty of Philosophy* [1847] quotation in Chapter 4 comes from Howard Selsam and Harry Martel, eds., *Reader in Marxist Philosophy* (New York: International, 1963), p. 188. For Hitler's views on history, even more chilling than the design failures of the Twin Towers, see Adolph Hitler, *Mein Kampf,* trans. Ralph Manheim (New York: Reynal, 1939), p. 390. Fukuyama's riff on his own work appears at www.marxists.org/reference/subject/philosophy/works/us/fukuyama.htm. See Niall Ferguson,

"Empires with Expiration Dates," *Foreign Policy*, September 1, 2006, p. 47, for the quote in the text.

Paul Boyer and Stephen Nissenbaum, *Salem Possessed: The Social Origins of Witchcraft* (Cambridge, MA: Harvard University Press, 1974), pp. 212, 150, 139. An informal survey of American history survey textbooks shows that the Putnam-Porter quarrel, with reference to *Salem Possessed*, is the gold standard for explanations of the Salem witchcraft crisis. Malcolm Gladwell's introduction to *The Tipping Point: How Little Things Can Make a Big Difference* (Boston: Little, Brown, 2000), is one of the most quoted modern discussions of historical causation. Gladwell's own Web page (www.gladwell.com/tippingpoint/index.html) repeats the key themes of the book and is the source of the quotations in the text. Thomas Kuhn, *The Structure of Scientific Revolutions* (Chicago: University of Chicago Press, 1962), pp. 182–91, explains paradigm shifting. I heard Thomas Kuhn talk about Copernicus and scientific revolutions when I was an undergraduate at the University of Rochester in 1962. The theory, now much criticized, remains a classic in many more fields than history of science.

Robert K. Merton, *Social Theory and Social Structure* (New York: Free Press, 1949), included the new term *self-fulfilling prophecy*. Merton was one of the most fruitful and frequently quoted thinkers of the mid–twentieth century, and his many contributions to our language—for example, *role expectation, insider,* and *focus group*—are still in use. See David Hume's *Treatise of Human Nature* (London: Noon, 1739), p. xiii, for his most commonly quoted explanation of the early application of scientific method.

For the quotations in Chapter 4 on the controversy over *Time on the Cross*, see Robert William Fogel and Stanley L. Engerman, *Time on the Cross: Evidence and Methods, A Supplement* (Boston: Little, Brown, 1974), p. 4; Herbert G. Gutman and Richard Sutch, "The Slave Family: Protected Agent of Capitalist Masters or Victim of the Slave Trade?" ch. 3 of *Reckoning with Slavery*, by Paul A. David et al. (New York: Oxford University Press, 1976), p. 96; Herbert G. Gutman, *Slavery and the Numbers Game*, rev. ed. (Urbana: University of Illinois Press, 2003), p. 38; Robert William Fogel and Stanley L. Engerman, "Explaining the Relative Efficiency of Slave Agriculture in the Antebellum South," *American Economic Review* 70 (1980): 672; and Robert William Fogel, *Without Consent or Contract: The Rise and Fall of American Slavery* (New York: Norton, 1989), p. 9.

The Rosenberg-Kessler Harris battle discussed in Chapter 4 played out in *EEOC v. Sears Roebuck Company*, U.S. District Court for the Northern

District of Illinois 628 F. Supp. 1264 (1986). Quotations are from the opinion of the court and from Thomas Haskell and Sanford Levinson's "Symposium on Academic Freedom: Academic Freedom and Expert Witnessing: Historians and the Sears Case," *Texas Law Review* 66 (1988): 1630, 1650. Kessler-Harris's reply appeared as "Academic Freedom and Expert Witnessing: A Response to Haskell and Levinson," *Texas Law Review* 67 (1988): 432. Haskell and Levinson's rejoinder is "On Academic Freedom and Hypothetical Pools: A Reply to Alice Kessler-Harris," *Texas Law Review* 67 (1989): 1594.

The standard work on Kinsey is James H. Jones, *Alfred Kinsey: A Public/Private Life* (New York: Norton, 1998). George Fitzhugh's comments, from *Cannibals All!,* were excerpted in Eric L. McKitrick, ed. *Slavery Defended* (Englewood Cliffs, NJ: Prentice Hall, 1963), p. 44.

Hitler's *Mein Kampf,* p. 212, introduced the "big lie," which I discuss in Chapter 5. Peter Sagal's delightful romp through "very naughty things and how to do them," *The Book of Vice* (New York: HarperCollins, 2007), p. 113, discusses the swiftboat episode. I discussed Michael Bellesiles's *Journal of American History* article in *Past Imperfect*, with quotations on pp. 145–51. For Woodrow Wilson's misrepresentations, see *A History of the American People, Documentary Edition* (New York: Harper, 1901) vol. 1, pp. 13, 28, 64, and vol. 10, pp. 17–18; Claude G. Bowers, *The Tragic Era, The Revolution after Lincoln* (New York: Literary Guild, 1929), p. 216; Allan Nevins and Henry Steele Commager, *A Pocket History of the United States* (New York: Harper, 1942), pp. 4, 5, 24, 53, 94, 248, and 249; Paul H. Buck, *The Road to Reunion, 1865–1900* (New York: Knopf, 1937), pp. 25–26, 33, 35, 294, 295, 309. E. Merton Coulter, *The South during Reconstruction, 1865–1877* (Baton Rouge: Louisiana State University Press, 1947), used Buck.

Full disclosure: I met both Buck and Coulter, the first at Harvard, in the 1960s, the second when I went to teach at Georgia, in 1978. Both small gentlemen, bowed with age, they were courteous and showed no awareness that what they had written could be seen as racist or biased in any way.

Scott Adams describes the weasel-zone in *Dilbert and the Way of the Weasel* (New York: Harper Business, 2002), p. 5. Albert Bandura, *Social Learning Theory* (Englewood Cliffs, NJ: Prentice Hall, 1977), explains how criminals learn to rationalize their conduct. "Bullshit" may involve lying, as Harry G. Frankfurt tells us in *On Bullshit* (Princeton: Princeton University Press, 2005), p. 9.

Arthur M. Schlesinger Jr., in *Journals, 1952–2000,* ed. Andrew Schlesinger and Stephen Schlesinger (New York: Penguin, 2007), pp. 838, 840, tells us about lying. The comments on Truman and Kennedy quoted in Chapter 6 appear on pp. 22, 57, and 334.

The quotation in Chapter 5 from John Demos, *The Unredeemed Captive: A Family Story from Early America* (New York: Knopf, 1994), is from pp. 189–90; Demos, "In Search of Reasons for Historians to Read Novels," *American Historical Review* 103 (December 1998): 1527, poses the novelistic alternative. T. H. Breen, *Imagining the Past: East Hampton Histories* (Athens: University of Georgia Press, 1996), pp. 14, 15, and Daniel K. Richter, *Facing East from Indian Country: A Native History of Early America* (Cambridge, MA: Harvard University Press, 2001), pp. 9, 13, explore the possibilities that a more open conversation between reader and author can dispel the anxiety about the uncertainties of history.

Regarding the discussion of experimental history in Chapter 5, see Laurel Thatcher Ulrich, *A Midwife's Tale, The Life of Martha Ballard, Based on her Diary, 1785–1812* (New York: Knopf, 1991), p. 33, and Martha Hodes, "Experimental History in the Classroom," AHA *Perspectives* 45 (May 2007): 38. Neither Ulrich nor Hodes would agree that they were advocating "lying," but calling invention "experimental" or doing what Ulrich does to fill in the gaps is artifice, surely. Rhys Isaac's "Discourse on Method" at the end of his *The Transformation of Virginia, 1740–1790* (Chapel Hill: University of North Carolina Press, 1982), is a model of its kind. The quotation in the text is from p. 325.

Dan Brown's revelations were reported in Dan Brown, "Witness Statement," *London Times*, Law News, March 14, 2006. For Frey, see thesmokinggun.com/archive/0104061jamesfrey1.html. Haley's *Roots* was outed in Philip Nobile's "Uncovering Roots," *Village Voice*, February 23, 1993. The true story of Rigoberta Menchú appears in Ron Robin's *Scandals and Scoundrels: Seven Cases That Shook the Academy* (Berkeley: University of California Press, 2004), pp. 166–92. See also Nancy Milford, "The False Memoir: All the Shouting about *A Million Little Pieces* Is Part of a Long Debate That Dates to the Origins of Writing," *Washington Post*, February 5, 2006, p. BW10, and Marie Arana, "The Way I Saw It: Chronicling a Life Requires the Imagination of a Storyteller," *Washington Post*, February 5, 2006, p. B03.

On puns in law reviews, see Thomas E. Baker's bibliography of law school humor in the *Drake Law Review* 51 (2002): 105–49, entitled "A Compendium of Clever and Amusing Law Review Writings," which includes a section on the punning titles. James Axtell's talk about teaching history is "The Pleasures of Teaching History," *History Teacher* 34 (2001), www.historycooperative.org/journals/ht/34.4/axtell.html.

H. Stuart Hughes was either a demigod or a demon, depending on one's politics, when I was a graduate student at Harvard. A superb slightly left-of-center European intellectual historian, he wore red ties to department meetings to infuriate his more conservative colleagues (so I was told). His comment on history, art, and science appears in H. Stuart Hughes, *History as Art and as Science: Twin Vistas on the Past* (Chicago: University of Chicago Press, 1975), p. 3.

Most of the quotations in Chapter 6 that do not have citations in the text come from my *Past Imperfect,* pp. 60–72, 115–21. The quotes from Harry Elmer Barnes's *The New History and the Social Sciences* (New York: Century, 1922), are on p. 13 (concessions to the first of many new histories) and p. 6 (on history and politics). David Donald, "Review Note," *American Historical Review* 74 (December 1968): 532, 533, fits into the long history of historical writing and criticism, inelegantly termed "historiography." Arthur Schlesinger, *The Vital Center* (Boston: Houghton Mifflin, 1949), pp. 1, 10, 249, 251, stirred great controversy at the time. His 1996 comment appears in *Past Imperfect,* p. 114. Dated but still the best survey of American historical writing and thought up to the 1960s is John Higham, *History: Professional Scholarship in America,* rev. ed. (Baltimore: Johns Hopkins, 1989).

Alan B. Spitzer, *Historical Truth and Lies about the Past* (Chapel Hill: University of North Carolina, 1989), pp. 97–115, deconstructs the Bitburg episode brilliantly. Quotations from Reagan appear on pp. 98 and 99. The newspaper smear of Burr first appeared in the *Gazette of the United States* on August 2, 1805, and the "Queries" were widely reprinted. John C. Calhoun's March 16, 1836, speech was reprinted in *The Works of John C. Calhoun* (New York: Appleton, 1851), vol. 2, pp. 626, 627. On Sheehy's mistake, see www.dailyhowler.com/h091598_2.shtml. Clarke's goof is lambasted in www.danieldrezner.com/archives/001188.html. For the (only, I'm happy to report) negative review of my *Great New York Conspiracy of 1741,* see Winthrop Jordan, "Review," *Law and History Review* 23 (2005): 212–13, "While this study gives a separate, helpful 'chronology' of events, the index is so incomplete as to be dangerous, especially for student use." Full disclosure: Winthrop Jordan was a superb historian of slavery, but we disagreed about the economic (me) versus the racial and sexual (him) origins and deployment of the institution. The full text of the Lincoln-Douglas debates of 1858 is at lincoln.lib.niu.edu/debates.html. The two speeches by President George W. Bush, in 2004 and 2006, are available at transcripts.cnn.com/TRANSCRIPTS/0405/21/se.01.html, and www.whitehouse.gov/news/releases/2006/01/200601310.html. The Donald Rumsfeld interview discussed in Chapter 6 is reported in David von Drehle, "Wrestling with History," *Washington Post* November 13, 2005, p. W12. The South Carolina abortion case is *The State, Respondent v. Regina D. McKnight*, 352 S.C. 635 (2003). Supreme Court opinions in the other cases can be found at lexis.com. The "Southern Manifesto" appears in *Congressional Record*, 84th Cong., 2nd sess., vol. 102, pt. 4 (March 12, 1956): 4459–60. I have taken the Southern Manifesto and the response of the southern newspapers to *Brown* from Waldo E. Martin Jr., *Brown v. Board of Education: A Brief History with Documents* (Boston: Bedford, 1998), pp. 204, 220–21.

The story of Sean Wilentz's part in the Clinton impeachment hearings is told in my *Past Imperfect*, pp. 122–27. John Kerry's hometown newspaper reference became the Web version of an urban rumor. See www.truthorfiction.com/rumors/e/endorsements.htm. Howard Dean was interviewed on December 6, 2005, on WOAI in San Antonio. The widely reported remarks appeared at www.cnn.com/2005/POLITICS/12/06/dean.iraq.1935. President Bush channeled President Truman on more than one occasion. For the West Point commencement address in 2006, see www.whitehouse.gov/news/releases/2006/05/20060527-1.html. For the 2002 speech, see www.whitehouse.gov/news/releases/2002/06/20020601-3.html. William Henry Seward warned about the irrepressible conflict in 1858; see www.nyhistory.com/central/conflict.htm.

Stephen Breyer's *Active Liberty: Interpreting Our Democratic Constitution* (New York: Knopf, 2005) is one of the most literate and persuasive essays on our law by anyone charged with interpreting it. This may be because Breyer has spent his entire career in academe and on the bench, and not in politics. For Haskell and Levinson's final remarks on the *Sears* case, see Haskell and Levinson, "On Academic Freedom and Hypothetical Pools," p. 1594. The AHA *Statement on Standards* as revised in 2004 and approved in 2005, is online at www.historians.org/pubs/Free/ProfessionalStandards.cfm.

On Ambrose, discussed in Chapter 7, see my *Past Imperfect*, pp. 180–89. In an interview on popular history, Laurel Thatcher Ulrich was quoted in Matthew Price, "Hollow History," *Boston Globe*, October 24, 2004, p. E1. For Herbert Spencer's "first principle," see his *Social Statics* (1855; repr., New York: Appleton, 1913), p. 55. For more on the National History Standards, including the quotes from Gary Nash, see my *Past Imperfect*, pp. 105–6.

James Kirkpatrick's less-than-epic poesy appeared in *The Sea-Piece: A Narrative, Philosophical, and Descriptive Poem in Five Cantos* (London: Cooper, 1750). The quotations come from pp. xxii, xxiii, xxiv. Stephen Oates described his travail in "I Stood Accused of Plagiarism," History News Network, April 15, 2002, hnn.us/articles/658.html. One of his accusers, Michael Burlingame, replied with line and verse quoted here; see "Michael Burlingame's Response to Stephen Oates," http://historynews-network.org/articles/article.html?id=648. The quotation from Oates's *Biography as High Adventure* (Amherst: University of Massachusetts Press, 1986), appears on p. 137. Posner's views are expressed in "Plagiarism—Posner Post" April 24, 2005, www.becker-posner-blog.com/archives/2005/04/plagiarismposne.html, and in Posner's *Little Book of Plagiarism* (New York: Pantheon, 2007).

The bible of game theory is *Contributions to the Theory of Games*, 4 vols., eds. H. W. Kuhn and A. W. Tucker (Princeton: Princeton University Press, 1950–59). I have used with profit Shaun P. H. Heap and Yanis Varoufakis's *Game Theory: A Critical Text*, 2nd ed. (London: Routledge, 2004), and Peter C. Ordeshook's *Game Theory and Political Theory: An Introduction* (New York: Cambridge University Press, 1986). Sylvia Nasar's *A Beautiful Mind: a Biography of John Forbes Nash, Jr., Winner of the Nobel Prize in Economics, 1994* (New York: Simon and Schuster, 1998) is an admiring biography.

The Micmac and the French offer their conflicting accounts of the encounter described in Chapter 8 in my *Sensory Worlds in Early America* (Baltimore: Johns Hopkins University Press, 2003), p. 4. My treatment of the philosophers in chapter 8 is confessedly episodic and anecdotal. I admit to source mining. See George Berkeley's *Treatise Concerning the Principles of Human Knowledge* (1734; repr., New York: Penguin, 1988), pp. 12, 49, 79, 89.

Derrida quotations come from *Speech and Phenomena*, trans. David B. Allison (Evanston: Northwestern University Press), p. 68; *Of Grammatology*, trans. G. C. Spivak (Baltimore: Johns Hopkins University Press, 1974), p. 158, and "As If It Were Possible" in Michel Meyer's *Questioning Derrida* (Aldershot: Ashgate, 2001), p. 105. On Derrida, I consulted John D. Caputo, *The Prayers and Tears of Jacques Derrida* (Bloomington: Indiana University Press, 1997); Peter Fenves, "Derrida and History," in *Derrida and the Humanities*, ed. Tom Cohen (Cambridge: Cambridge University Press, 2001), pp. 271–92; Christopher Norris, *Deconstruction: Theory and Practice* (London: Routledge, 2002); Barry Stocker, *Routledge Philosophy*

Guidebook to Derrida on Deconstruction (London: Routledge, 2006), and the essays in Jack Reynolds and Jonathan Roffe, eds., *Understanding Derrida* (New York: Continuum, 2004).

Richard J. Evans's take on the deconstructionists is far easier to read. In other words, good philosophy of history is argument that can be shared with non-experts. See *In Defense of History* (New York: Norton, 1999), p. 83. His lamentation on the philosophy of history appears on p. 9. But he agrees that "the theory of history is too important to be left to the theoreticians" (p. 12). This formulation of the duty of historians to examine their own discipline (arrived at independently by both him and me) originates from Georges Clemenceau's famous epigram, "La guerre! C'est une chose trop grave pour la confier à des militaires" (War is too important to be left to the generals). David D. Roberts's comment on deconstruction appears in his *Nothing but History: Reconstruction and Extremity after Metaphysics* (Berkeley: University of California Press, 1995), pp. 180, 181.

John Tosh's plea for historical awareness appears in *The Pursuit of History*, p. 22. "Wuz you dere?" was the communist refutation of scholarship contrary to the teachings of Marx and Lenin, according to the official party line. My parents, good socialists, hated it.

Gilbert Ryle, *The Concept of Mind* (London: Hutchinson, 1949), p. 16, offers the now-classic query "But where is the university?" A. J. Ayer's classic work *Language, Truth, and Logic* first appeared in 1936. I have used the later edition (London: Gollancz, 1946), pp. 100, 101, 102.

The definition of pragmatism from its founder, Charles Sanders Peirce, appears in Philip P. Wiener, ed., *Charles Sanders Peirce: Selected Writings* (New York: Dover, 1966), p. 183. William James's lectures on pragmatism, in the 1906–7 academic year, became the classic *Pragmatism*. The quotation is from Giles Gunn, ed., *William James: Pragmatism and Other Writings* (New York: Penguin, 2000), p. 113. Not only is John Dewey's *Democracy and Education: An Introduction to the Philosophy of Education* (New York: Macmillan, 1916) a classic, but it influenced the physical and psychological shape of education in New York City. Desks and chairs once bolted to the floor became movable as teachers turned classrooms into miniature democratic committees and students learned to work in teams. The quotation appears on p. 94. Dewey's presentism blossoms in his essay "Historical Judgments" in *Logic: The Theory of Inquiry* (New York: Holt, 1938), 235. A close and persuasive reading of Dewey's presentism is William H. Dray, *On History and Philosophers of History* (Leiden: E. J. Brill, 1989), 164–83.

Kurt Gödel is so difficult to follow that only a few brave souls (outside the community of mathematicians) have ventured to follow his tracks. See Rebecca Goldstein, *Incompleteness: The Proof and Paradox of Kurt Gödel* (New York: Norton, 2005). The Gödel quotation is from the book's frontispiece. David Horowitz weighs in on the majority-minority question in his *Unholy Alliance: Radical Islam and the American Left* (New York: Regnery, 2006). The quotation comes from the blurb for the book at the frontpagemagazine.com bookstore page, www.donationreport.com/init/controller/ProcessEntryCmd?key'D8QoU3WoR8. Richard Dawkins, "God's Utility Function," *Scientific American,* November 1995, p. 85, is the source for the lack of pattern in genetic activity.

Benoit B. Mandelbrot explains himself and his theory in *The Fractal Geometry of Nature* (San Francisco: W. H. Freeman, 1982). A popular version appears in James Gleick, *Chaos: Making a New Science* (New York: Viking, 1987). Georges Santayana, *The Life of Reason* (New York: Scribners, 1906), vol. 1, pp. 1–2, asks the question that will drive the five-volume survey and, on p. 2, admits that the philosopher's ambition is to speak for the entire race.

The quotation from Lord Acton in Chapter 9 is from *Lectures on Modern History* (New York: Macmillan, 1952), p. 24. O'Sullivan's Manifest Destiny can be found at www.mtholyoke.edu/acad/intrel/osulliva.htm. Theodore Roosevelt speaks in *The Man in the Arena: Selected Writings of Theodore Roosevelt* (Ferndale, Penn.: Forge, 2004), p. 20. U. B. Phillips's *American Negro Slavery* (1918; repr., New York: Appleton, 1929), pp. 454, 455, espoused the racialist view of slave character.

The discussion of the Lipstadt-Irving case appears in Jamil Zinaldin, "The Price of Truth," *AHA Perspectives,* January 2002, and Deborah Lipstadt, *History on Trial: My Day in Court with David Irving* (New York: Harper Collins, 2005), with the quotations from pp. 289–90. The judicial ruling was widely reported in the British press. See, e.g., David Pallister, "The Judgment: Judge Condemns Deliberate Falsification of Historical Record," *Guardian* (London), April 12, 2000, p. 6.

Augustine's *City of God* is grim reading for the sinner. The quotation is from Augustine, *On the Two Cities* (New York: Ungar, 1957), p. 66. For the historians of religion, see Edward Whiting Fox, "Editor's Introduction" to E. Harris Harbison, *The Age of Reformation* (Ithaca: Cornell University Press, 1955), pp. viii, ix; Harbison, *Age of Reformation*, p. 55; Arnold J. Toynbee, *A Study of History,* vol. 4, *The Breakdown of Civilizations* (1939; repr., New York: Oxford University Press, 1962), p. 227, which casts a skeptical eye on all religion.

Excerpts from Johnson and Mather texts are reproduced in Perry Miller and Thomas H. Johnson, eds., *The Puritans: A Source Book of Their Writings* (New York: Harper, 1938), pp. 144, 163; Michael P. Winship, *Making Heretics: Militant Protestantism and Free Grace in Massachusetts, 1636–1641* (Princeton: Princeton University Press, 2002), p. 230. To be fair and forthcoming, I should admit that Michael Winship is my colleague and I have spent much time with him listening and learning. Winship's take on theology is the opposite of George M. Marsden's, but when they set about their scholarly labors they converge. See Marsden, *Jonathan Edwards: A Life* (New Haven: Yale University Press, 2003), p. 502. The other quotations are from Sidney E. Ahlstrom, *A Religious History of the American People* (New Haven: Yale University Press, 1972), 1096, 13.

Steven Pinker's essay on the short-lived Harvard College curriculum requirements that I discuss in the Conclusion is "Less Faith and More Reason," *Harvard Crimson* October 27, 2006. Lawrence M. Krauss added his "amen" to Pinker in "Reason, Unfettered by Faith," *Chronicle of Higher Education,* January 12, 2007, p. B20. The last Krauss quotation comes from his *Hiding in the Mirror: The Mysterious Allure of Extra Dimensions, From Plato to String Theory and Beyond* (New York: Viking, 2005), p. 12. Stephen J. Gould's views appear in Gould, "Nonoverlapping Magisteria," *Natural History* 106 (March 1997): 16–22. Ralph Waldo Emerson, "The American Scholar," address to the Phi Beta Kappa Society of Harvard College [1837], reprinted as *The American Scholar* (New York: New York Public Library, 1901), p. 14.

A friend, reading this essay, was shocked that it made no mention of Michel Foucault. Foucault references are a staple of history dissertations these days, and I decided that I did not want to be left out of the mob, as it were. Roberts's *Nothing but History*, p. 184, offers a most succinct and sympathetic summary of Foucault: "Foucault has been a major source of the postmodern notion that 'man,' which once seemed the transcendent and enduring subject, dissolves into impersonal systems that are historically specific." Foucault himself taught us to look for the discontinuities, the interruptions that are the stuff of real lives. Instead of movements and progress, we need to probe how our own ruling assumptions govern not only our view of the past but how we constructed that past. But there is a little too much self-reflection in this for me. A sample, an apology of sorts, appears in Foucault's *Archaeology of Knowledge* (London: Routledge Classics, 2002), p. 18: "I console myself with the thought that . . . in order to carry out its task [this work] had first to free itself from these various methods and forms of history. . . . Hence the cautious stumbling manner of this text: at every turn, it stands back, measures up what is before it, gropes towards its limits, stumbles against what it does not mean, and digs pits to mark out its own path. At every turn, it denounces any possible confusion. It rejects its identity, without previously stating: I am neither this nor that." Fair enough.

Index

Puritanism, 22, 172-173
Puritans, 172–173

Quoting out of context, 112, 120–123

Race, 48, 92
Radicalism, 55
Rand Corporation, 138
Randall, J.G., 52
Rationalization, 93
Ravitch, Diane, 131
Reagan, Ronald, 111–112
Reason, 11–19
Reconstruction, 92
Reductionists, 70
Reformation, the, 171
Regression fallacy (statistical fallacy),
    81–83
Rehnquist, William, 40
Relativism, 3, 167
Republican Party, 52, 112
Rhetoric, 58
Rhetorical question, 57–60
Rhodes, James Ford, 9–10
Richter, Daniel, 96
Ritual, 29
Roberts, Cokie, 137
Roberts, David, 151
Robinson, James Harvey, 10
Roe v. Wade (1973), 40, 83, 119, 125
Roosevelt, Franklin D., 26, 28, 36, 95, 110
Roosevelt, Theodore, 166
Rosenberg, Rosalind, 81
Rosenthal, David, 133
Roth, Philip, 54–55
Royalties, 133
Rules of thumb, 44–46
Rumsfeld, Donald, 117
Ryle, Gilbert, 151

Saint Augustine, 170–171
Salem witchcraft crisis, 55, 73–74

Sampling, 26
Santayana, Georges, 161
SAT, 47
Schlesinger, Arthur Jr., 94, 110
Science, 2, 37
Scientific method, 15, 68, 153
Self-fulfilling prophecy, 76
Semantic error, 101
Seward, William Henry, 123
Shaggy-dog story, 62–63
Shapiro, Barbara J., 9
Sheehy, Gail, 115
Sheridan, Philip, 43
Skeptic's fallacy, 50
Skokie, Ill., 158
Skyscrapers, 66
Slavery, 30–31, 48, 64, 78-79, 85, 99,
    114, 155, 166–167, 176–177
Slippery slope, 118–120
Smithsonian Institution, 110 111
Social sciences, 10, 107
Socrates, 11, 58–59
Souter, David, 125
South Carolina, 52
Southern "Manifesto", 119–120
Special pleading, 117
Speculation, in history, 61
Spencer, Herbert, 129
Spoonerism, 102
Stamp Act of 1765, 64
Statement on Standards (AHA),
    126–127, 139, 142
Statistics, in history, 78–84
Stereotyping, 36–37
Sterne, Laurence, 28, 96, 113
Stewart, Potter, 44
Stoll, David, 100
Stone, Geoffrey R., 56
Straw man, 115–117
Subjectivity, 18
"Survival of the fittest," 129
Susman, Warren, 108

About the Author

PETER CHARLES HOFFER is Distinguished Research Professor of History at the University of Georgia and the author of numerous books, most recently *Past Imperfect: Facts, Fictions, and Fraud in American History from Bancroft and Parkman to Ambrose, Bellesiles, Ellis, and Goodwin; The Treason Trials of Aaron Burr;* and *Seven Fires: The Urban Infernos That Reshaped America.*

DATE DUE